American Heritage Landmarks

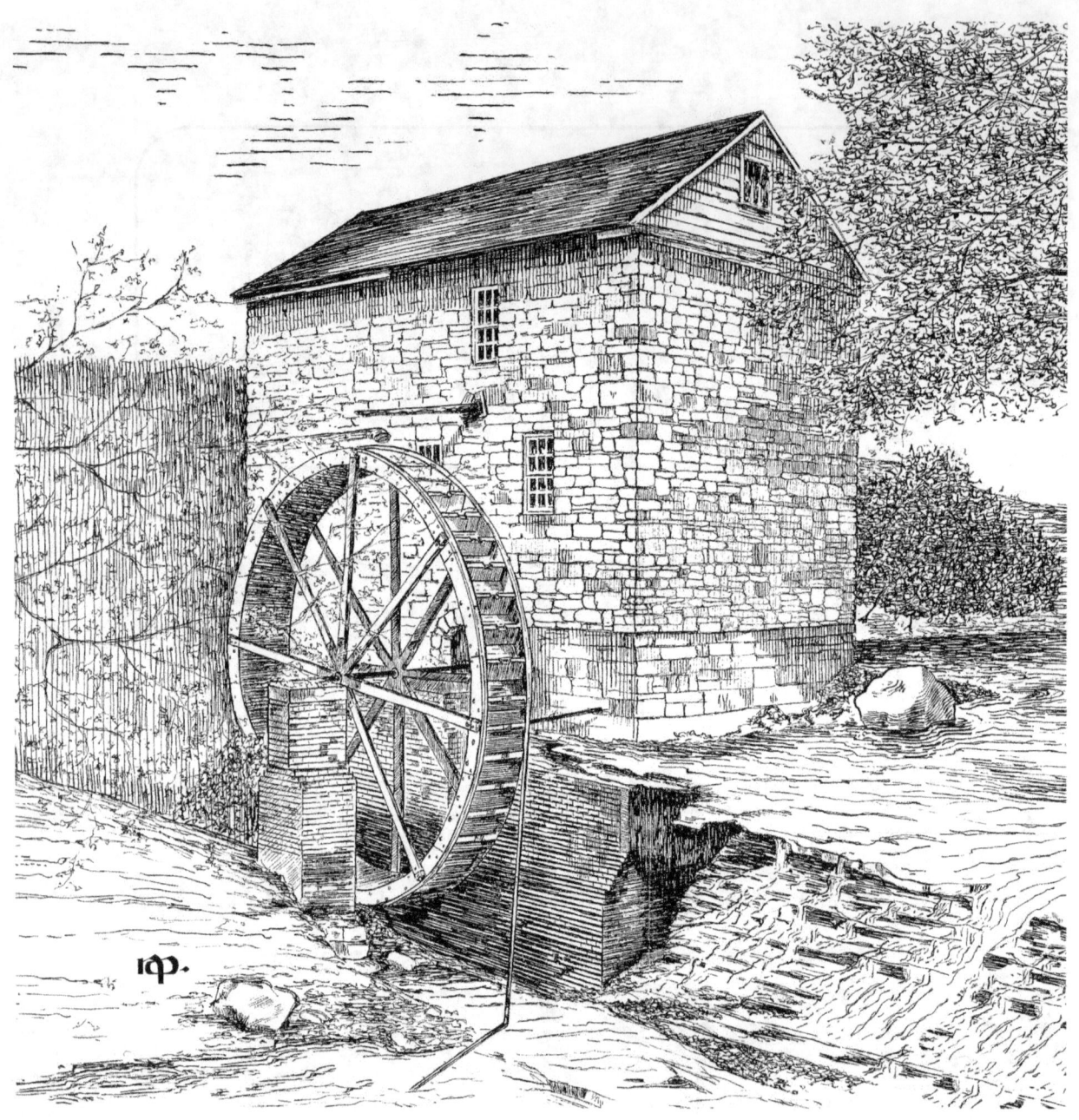

American Heritage Landmarks

Pen & Ink Art

Written & Illustrated

by Robert A. Powell

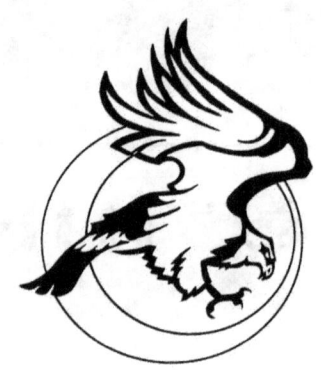

Published & Distributed by:
Silverhawke Publications
Bayonet Point, Florida 34667

ISBN 978-14954948-7-1
Copyright 2010 by Robert A. Powell

Landmarks of our Heritage!

This unique volume of art and history includes distinctive pen & ink drawings of the American Flag and significant landmarks from our proud and noble heritage, both natural and man-made. These are subjects that have played a major role in the development of this great country.

American Heritage Landmarks is a collection of pen & ink drawings that represent the extremely diverse history that made America the greatest nation on planet Earth. It is the effort of one artist to preserve vital bits and pieces of that history and heritage to be appreciated by the current and future generations.

Many of these drawings have captured an eternal place in the hearts of many Americans in various ways through the years. Some subjects still look the same as when they were actually drawn, while others have evolved in some way, and some no longer exist; however, all will remain captured in time along with the significance to their place in history.

Some of the most popular subjects in United States history, as well as some more obscure are depicted. All of these have played a significant role in the making of America.

There is a brief description about each subject; a story that offers the basic facts as to why that subject is considered to be worthy of preserving.

For easiest organization the topics are listed in the Table of Contents in alphabetic order according to the most common title used for that subject.

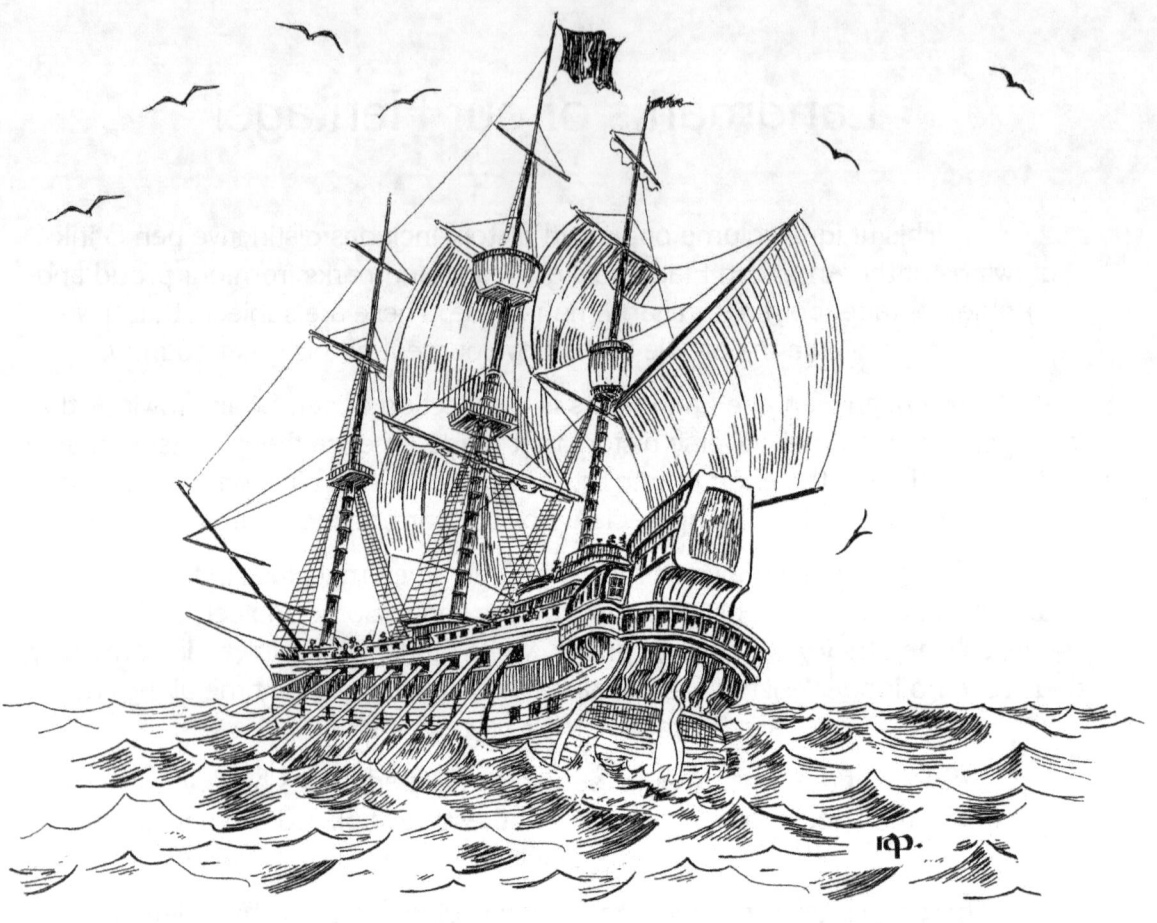

Getting to America in the first place was no easy task!

Table of Contents

American Flag 8
Abbey of Gethsemani 10
Admiral Farragut Academy 12
Alamo 14
Arlington National Cemetery 16
Ashland - Henry Clay Home 18
Audubon Museum 20
Belle of Louisville 22
Booker T. Washington Home 24
Brooker Creek Preserve 26
Butcher Hollow Home 28
Cape Florida Lighthouse 30
Cape Hatteras Lighthouse 32
Carl Sandburg Home 34
Cass Scenic Railway 36
Chained Rock 38
Clara Barton Home 40
Claude Moore Colonial Farm 42
Coal Marker at Baxter 44
Columbus-Belmont Battlefield 46
Cumberland Falls 48
Cumberland Gap Iron Furnace 50
Cumberland Gap Twin Tunnels 52
Farmington 54
Fort Jefferson 56
Fort McHenry 58
French Quarter 60
George Rogers Clark Memorial 62
George Washington Birthplace 64
Glenmont - Edison Home 66
Gold Vault at Fort Knox 58
Golden Gate Bridge 70
Graceland 72
Grand Canyon 74

Harry Truman Home 76
Hoover Dam 78
Independence Hall 80
Jefferson Davis Monument 82
Jefferson Memorial 84
JFK Birthplace 86
John Brown's fort 88
Kentucky's Floral Clock 90
Kingdom Come Gazebo 92
Lincoln Memorial (Kentucky) 94
Longfellow Home 96
Mansfield Mill 98
McHargue Millstones 100
Martin Luther King Birthplace 102
Mount Rushmore 104
Natural Bridge (Kentucky) 106
New River Rafting 108
Norris Dam 110
Orlando Train Depot 112
Paul Revere - Old North Church ...114
Point Park 116
Prickett's Fort 118
Sponge Docks at Tarpon Springs 120
Springwood - Home of FDR..........122
Old Talbott Tavern 124
Tipton-Haynes Farm 126
U.S. Navy Memorial 128
United States Capitol 130
USS Arizona Memorial 132
USS Constitution 134
USS Harlan County 136
Wright Brothers Cycle Shop 138
Zachary Taylor Home 140

The American Flag

The national flag of the United States of America, often referred to as the American Flag, has become a powerful symbol for freedom.

It is proudly flown by individuals, businesses and government offices on numerous different occasions.

Desecration of the American flag is considered to be a public outrage, yet that inappropriate action remains protected as freedom of speech.

The American Flag consists of thirteen equal horizontal stripes of red (at top and bottom) alternating with white; with a blue rectangle in the canton (referred to specifically as the "union") bearing fifty small, white, five-pointed stars. The stars are arranged in nine offset horizontal rows of six stars (top and bottom) alternating with rows of five stars.

The 50 stars on the flag represent the 50 states of the United States of America and the 13 stripes represent the thirteen British colonies that declared their independence from the Kingdom of Great Britain and became the first states in the Union.

Nicknames for the flag include the "Stars and Stripes", "Old Glory", and "The Star-Spangled Banner".

The true meaning of the flag came to the surface nearly 100 years after it was first created. In December 1860, Major Robert Anderson moved the U.S. garrison from Fort Moultrie to Fort Sumter in Charleston Harbor. This was considered to be the opening move of the Civil War. It was this war that would ultimately determine how secure the philosophy of a group of states "united" under one banner might actually work as a nation.

The American flag was used prominently throughout the North to symbolize nationalism and rejection of secessionism.

The overall design of the flag has remained the same, but it has been officially modified 26 times since it was originally adopted in 1777.

The 48-star flag was in effect for 47 years. The 49-star version became official on July 4, 1959. The 50-star flag was officially ordered by President Eisenhower on August 21, 1959, and has remained unchanged since.

On June 14, 1777, the Second Continental Congress passed the Flag Resolution which stated: "Resolved: That the flag of the thirteen United States be thirteen stripes, alternate red and white; that the union be thirteen white stars, in a blue field to represent a new constellation."

Flag Day is observed on June 14 of each year, and tradition holds that the new flag was first hoisted in June 1777 by the Continental Army at the Middlebrook encampment.

The first official U.S. flag flown during battle was on August 3, 1777 during the Siege of Fort Stanwix.

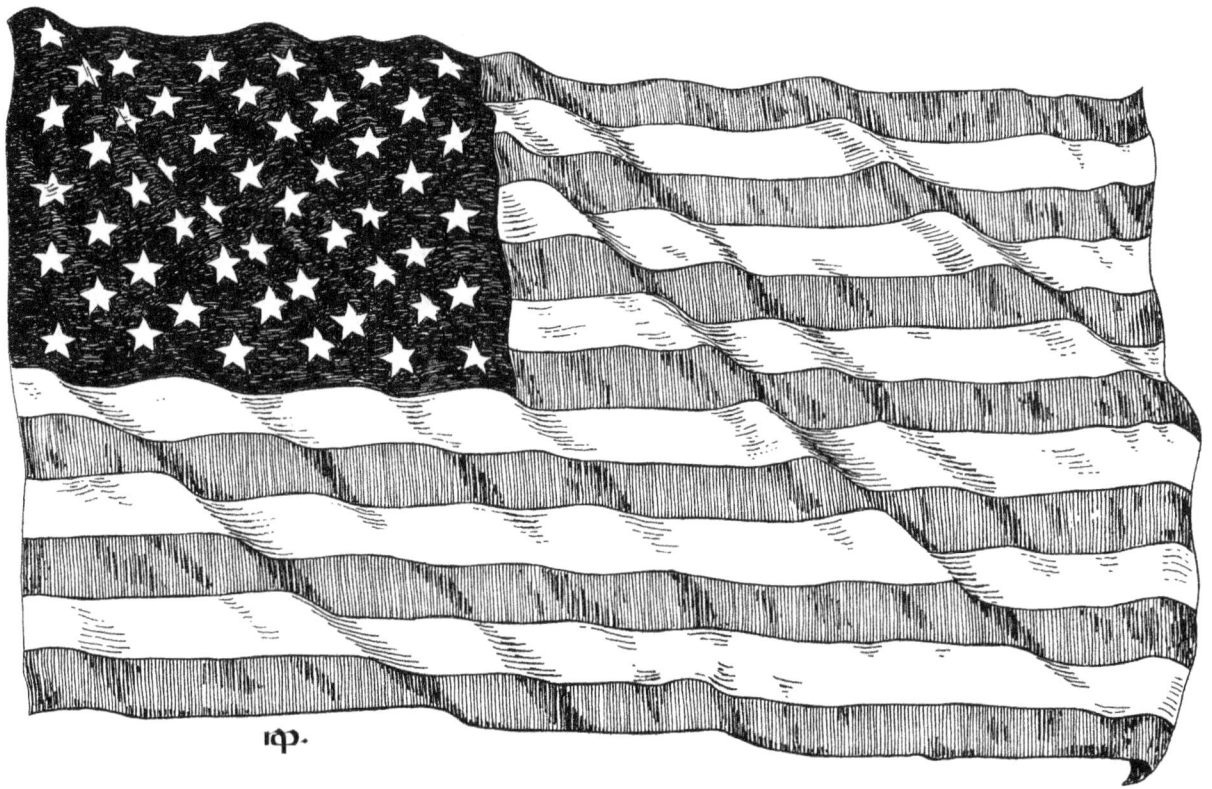

The Star Spangled Banner
Written in 1814 by Francis Scott Key

O say can you see by the dawn's early light,
What so proudly we hailed at the twilight's last gleaming,
Whose broad stripes and bright stars through the perilous fight,
O'er the ramparts we watched, were so gallantly streaming?
And the rockets' red glare, the bombs bursting in air,
Gave proof through the night that our flag was still there;
O say does that star-spangled banner yet wave,
O'er the land of the free and the home of the brave?

On July 27, 1889, Secretary of the Navy Benjamin F. Tracy signed General Order #374, making "The Star-Spangled Banner" the official tune to be played at the raising of the flag. By a law signed on March 3, 1931 by President Herbert Hoover, "The Star-Spangled Banner" was adopted as the national anthem of the United States of America.

Abbey of Our Lady of Gethsemani

New Haven, Kentucky

Abbey of Our Lady of Gethsemani was founded in 1848 near Bardstown, Kentucky, by a group of Trappist Monks from Melleray, France.

Trappists are a part of the Order of Cistercians of the Strict Observance that came into existence in 1664 at the Abbey at La Trappe in France.

In 1847, Dom Maxime, Abbot of the Abbey of Melleray in France, sent two monks to Kentucky to find a tract of land on which the Order could build a monastery in the new world.

Bishop Benedict Joseph Flaget in Louisville guided the pair to Nelson County, to a tract of land owned by the Sisters of Loretto. The area was called Gethsemani. The two monks were able to contract a deal for the land.

Gethsemani is considered to be the motherhouse of all the Trappistine monasteries in the United States. It is the oldest monastery in the U. S. that is still in operation.

Following the Rule of St. Benedict, the Trappist monks live a pensive, contemplative life of faithful prayer and work. The monastery is situated on a working farm of 2,000 acres.

The monks support themselves and their abbey through its store.

Gethsemani Farms offers onsite and by mail order handmade Trappist cheeses, fruitcake, and bourbon fudge.

Gethsemani was home to Trappist monk, social activist and author Thomas Merton from 1941 until his death in 1968. Merton wrote poetry, and many of his 70 books address issues of spirituality, social justice and a quiet pacifism in the modern age.

In his autobiography ***The Seven Storey Mountain*** Merton reflects on his upbringing and experiences as a teen, and what drove him on a search to find faith in God that compelled him to convert to Roman Catholicism at the age of 23. It became a best-seller, and gained Merton millions of followers.

The Cistercians were founded after a reformation of the Benedictine Order; oldest in the Roman Catholic Church.

This meditative order of monks fasts continually and takes the vow of silence, chastity and poverty.

The Abbey was completed and consecrated in 1866. The buildings form an immense quadrangle.

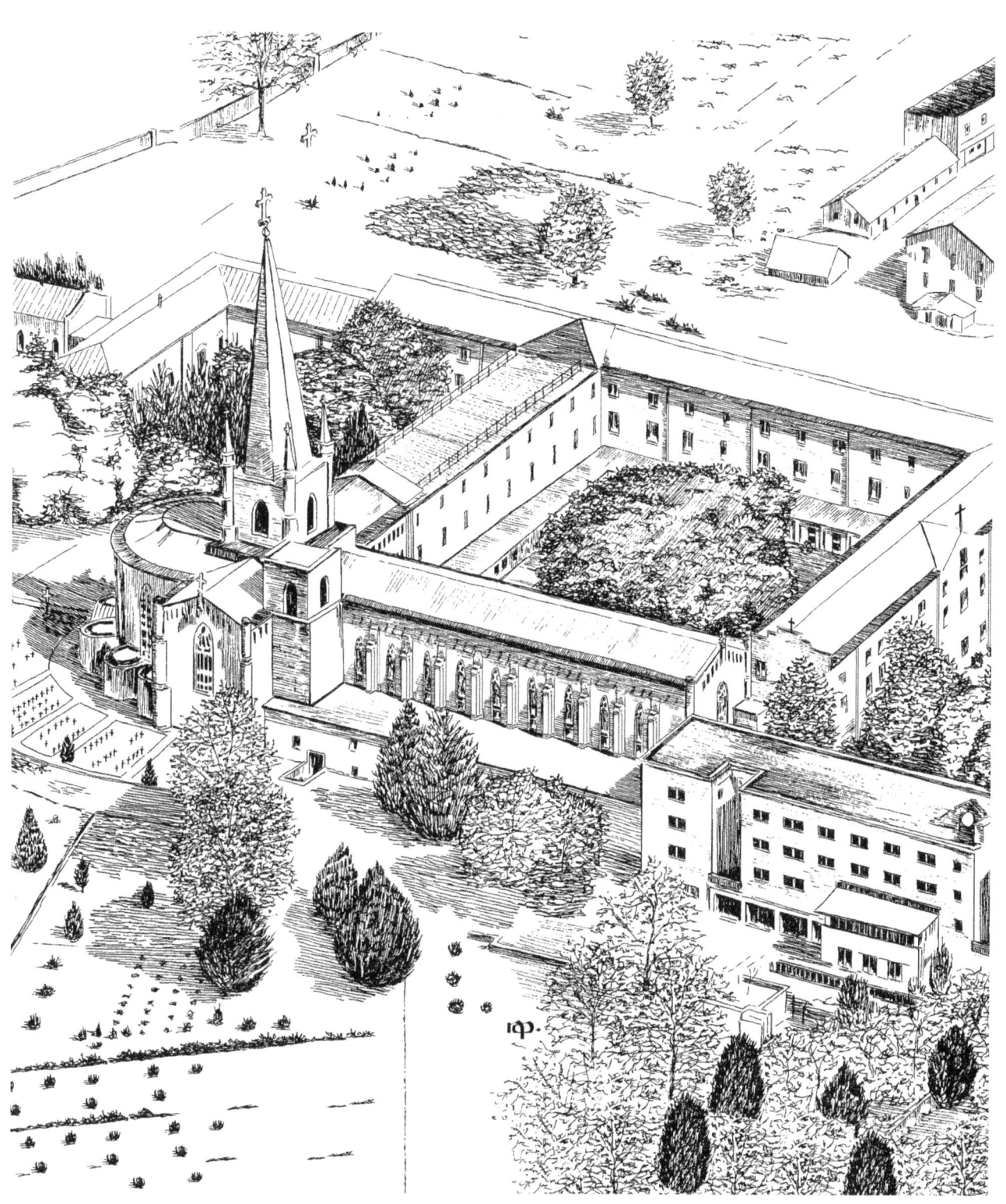

Abbey of Our Lady of Gethsemani

Admiral Farragut Academy

St. Petersburg, Florida

The Admiral Farragut Academy in St. Petersburg occupies the former Jungle Country Club Hotel and 55 acres of campus on Boca Ciega Bay.

Completed in 1925, this sprawling Mediterranean Revival structure was the centerpiece of Walter Fuller's Jungle Subdivision. In 1945 the Hotel was transformed into the Florida home for Admiral Farragut Academy.

The Academy was founded in Pine Beach, New Jersey in 1933 under the leadership of Adm. S.S. Robison, USN, former Superintendent of the United States Naval Academy and Brigadier General Cyrus Radford, USMC.

It is named after Admiral David Glasgow Farragut, the senior officer of all the U.S. Navy forces during the American Civil War.

This academy was America's first preparatory school with naval training. The Florida school was established in St. Petersburg in 1945.

At that time, all hotels in the area were being converted from military barracks back to civilian use. The Academy moved into the Jungle Country Club Hotel.

An independent coeducational day and boarding school, it quickly earned distinction as a Naval Honor School. It is authorized to nominate graduates to compete for special appointments to the various service academies.

Student population is made up of approximately 450 cadets in all grades Kindergarten through 12 as well as a post graduate year.

In 1989 the schools both became coeducational; in 1992 they became two separate schools; and in 1994 the New Jersey school closed.

The Admiral Farragut Academy is the alma mater of two of the twelve men who walked on the moon, Admiral Alan Shepard, class of '41 and Brigadier General Charles Duke '53.

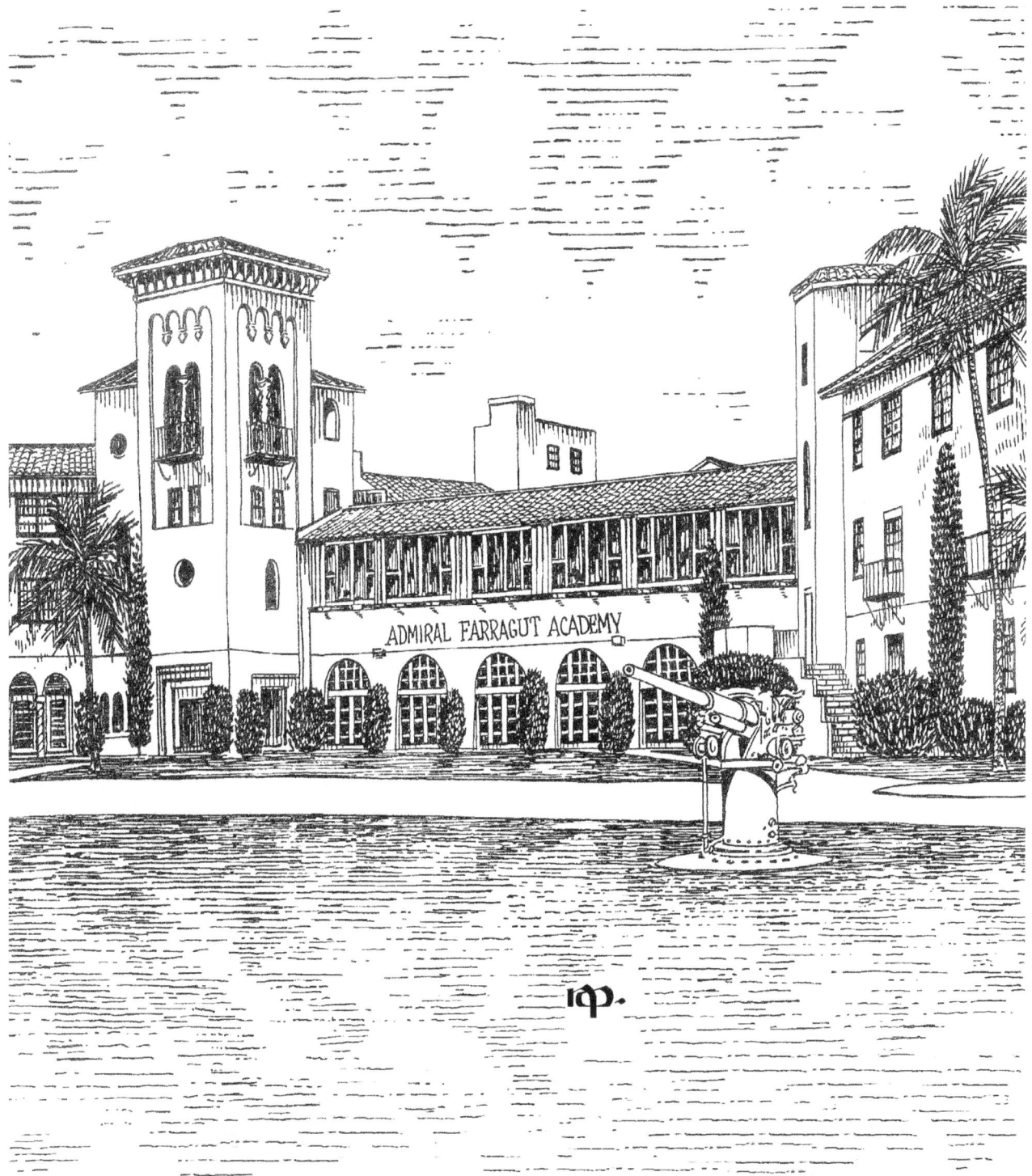

Admiral Farragut Academy

The Alamo

San Antonio, Texas

The Alamo in San Antonio became the "cradle of Texas Liberty" in 1836, when a brave band of 189 Texas volunteers defied a Mexican army of thousands.

Originally known as Mission San Antonio de Valero, The Alamo was a Roman Catholic mission and fortress compound. It was the site of the Battle of the Alamo in 1836. It is now a museum in Downtown San Antonio.

Built by Spanish Franciscan priest Antonio de Olivares and the Payaya Indians, the Alamo was part of the origin of San Antonio. It was built for the education of Native Americans after their conversion to Christianity.

The mission was secularized In 1793, and soon abandoned. Ten years later, it became a fortress housing the Mexican Army until December 1835, when it was surrendered to the Texian Army. A relatively small number of soldiers occupied the compound.

On February 23, 1836 Mexican General Santa Anna led a large force of Mexican soldiers into San Antonio. The siege ended on March 6, when the Mexican army attacked the Alamo, which was defended by Texians under leadership of Colonel James Bowie; all or almost all of the defenders were eventually killed.

General Sam Houston ultimately defeated the Mexican army to end the Texas Revolution. The brave resistance of those defenders of the Alamo is credited with distracting the Mexicans so the Americans could properly prepare to roust them from Texas.

In 1849, several years after Texas was annexed to the United States, the US Army rented the facility for use as a quartermaster's depot; however they abandoned the mission in 1876 after Fort Sam Houston was established.

The Alamo chapel was sold to the state of Texas. In 1892, the Daughters of the Republic of Texas (DRT) began trying to preserve the Alamo. Texas governor Oscar Colquitt briefly took the complex under state control and began restorations in 1912; the site was given back to the DRT later that same year.

In 1914, a silent film *The Siege and Fall of the Alamo* became the first feature film about the legendary battle of 1836. It was also the first and only such film shot at the Alamo.

The Alamo welcomes over four million visitors each year, making it one of the most popular historic sites in the U.S. The Long Barracks contains a small museum of paintings, weapons, and other artifacts from the era of the Texas Revolution, and a large diorama recreates the compound as it existed in 1836. The large mural, known as the Wall of History, portrays the history of the Alamo complex.

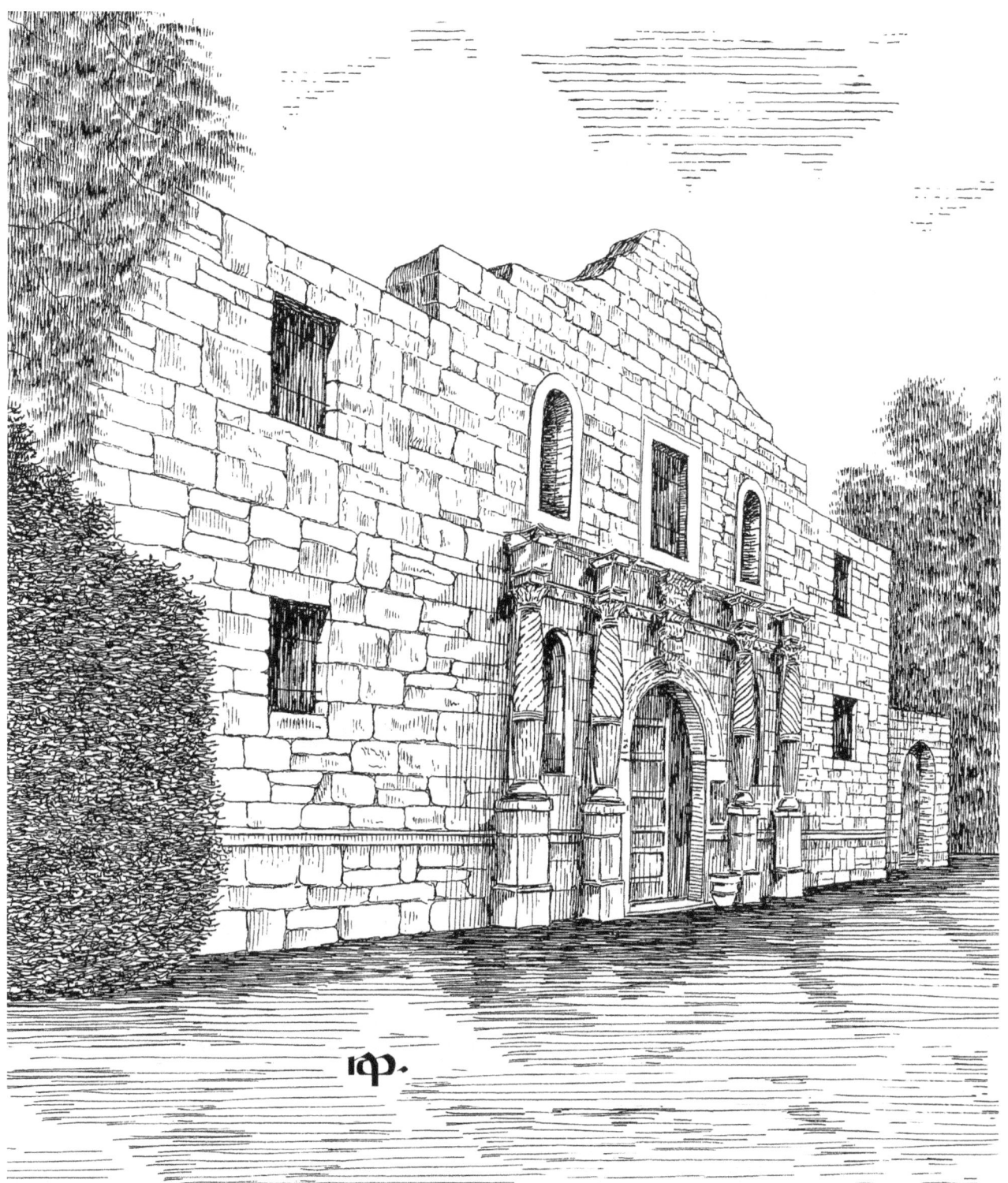

The Alamo

Arlington National Cemetery

Civil War Section - Arlington, Virginia

The Civil War Section of Arlington National Cemetery overlooks the capital city. The Tomb of the Civil War Unknowns was one of the first grave sites at Arlington.

What has become the world-wide symbol to honor America's dedication to freedom and the soldiers who died to protect it, was created in a personal vendetta against the South.

Arlington National Cemetery is located on Confederate General Robert E. Lee's confiscated estate. Days after resigning from the U.S. Army in 1861, to take command of Virginian forces in the Civil War, Lee left the Arlington estate where he had married and lived for 30 years; never to return.

After Virginia seceded from the Union on May 23, 1861, Union troops crossed the Potomac and occupied the 200-acre property and house.

In 1778 John Parke Custis bought the 1,100 acre tract of land, but died during the American Revolution and his infant son was adopted by George and Martha Washington. In 1802 he built the home and named it Arlington. His only child to reach adulthood was Mary, who married Robert E. Lee.

With Washington, D.C., teeming with dead soldiers, Gen. Montgomery C. Meigs proposed Arlington as the location of a military cemetery. In 1866, General Meigs ordered that the remains of all the unidentified soldiers found in or near Washington were to be gathered and placed in a common vault located in the Lee Rose Garden beside the Arlington House.

Both Union as well as Confederate soldiers are among the 2,111 unknown bodies in the tomb.

A Supreme Court ruling in 1882, more than a decade after Robert E. Lee's death, declared that the U.S. government had seized the estate illegally, and ordered it returned to the Lee family in the same condition as when it was confiscated.

The ruling could have required the exhumation of all the soldiers buried there, but instead Lee's son officially sold the property to the United States for $150,000 in 1883.

Arlington is the only national cemetery that holds servicemen from every war in U.S. history. The first burial at Arlington did not occur until 1864, but the burial ground holds the remains of those who fought in every war, including the Revolution.

Soldiers killed in the Revolutionary War as well as from the War of 1812 have been reburied at Arlington.

It is considered the highest honor a soldier can achieve; to be buried at Arlington National Cemetery. Truly the nation's most Sacred Shrine.

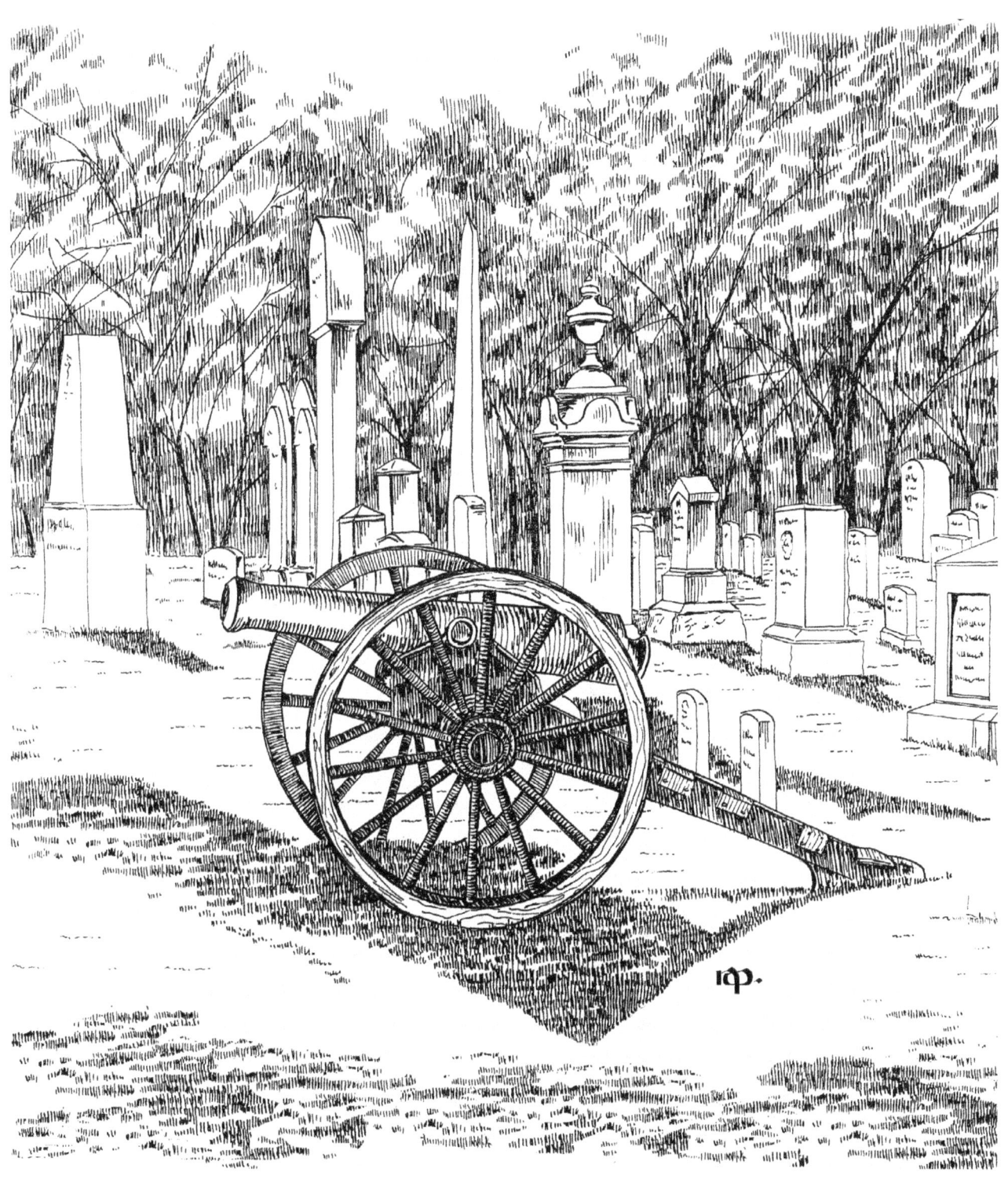

Arlington National Cemetery

Civil War Section

Ashland

Home of Henry Clay • Lexington, Kentucky

Henry Clay built his home in 1805 at the eastern edge of the thriving city of Lexington. Clay was born April 12, 1777, in Virginia; he came west as a young man, married Lucretia Hart and settled here where he made his very impressive mark in history.

The central portion was erected on a 125-acre tract of land Clay purchased from Cuthbert Banks. He later added several hundred acres to his estate and two wings to the house.

Henry Clay and his wife Lucretia lived at Ashland for many years, where they reared their 11 children. Clay was actively engaged in law and politics for his entire life. He served as a Kentucky Representative, U.S. Senator, Secretary of State and three times a candidate for the president of the United States.

He died in Washington, D.C. June 29, 1852, and was returned with great pomp and circumstance for burial in the Lexington Cemetery. A monument was erected with private funds by the Henry Clay Monument Association, organized shortly after his death.

The cornerstone was laid July 4, 1857, and a 120 feet high column with Clay's figure on top was completed in 1861. He looks over the city.

His son, James Clay, purchased Ashland in 1856 and razed the old mansion, which had become unsafe for habitation. The house was rebuilt on the exact same site with much of the materials from the old structure. The new Ashland was completed in 1857.

This Ashland site was home to five generations of the Clay family.

It was sold to Kentucky University in 1866 and housed a part of the Agricultural and Mechanical College.

Ashland became a national shrine in 1950, and was designated a National Historic Landmark in December 1960.

Following an extensive three-year renovation between 1990 and 1993, many discoveries were made and many pieces belonging to the Clay family were returned to the home.

Now situated in the very heart of Lexington, the Ashland plantation at one time covered more than 600 acres. Today the shrine includes twenty acres of the original estate, which contain the home, gardens and dependencies of Ashland.

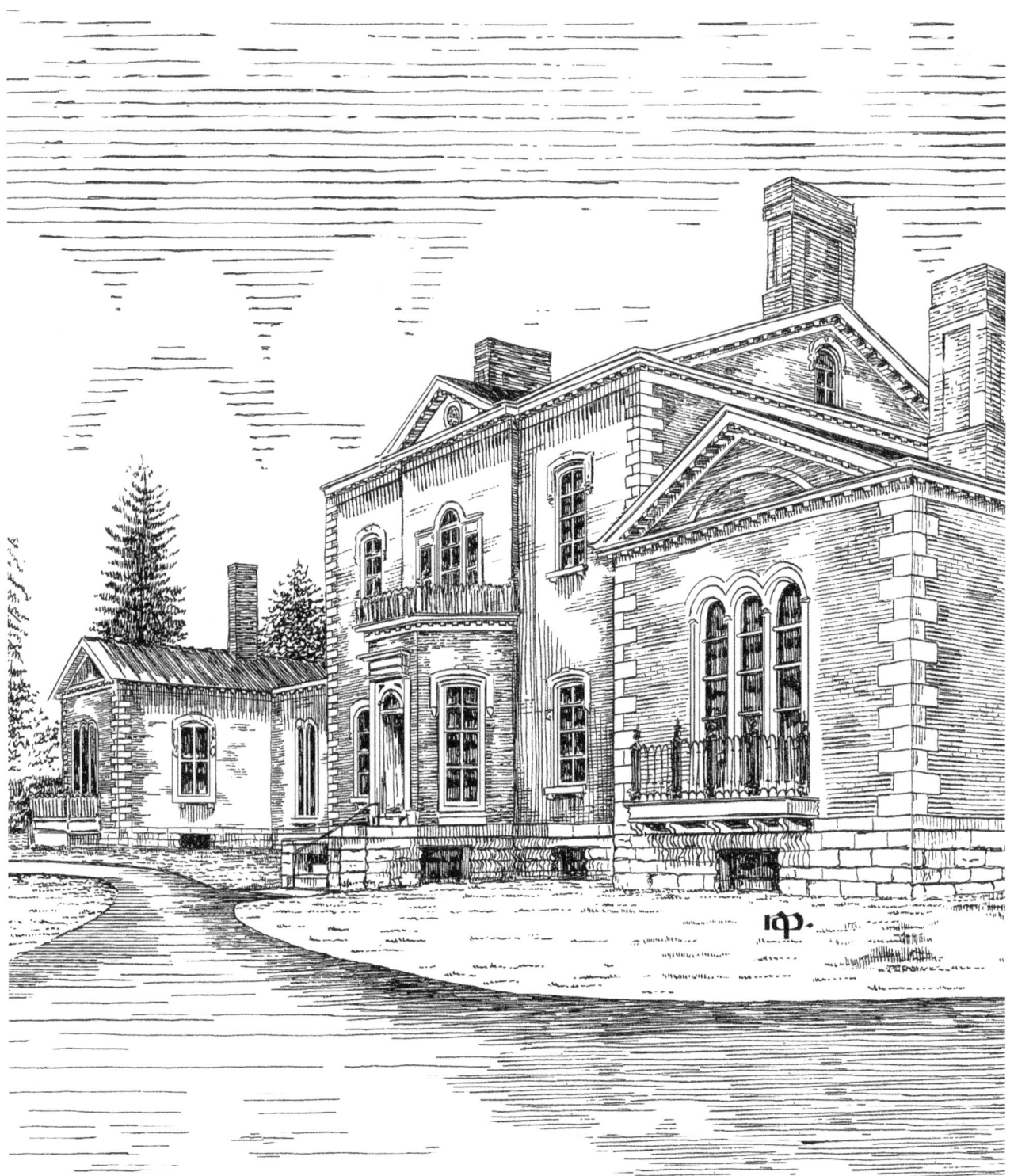

Ashland

Home of Henry Clay

Audubon Museum

Henderson, Kentucky

Audubon Museum is the center piece for the John James Audubon State Park. This is a 692-acre wildlife sanctuary donated by the citizens of Henderson in memory of the famed ornithologist who roamed throughout Kentucky in the early 1800s.

Audubon (1779-1851) was one of the few Kentucky's artists to establish a wide reputation through his paintings of local subjects. He lived at Henderson and also Louisville for several years, gathering material for his monumental *Birds of America*. The park includes one of his favorite haunts, Wolf Hill, where he studied the birds.

The internationally acclaimed Audubon Museum design is of French heritage. The style permits inclusion of small niches in the museum tower for nesting birds.

The Museum proudly displays one of the world's largest collections of original Audubon art that made the wildlife artist a legend. But it is the personal artifacts and memorabilia that portray the often difficult life of Audubon; more a starving artist than artistic success.

The museum's four exhibit halls chronicle Audubon's life, including his 1810-1819 residence in Henderson.

Highlights of the collection include the *American Bald Eagle* oil, a four-volume edition of the *Birds of America*, a personal seal, handwritten journals, the silver service Audubon sent from England to his devoted wife, Lucy.

The park was listed on the *National Register of Historic Places* in 1988. In 1990 the Kentucky General Assembly allocated $2.5 million for a thorough renovation of the museum and the additional 9,500-square-foot nature center to promote the study of nature.

In the spring of 1992, the largest renovation in the Museum's 54-year history began and in December 1993 the refurbished and expanded museum reopened to the public.

Observers have identified nearly 200 species of birds, 150 varieties of wildflowers, 50 different kinds of trees and numerous shrubs within the park.

Audubon came to the area in 1810, first as a partner in a general store, later running a grist mill.

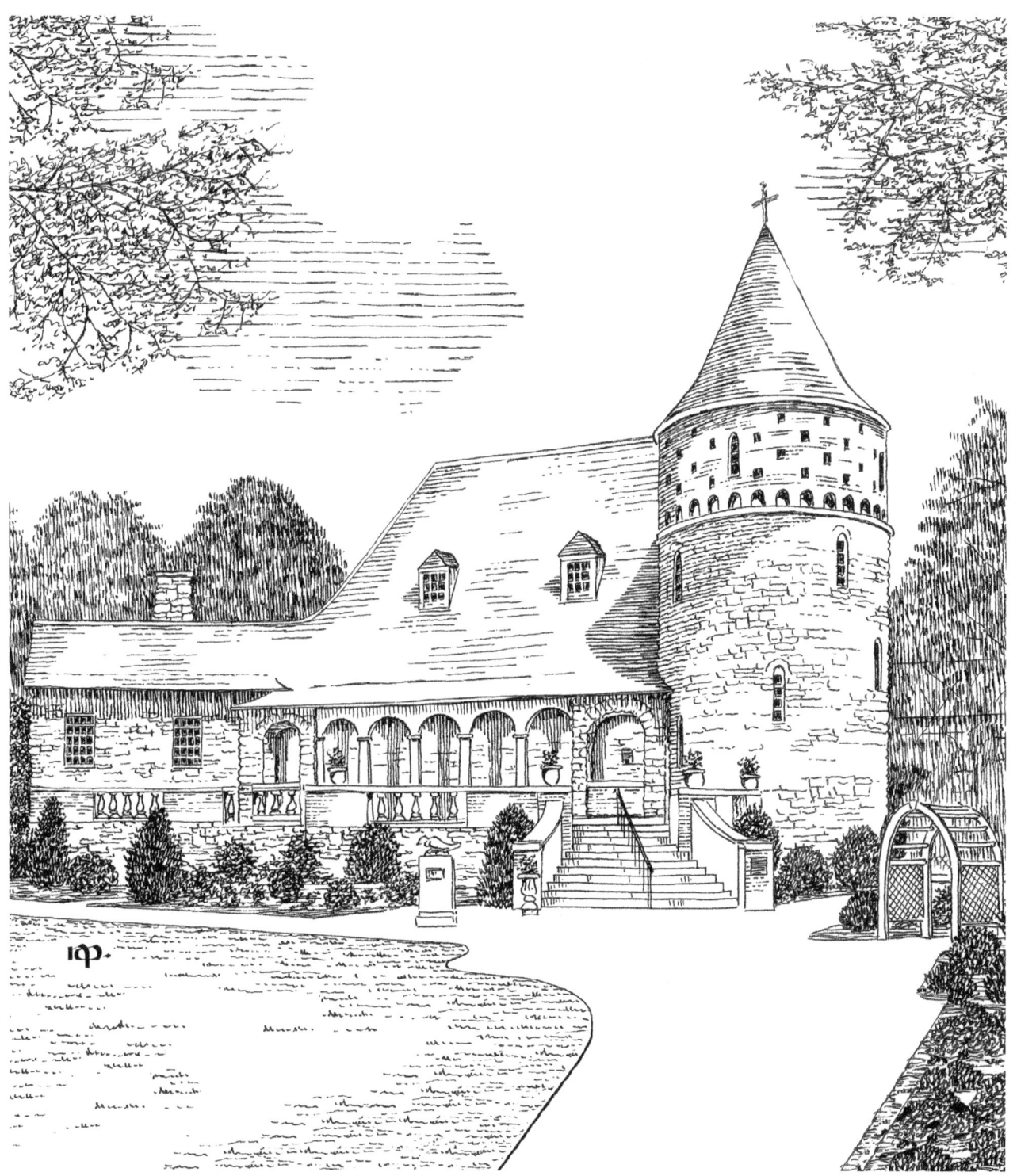

Audubon Museum

Belle of Louisville

Louisville, Kentucky

Belle of Louisville is recognized as the oldest river steamboat in operation; it was placed on the *National Register of Historic Places* in 1972 and was then designated as a U.S. National Historic Landmark in 1989.

Out of more than 85,000 sites on the *National Register,* only about 2,500 are designated as National Landmarks; officially recognized by the United States government for its national-level historical significance.

Owned and operated by the city of Louisville, The Belle is moored at the downtown wharf next to Riverfront Plaza/Belvedere; a public area situated on the Ohio River.

The Belle gained a great deal of her popularity and fame in the annual riverboat race that began a tradition in 1963 (against the Delta Queen) and quickly became a favorite part of the annual *Kentucky Derby Festival*.

Originally named the Idlewild, she was built by James Rees & Sons Company in Pittsburgh, Pennsylvania for the West Memphis Packet Company in 1914 and was first put into service on the Allegheny River.

Constructed with an all-steel superstructure and asphalt main deck, the steamboat is said to hold the record in her class for miles traveled, actual years in operation, and number of places visited.

She came to Louisville in 1931 as an excursion boat, but was sold and renamed Avalon in 1947. She operated all along the Mississippi, Missouri, St. Croix, Illinois, Kanawha, Ohio and Cumberland Rivers.

In 1962, Jefferson County Judge Marlow Cook bought her at auction and brought her back to Louisville where she was completely renovated and re-christened Belle of Louisville.

On October 18, 2014, the Belle of Louisville will be 100 years old.

As a celebration of this unique and outstanding accomplishment, a 5-day riverboat festival to be named "The Belle's Big Birthday Bash" will be held in Louisville, Kentucky, all along the Waterfront Park.

During that week, eight riverboats from across the country will join Belle of Louisville to help celebrate her 100th year on the river.

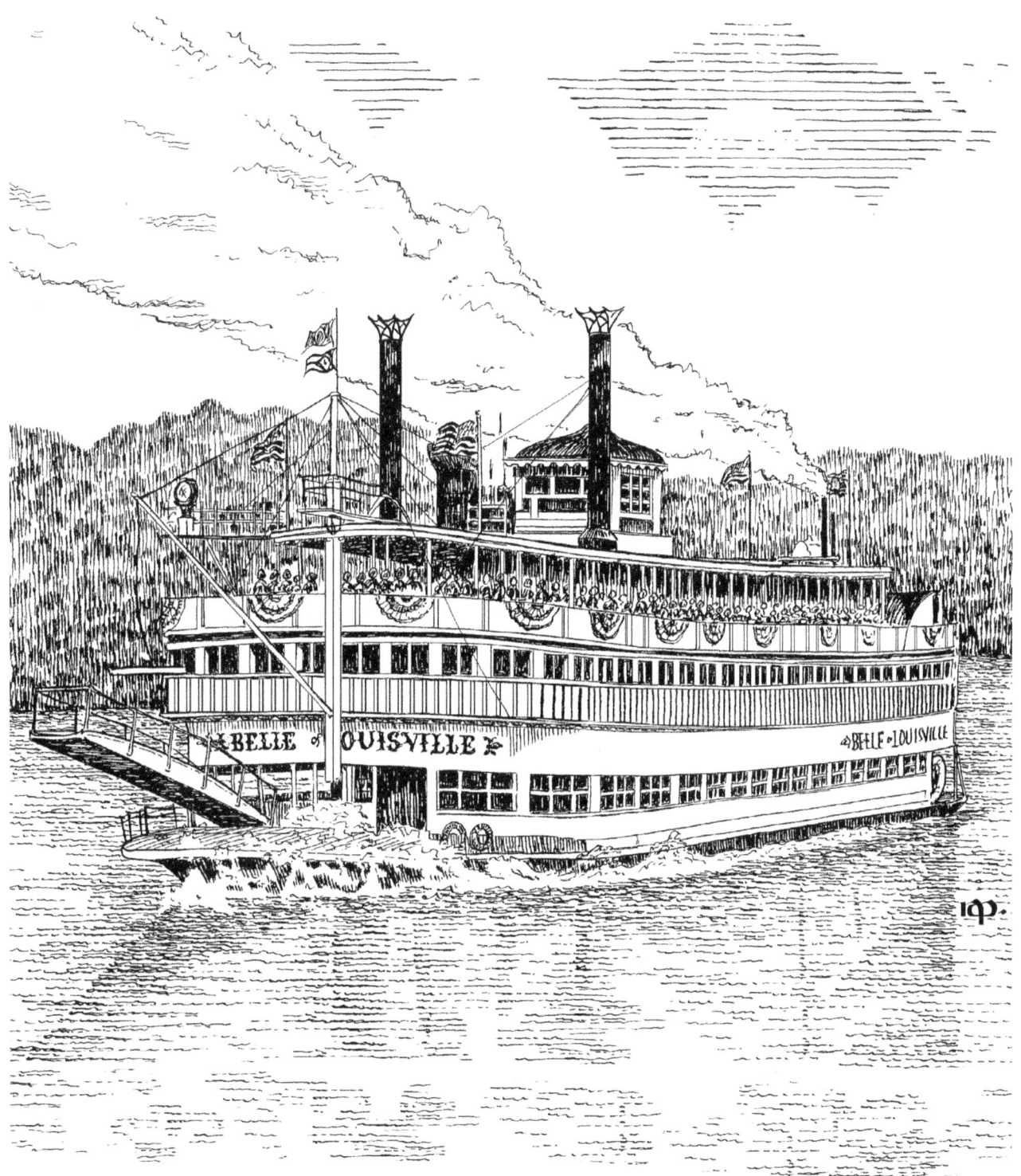

Belle of Louisville

Booker T. Washington Birthplace

Piedmont, Virginia

Booker T. Washington National Monument commemorates the birth place of America's most prominent African-American educator and orator of the late nineteenth and early twentieth centuries.

Washington was born in slavery April 5, 1856 in a small cabin on the Burroughs tobacco farm in Piedmont, Virginia. His mother was a cook, his father a white man from a nearby farm.

It was illegal to educate slaves, but he went to school each day to carry the school books and materials for one of James Burroughs' daughters.

Booker T. Washington was born during a time when the United States of America was trying to work toward a solution dealing with slavery.

Since the beginning, the colonies and most of the territories that became the United States had developed by agrarian economics that utilized slave labor to some extent.

By the early 1800s, factories had become the major economic system of the Northern States while the Southern States remained agrarian.

As slavery ceased to exist in most of the Northern States, abolitionists began to demonstrate and influence state governments pushing toward the emancipation and sometimes even the relocation of slaves, former slaves and their descendants.

In April 1865 the Emancipation Proclamation allowed the freedom of all slaves, and Booker's family joined his stepfather in West Virginia.

At the age of 16 he walked 500 miles back to Virginia in order to attend Hampton Institute, where he eventually became a teacher.

Later he was principal and guiding force behind the Tuskegee Institute in Alabama and became recognized as the nation's foremost black educator.

He died in 1915 at the age of 59.

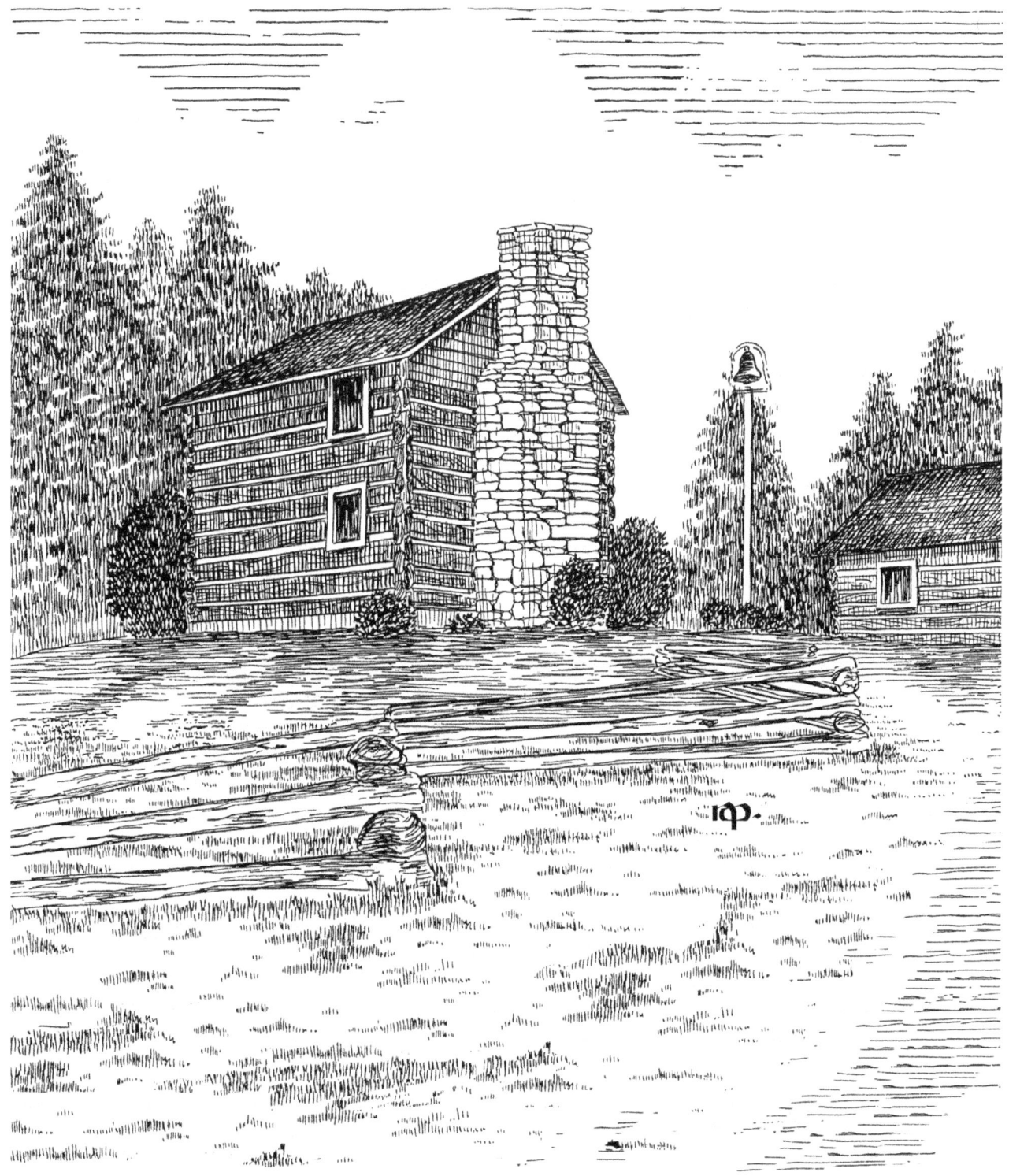
Booker T. Washington Birthplace

Brooker Creek Preserve

Tarpon Springs, Florida

Brooker Creek Preserve is an 8,500-acre wilderness area located in the northeastern corner of Pinellas County. Bordered by Pasco County to the north and Hillsborough County to the east, the Preserve is roughly seven miles long and one and one-half miles wide and lies within the rapidly developing East Lake region of Pinellas County.

The Brooker Creek Preserve is a wilderness island surrounded on all sides by urban development. It is not a park, but a wilderness area.

Management for the Preserve rests with the Pinellas County Department of Parks and Conservation Resources.

The Preserve provides a unique refuge for native flora and fauna as well as an opportunity for citizens to explore the natural beauty of wild Florida.

It also serves to protect quite a significant portion of the Brooker Creek Watershed. A complex of hiking and equestrian trails provides visitors an opportunity to explore the Preserve's many ecosystems.

Pinellas County Extension at the Brooker Creek Preserve Environmental Education Center offers a variety of educational and interpretive programs for the public.

The goal of these programs is to empower citizens to make informed decisions about natural and cultural resources; especially within the region.

Center programs interpret all the natural and cultural history of the area in order to demonstrate the balance of nature in Florida.

A watershed is an area of land that water flows across as it moves toward a common body of water, such as a lake, stream, river or coast.

All land is part of a watershed; it can be very large, draining thousands of square miles, or very small, draining only a few acres to a small pond.

The Brooker Creek watershed is home to more than 750 species of plants and animals. Although they are free to roam within or even leave the area, they are indigenous.

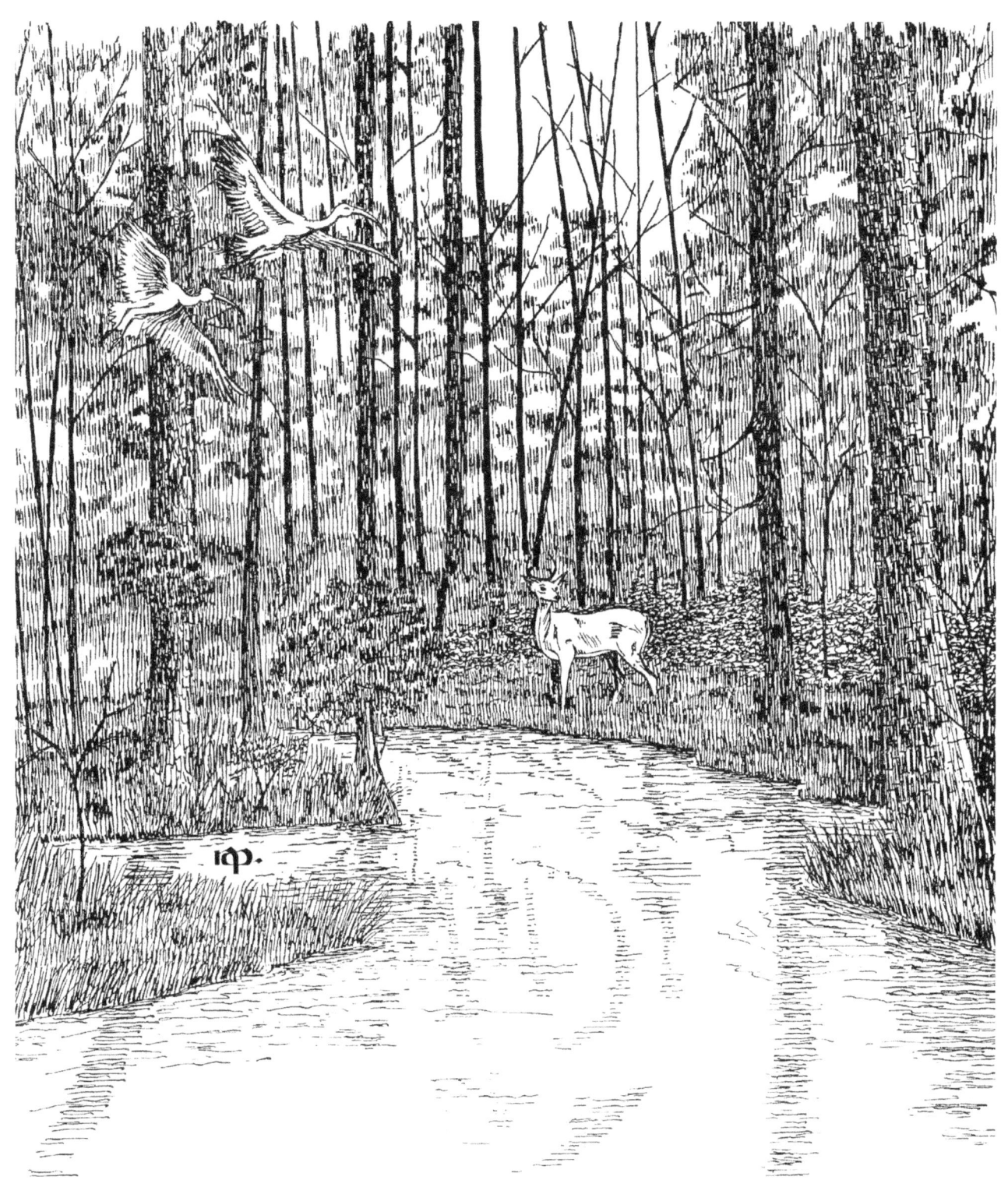

Brooker Creek Preserve

Butcher Hollow Home

Loretta Lynn Birthplace • Johnson County, Kentucky

The home of Loretta Lynn is one of the few reminders of the once prosperous community of Van Lear. Since the close of the Van Lear Coal Mines in the 1950s, Butcher Hollow has been nearly deserted.

This obscure mountain community became the symbol of hope and pride to all residents and former residents of Appalachia in the 1970s, when Loretta Lynn belted,

"Well, I was born'd a coal miner's daughter ... In a cabin on a hill in Butcher Holler"

It merited Loretta Lynn with the everlasting respect of anyone who was connected with coal mining and/or mountain life.

At one time the mountainsides around Butcher Hollow were home to scores of men who dug coal by night and scraped crops out of the unyielding land by day. Ted and Clara Webb had eight children.

Loretta Webb was only 13 when Mooney Lynn (22) married her and took her out of Butcher Hollow.

They had known each other for only one month. She was a mother by the age of 14 and was a grandmother at the age of 28.

Butcher Hollow was so isolated and poverty was so much a way of life that Loretta did not realize she was poor until she no longer was. At the age of 12 she had never been in an automobile, to a movie, talked on the telephone, worn a "store bought" dress, tasted steak or even hamburger.

Butcher Hollow is a part of the community of Van Lear, which was constructed by the Consolidation Coal Company in the early part of the 20th century. Van Lear was named for Van Lear Black, a director for the company.

The Van Lear post office was established in 1909. Butcher Hollow is not an independent town or village.

A hollow in any Eastern Kentucky community is much like a street or road in a city.

Loretta Lynn is truly one of the few legitimate overnight successes in show business. A month after Mooney had given her a guitar, she had learned to play without lessons, written her own songs, and recorded a song which became a number one hit and landed her a major recording contract.

Hundreds of tourists visit Van Lear each year to see the childhood home of Loretta Lynn, Crystal Gayle, and her siblings. Herman Webb, one of Lynn's brothers, gives tours of the house for a fee of five dollars.

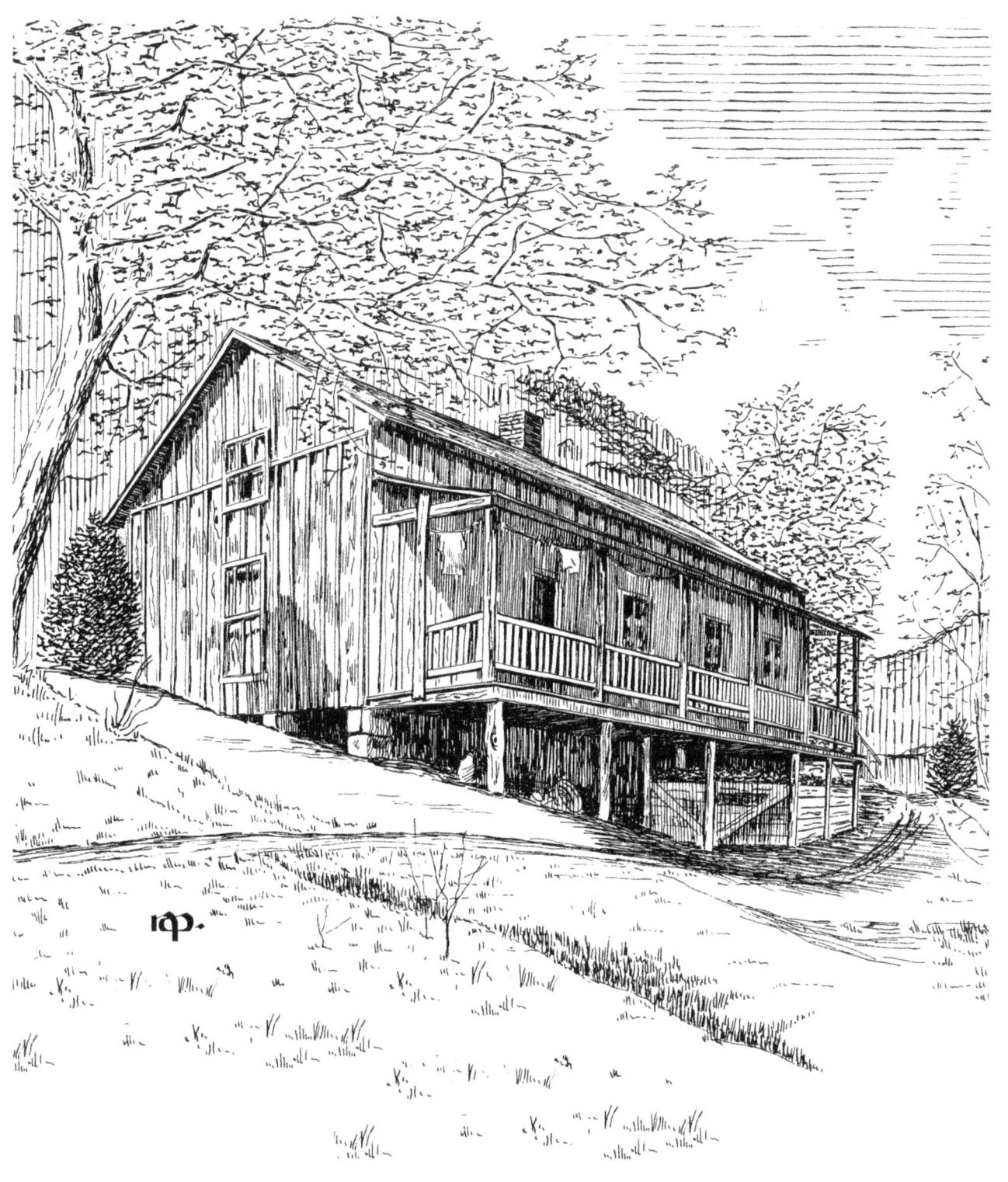

Butcher Hollow Home

Cape Florida Lighthouse

Key Biscayne, Florida

The oldest structure in South Florida is located on the southern tip of a barrier island just south of Miami Beach called Key Biscayne.

It is the Cape Florida Lighthouse, built in 1825 as part of a network of navigational aids built along the eastern seaboard of Florida by the government to help prevent shipwrecks that were caused by sandbars and the uncharted, submerged reefs.

The original tower had withstood numerous hurricanes, but was heavily damaged during the Second Seminole War in 1836.

The lighthouse was a gathering place for refugees of Indian attacks, and in July of 1836 the Indians set fire to the wooden door, forcing the people to the top of the tower.

To prevent Indians from coming up, John Thompson set off a lusty explosion with gun powder to destroy the wooden stairway. He was rescued several days later, but the tower was not rebuilt until 1845.

To improve the effectiveness, the tower was raised from 65 feet to its current height of 95 feet in 1855.

During the Civil War the lighthouse lamp was destroyed by Confederate sympathizers so it could not be used by the Union sailors who controlled the surrounding waters.

It was relit in 1867 and went out of active service officially in 1878.

On June 15, 1978, 100 years after it was extinguished, the lighthouse was put back into use by the U.S. Coast Guard to mark the Florida Channel, the deepest natural channel into Biscayne Bay. They decommissioned it in 1990.

The lighthouse is now open to the public as part of the Bill Baggs Cape Florida State Park; the light was relit in 1996. It is owned and operated by the Florida Department of Environmental Protection.

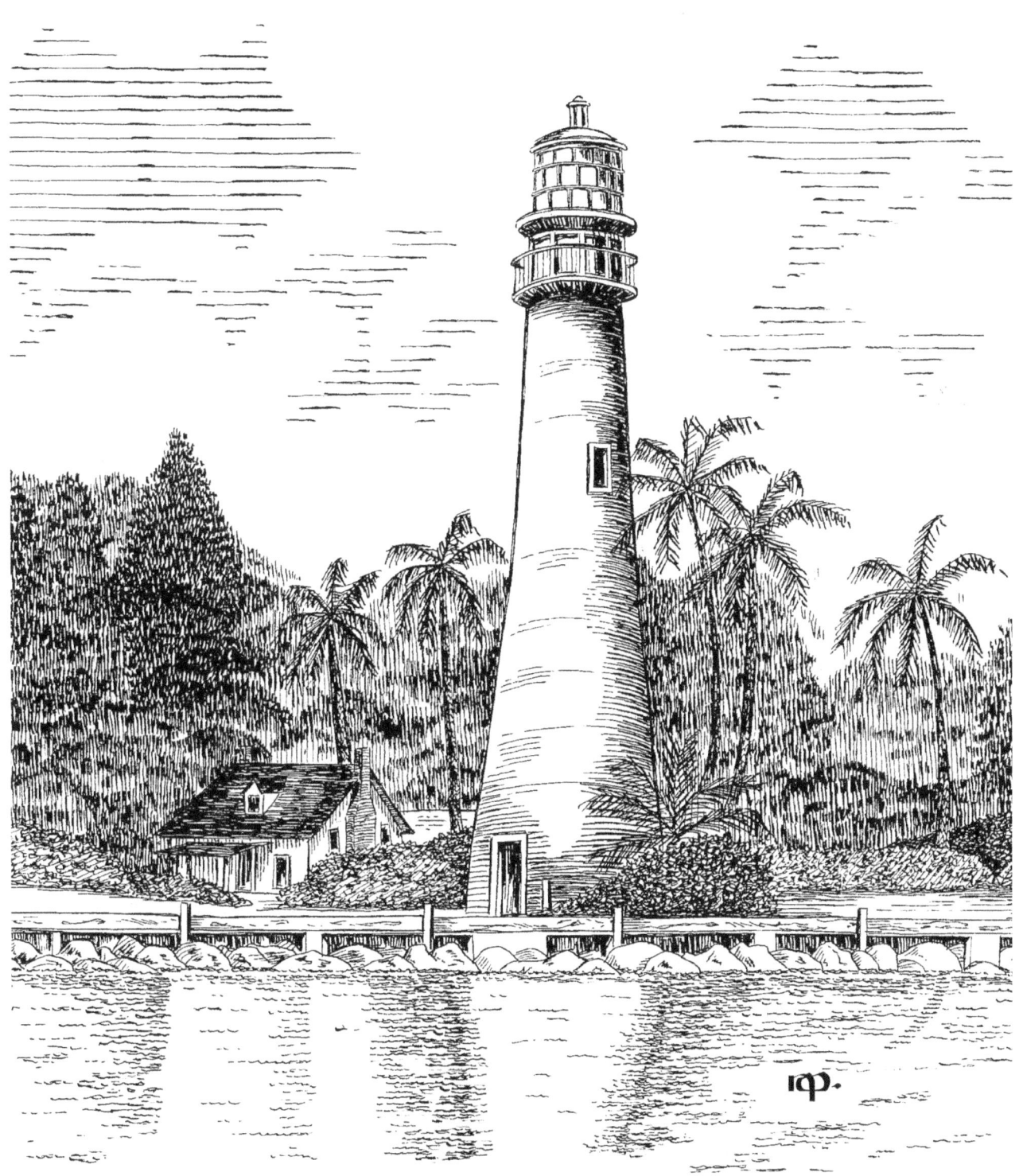

Cape Florida Lighthouse

Cape Hatteras Lighthouse

Buxton, North Carolina

Cape Hatteras Lighthouse is the tallest lighthouse tower in the United States. It was activated in 1870 to replace a structure which had served as a navigational aid for 70 years.

Cape Hatteras Light is located on Hatteras Island in the Outer Banks in the town of Buxton, North Carolina and is the focal point of the Cape Hatteras National Seashore.

The Outer Banks are a group of islands that separate the Atlantic Ocean from the coastal sounds and inlets. The Atlantic currents in this area made for excellent travel for ships, except in the area of Diamond Shoals, just offshore at Cape Hatteras.

The warm Gulf Stream ocean current collides here with the colder Labrador Current, creating conditions for powerful ocean storms and sea swells. The large number of ships that ran aground because of these shifting sandbars, including the Civil War ironclad warship USS Monitor, gave this area the nickname "Graveyard of the Atlantic."

The U.S. Congress authorized the erection of a lighthouse here in 1797. Structural problems caused it to be replaced by the current one in 1870.

Its 210 foot height makes it the tallest brick lighthouse structure in the United States and 29th in the world. But since its base is situated almost at sea level, it is only the 15th highest light in the United States.

It was originally located 1,500 feet from the water, and the distinctive black & white candy-cane design made it a most prominent landmark along the entire Carolina coastline.

In 1935 it was discovered that due to seaside erosion, the water was only 100 feet away from the base of the massive lighthouse.

The only solution was to move or replace the lighthouse. It was finally moved away from the water's edge during the summer of 1999 at an approximate cost of $12 million.

The Cape Hatteras Lighthouse is the tallest masonry structure ever known to be moved (200 feet tall and weighing 5,000 tons).

Adjacent to the Cape Hatteras Light is the Hatteras Island Visitor Center and Museum of the Sea. It is operated by the National Park Service. Exhibits include the history, maritime heritage and natural history of the Outer Banks and the lighthouse.

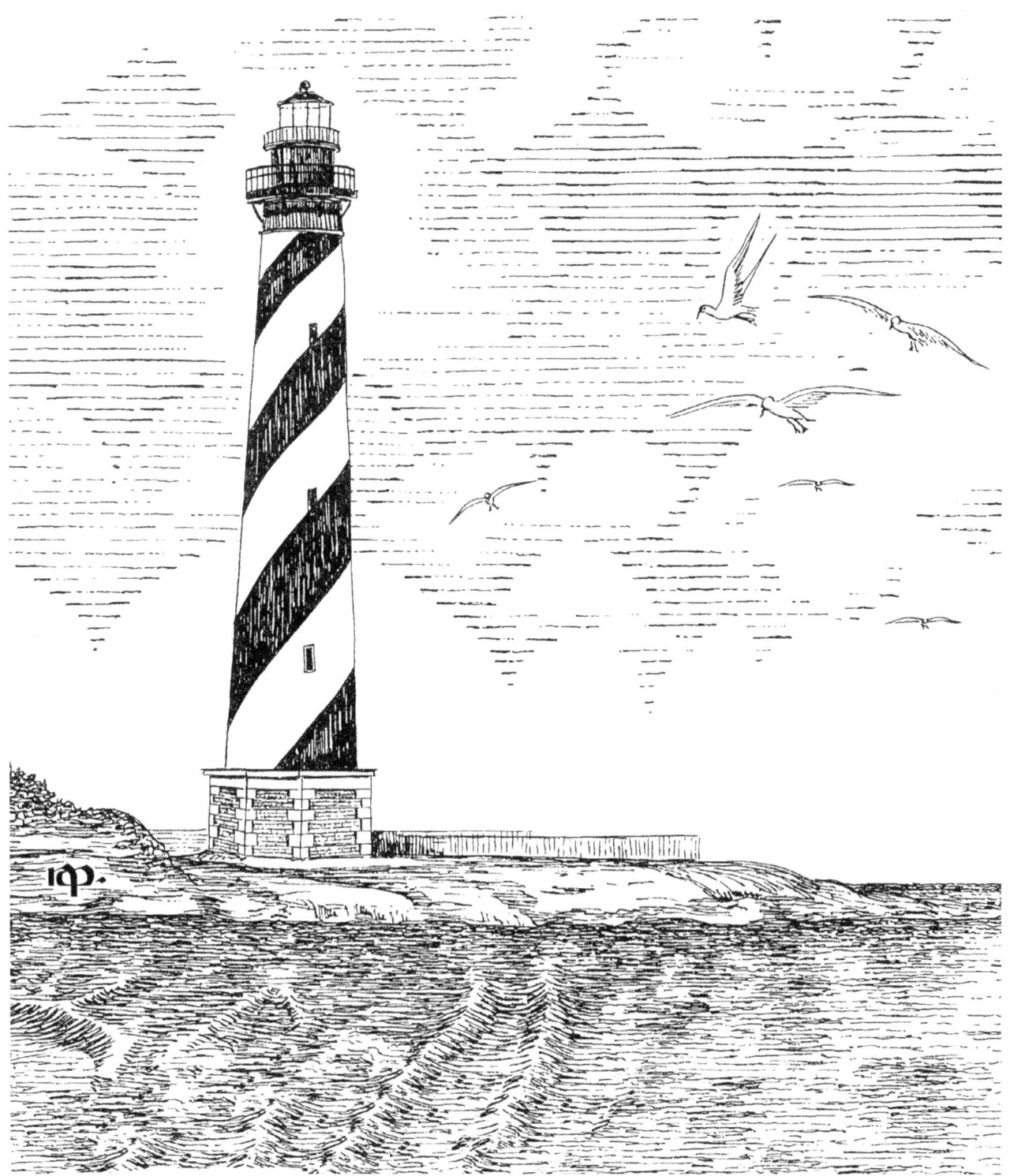

Cape Hatteras Lighthouse

Carl Sandburg Home

Flat Rock, North Carolina,

The Carl Sandburg Home National Historic Site is located in the village of Flat Rock, near Hendersonville, North Carolina. It preserves the Connemara Farms, home of Pulitzer Prize-winning poet and writer Carl Sandburg.

Sandburg was born in Galesburg, Illinois January 6, 1878. The family was poor, and he left school at age thirteen to work. After serving in the Spanish-American War, he returned to school and worked his way through Lombard College in Galesburg.

After college Sandburg moved to Milwaukee, where he met and married Lillian Steichen. The couple moved to Chicago, and he became an editorial writer for the Chicago Daily News.

Harriett Monroe published his poetry in her new magazine, and it was very popular; however, his fascination with Abraham Lincoln caused him to do extensive research for 30 years and eventually produce six large volumes.

He was awarded a Pulitzer Prize in history for his Lincoln books in 1939 and then received a second Pulitzer for poetry in 1950.

Mrs. Sandburg had been looking for a new farm in a warmer climate to raise her Chikaming dairy goats. They were both impressed with Connemara.

They purchased the farm in 1945, and moved to North Carolina.

It provided the peace and solitude required for his writing and the more than 30 acres of pastureland required for his wife to raise her champion dairy goats. Sandburg spent the last twenty-two years of his life on this farm and published more than a third of his works while he resided here.

Sandburg died at this house in 1967. After his death, Lillian sold the farm to the government to preserve the house as a memorial to her husband. Mrs. Sandburg signed a deed of gift in June 1968, and in October President Johnson approved a congressional act making it an historic site.

The home officially opened to the public in 1974, and the Carl Sandburg National Historic site now attracts more than 26,000 visitors a year. The U.S. government designated the goats an historic herd.

The National Historic site includes the Sandburg residence, the goat farm, sheds, rolling pastures, mountainside woods, 5 miles of hiking trails on moderate to steep terrain, two small lakes, several ponds, both flower and vegetable gardens, as well as an apple orchard.

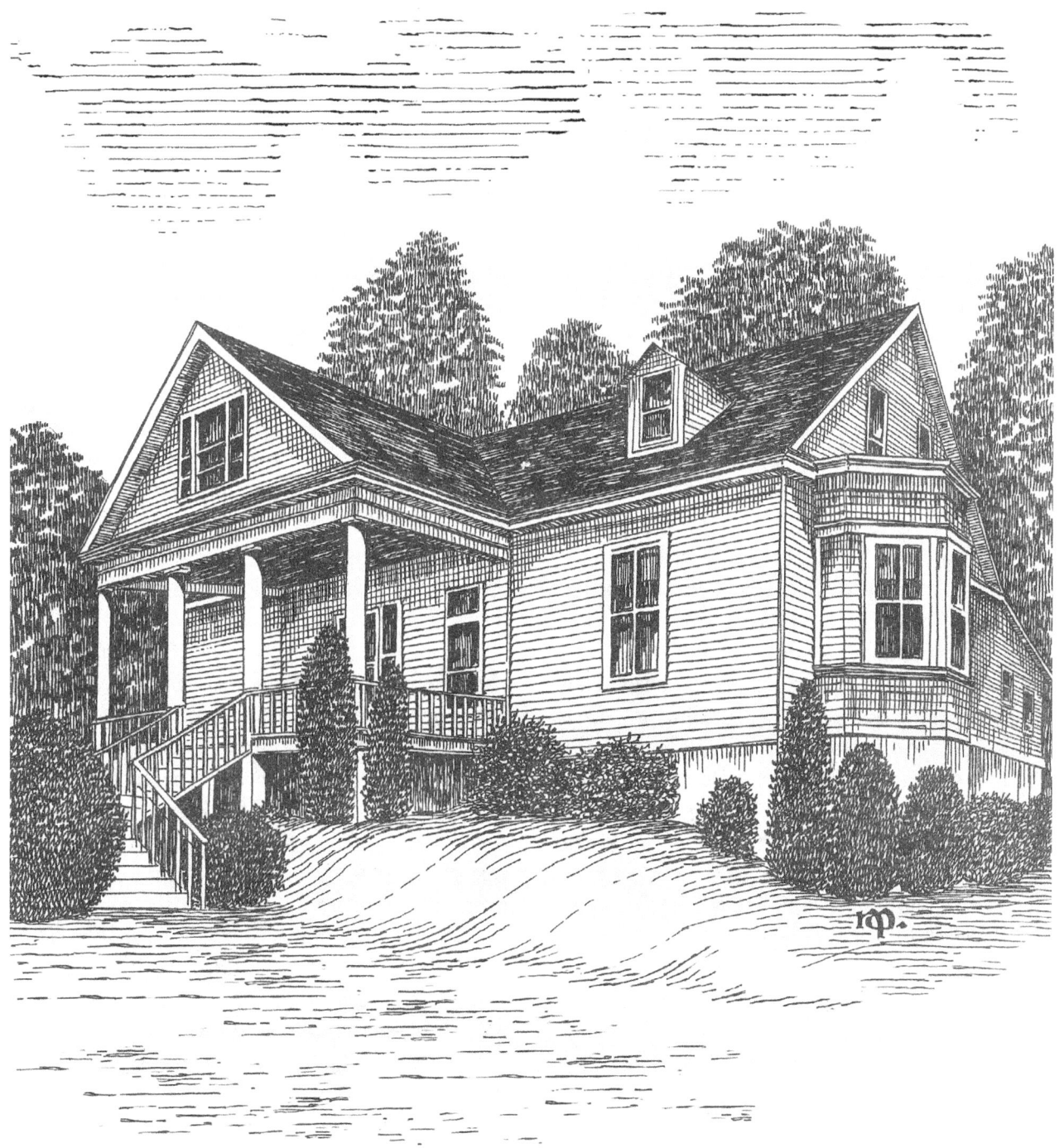

Carl Sandburg Home

Cass Scenic Railroad

Cass, West Virginia

Nestled in the mountains of West Virginia, Cass Scenic Railroad State Park offers excursions that transport visitors back in time to relive an era when steam-driven locomotives were an essential part of everyday life.

Located in Pocahontas County, West Virginia, the park consists of the Cass Scenic Railroad, an 11-mile long heritage railroad that is owned by the state of West Virginia; the former company town of Cass, and a portion of the summit of Bald Knob, highest point on Back Allegheny Mountain.

The town of Cass remains relatively unchanged since its founding in 1901. The restored company buildings add to the charm and atmosphere. The Cass Scenic Railroad uses the same line built in 1901 to haul lumber from the mountains to the mill in Cass.

The town was founded by the West Virginia Pulp & Paper Company. Cass was built as a company town to serve the needs of the men who worked in the nearby mountains cutting spruce and hemlock for the West Virginia Spruce Lumber Company, a subsidiary of WVP&P.

At one time, the sawmill at Cass was the largest double-band sawmill in the world. It processed an estimated 1.25 billion board feet of lumber during its lifetime.

The locomotives are the same ones used here and in the rain forests of British Columbia for more than half a century. Old logging flat-cars have been refurbished and converted into passenger cars. Hundreds of pounds of steam pressure start the wheels turning to move the locomotive.

The train travels through the scenic mountains to Whittaker Station, where there is a 1940s logging camp.

The Lidgerwood tower skidder is one of two examples known to exist anywhere in the world. These huge railcar-mounted machines carried logs out of the woods on aerial cables high in the air for distances up to 3000 feet.

There are different trips available ranging up to four and one-half hours, where the engines are required to take on additional water at a spring, before climbing to Bald Knob, the 2nd highest point in West Virginia, at an altitude of 4,842 feet.

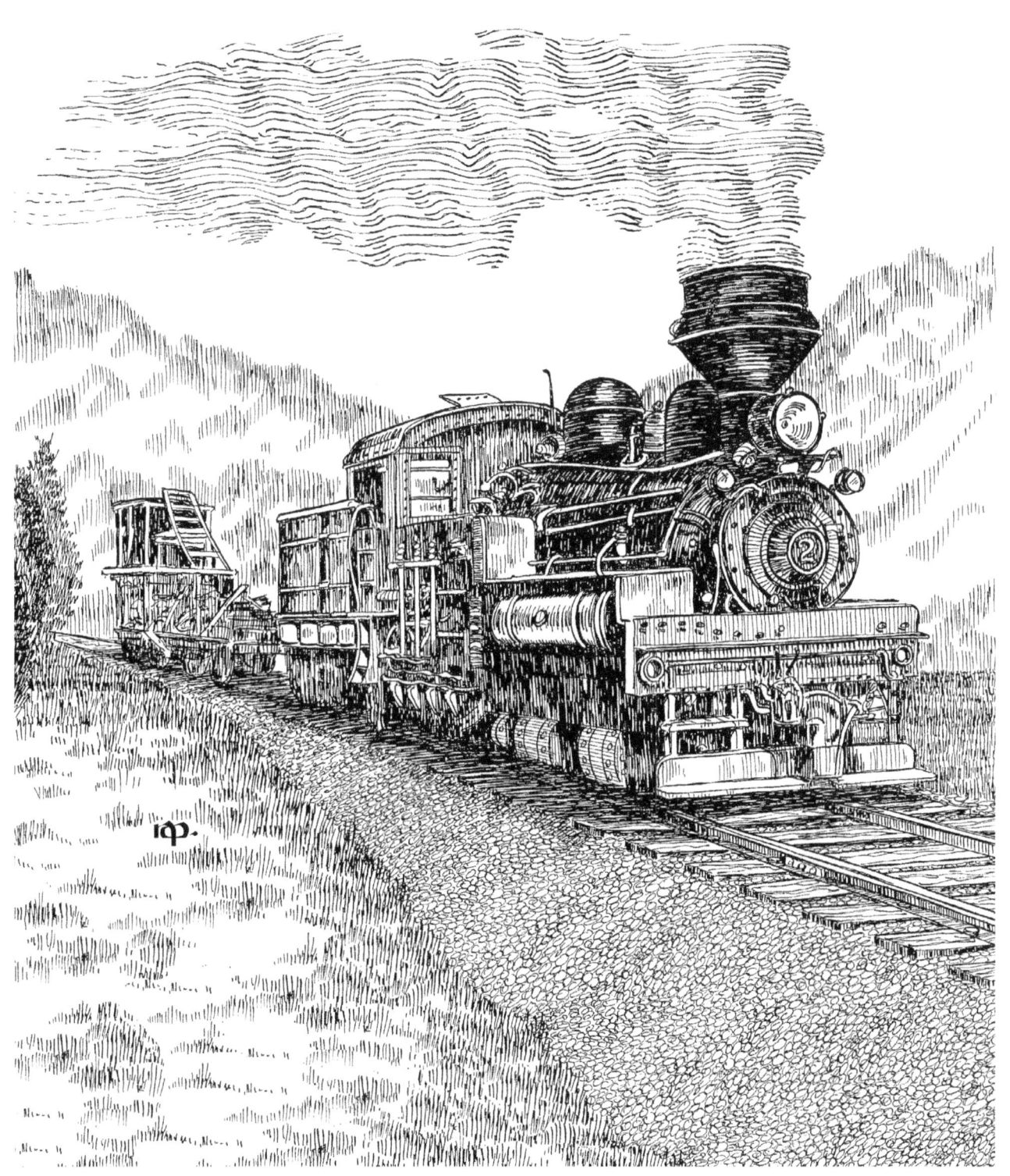

Cass Scenic Railroad

Chained Rock

Pineville, Kentucky

Sitting high above Pineville in southeastern Kentucky, an enormous chain spans the gap between a great boulder and Pine Mountain.

This landmark was spawned from a myth, that the giant rock would come crashing down to destroy the town.

In the 1930s a group of citizens in Pineville created a story which was carried in more than 6,000 newspapers across the nation and brought droves of visitors to this secluded area.

Pat Caton proposed to the Pineville Kiwanis Club to chain the threatening boulder. His plan was accepted and a group was formed, which soon became known as the Chained Rock Club.

A chain weighing nearly 3,000 pounds was located nearby in Virginia on an obsolete steam shovel. The owner, W.B. Paynter of Middlesboro donated the chain for the project, and it was transported to the foot of Pine Mountain. At this point Arthur Asher, a logging operator, and Tom Hodd, a mule skinner, took charge.

Three mules pulled the enormous chain halfway up the mountain before they gave completely out. Then the Kiwanians, a group of Boy Scouts, the Civilian Conservation Corps and several interested onlookers took over.

Holes were hand drilled into the rock and pins that were more than an inch wide and 24 inches long were inserted. A set of triple block and tackle ropes were fastened to the chain and fifty men and a mule team pulled the chain across the breach.

The chain was secured with iron rods in the large boulder. The task was completed June 24, 1933.

A telegram of appreciation was immediately sent to the group by Kentucky Governor Ruby Laffoon, and the press gave national coverage.

Chained Rock is now part of Pine Mountain State Resort Park. The park opened in 1924 as Kentucky's first state park. Each spring, the park hosts the annual Kentucky Mountain Laurel Festival; as it has since the festival's inception in 1931.

When Pine Mountain State Resort Park was established in 1926, it was named Cumberland State Park. The name was changed in 1938 in order to avoid confusion with the newly formed Cumberland Falls State Resort Park.

The beautiful park serves as one of southeastern Kentucky's premier state parks, and the Chained Rock continues to draw droves of curious spectators.

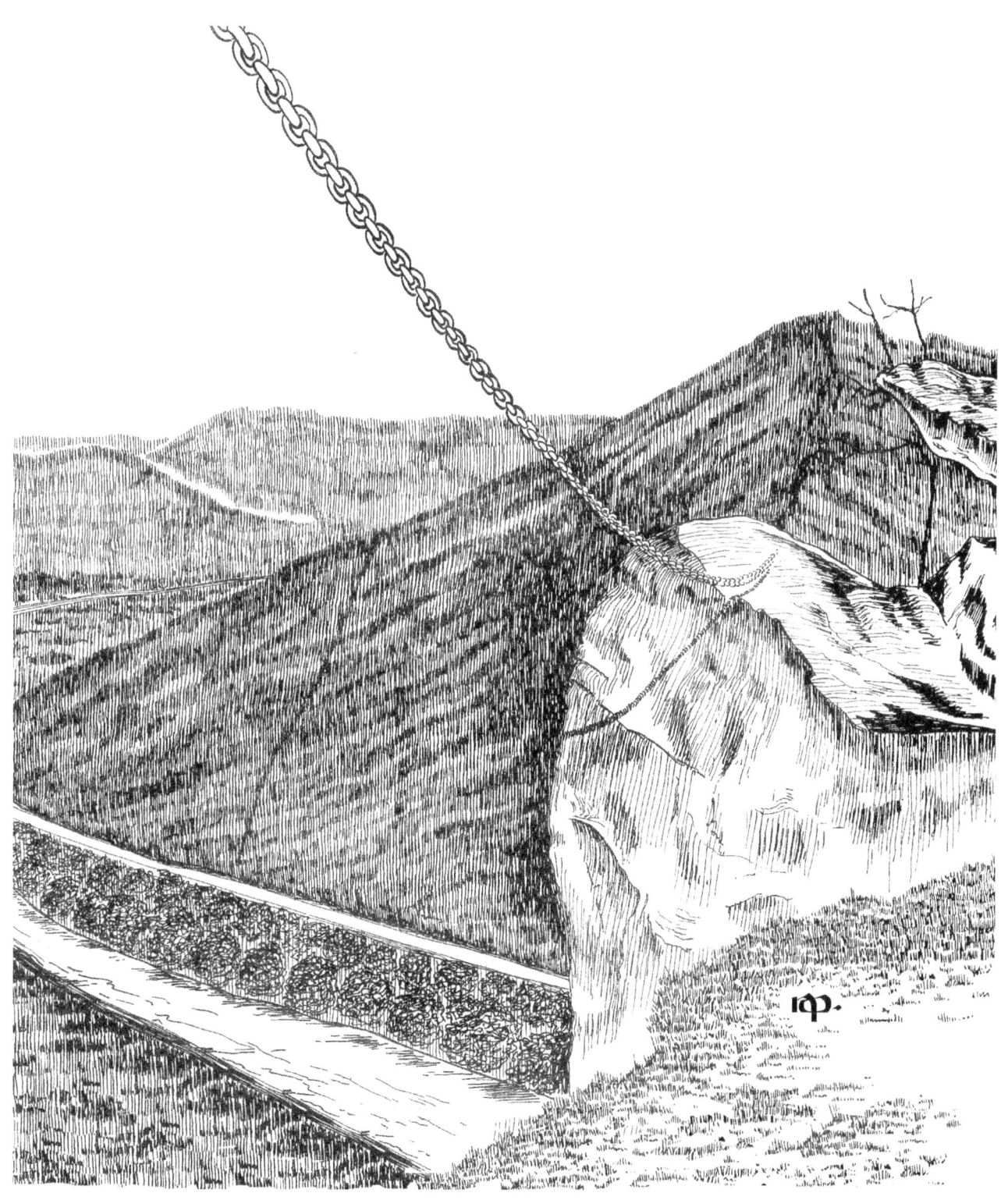

Chained Rock

Clara Barton House

Glen Echo, Maryland

The Clara Barton National Historic Site, which includes the Clara Barton House, was established in 1974 to interpret the life of Clara Barton (1821–1912), an American pioneer teacher, nurse, and humanitarian who was the founder of the American Red Cross.

The site is located just two miles northwest of Washington D.C. in Glen Echo, Maryland.

This was the first national historic site dedicated to the accomplishments of a woman. It preserves the history of the American Red Cross. Clara Barton spent the last 15 years of her life in her Glen Echo home, and it served as an early headquarters of the American Red Cross as well as her home.

The United States National Historic Site protects 9 acres of land at her Glen Echo house including the 38-room former residence of Barton. The site is managed by the George Washington Memorial Parkway.

The enormous frame house was partially constructed from lumber that was salvaged from the emergency buildings built by the Red Cross at Johnstown, Pennsylvania in the wake of the Johnstown Flood of 1889.

The lumber of various dismantled buildings was brought to Washington via the Chesapeake and Ohio Canal to avoid flooding the local market in the Johnstown area.

The lumber was stored on a lot owned by Barton in Washington D.C. until early in 1891 when construction began on land that was donated by Edwin and Edward Baltzley.

The house was designed by Dr. Julian B. Hubbell, the first field agent of the American Red Cross. Hubbell oversaw the construction work. The original structure included a massive stone front. In 1897, when Barton moved into the house, the central part of the stone facade was dismantled, creating flanking stone towers.

The Clara Barton House was listed on the National Register of Historic Places in 1974.

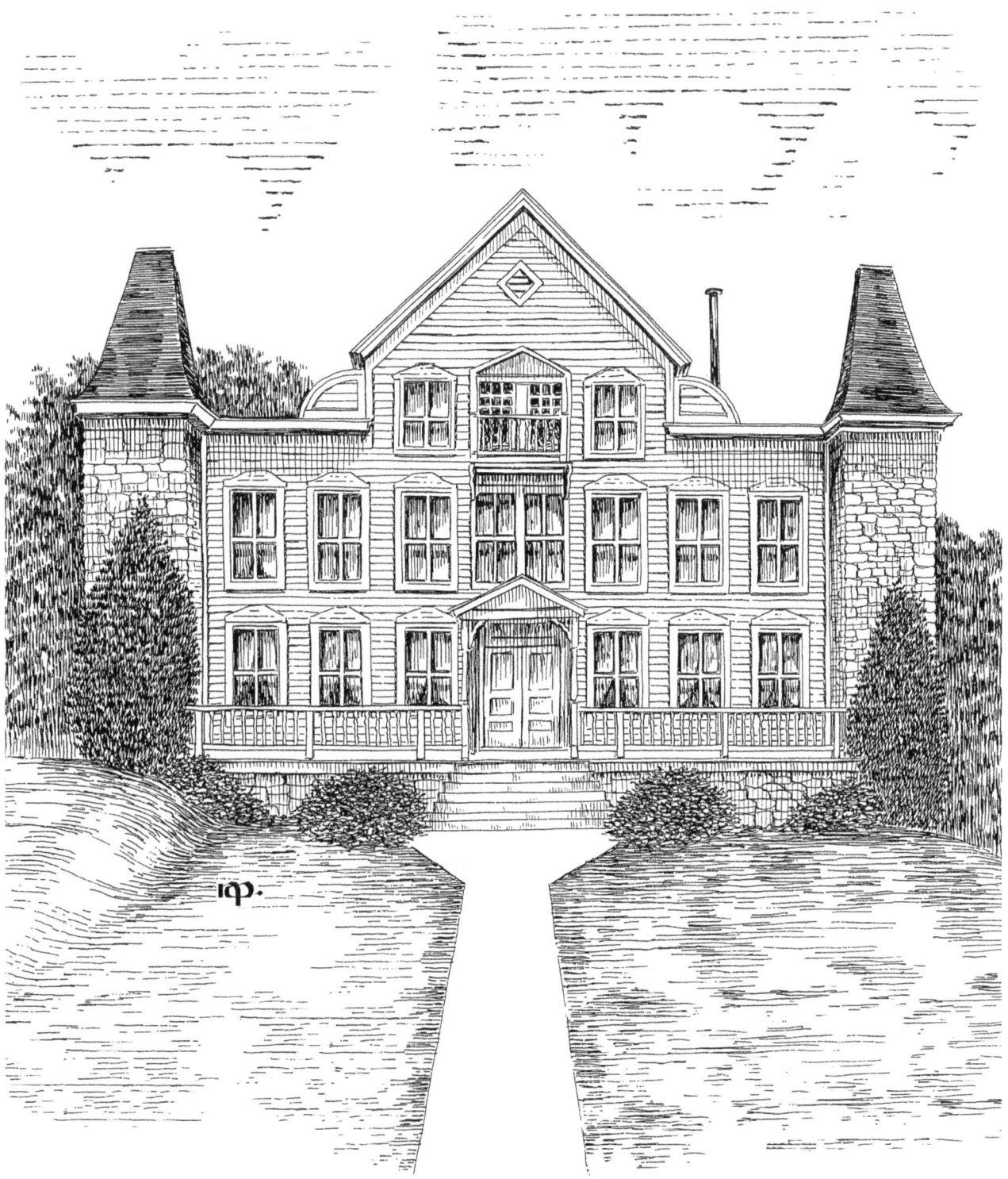

Clara Barton House

Claude Moore Colonial Farm

Langley, Virginia

The Claude Moore Colonial Farm at Turkey Run, Virginia is a living history site which demonstrates life on a small farm in northern Virginia prior to the American Revolutionary War.

Staff and volunteers dress in period clothes, work the farm, and answer questions about the 18th century farm and family. The mission of Turkey Run is to recreate the life of 1771 tenant farmers. The vast majority of Virginians in 1771 were tenant farmers who grew tobacco to pay their rent and grew their own food to eat.

The property includes twelve acres planted with corn, tobacco, wheat, flax, rye, barley; a kitchen garden and an orchard. The small log house was the family dwelling; meals are prepared over the hearth fire with food raised on the farm.

Turkey Run is the only privately run park in the U.S. National Park Service. The Friends of Claude Moore Colonial Farm at Turkey Run Inc., a privately funded foundation, pays for all activities on the farm, while the land is owned by the NPS. An annual stipend is provided from the Park Service.

The Farm is located in Langley, Virginia, next to George Bush Center for Intelligence and behind the Turner-Fairbank Highway Research Center.

Originally named Turkey Run Farm when it opened in July 1973 as a National Park Service operation, it was renamed in 1981 for Dr. Claude Moore, whose large bequest at the time of his death allowed the farm park to establish itself as the only autonomous site in the park system.

The Farm operation has expanded its facilities over the years. The Gate House Giftshop was built to replace the old on-your-honor admission fee drop box and an event deck and the Bounty Garden were all added at the front parking lot during the last decade.

An access road was cut through the upper pasture so that access to the farm office no longer passes through the security gate of the Federal Highway Administration headquarters, behind the CIA grounds.

Turkey Run is run by a small paid professional staff, supplemented by many volunteers.

The interpretive staff includes preteens and teenagers who portray the farm children. Staff and volunteers demonstrate living history so visitors feel as if they've stepped back in time.

The Farm's heirloom crops and heritage breed livestock are carefully researched to provide as accurate an atmosphere as possible.

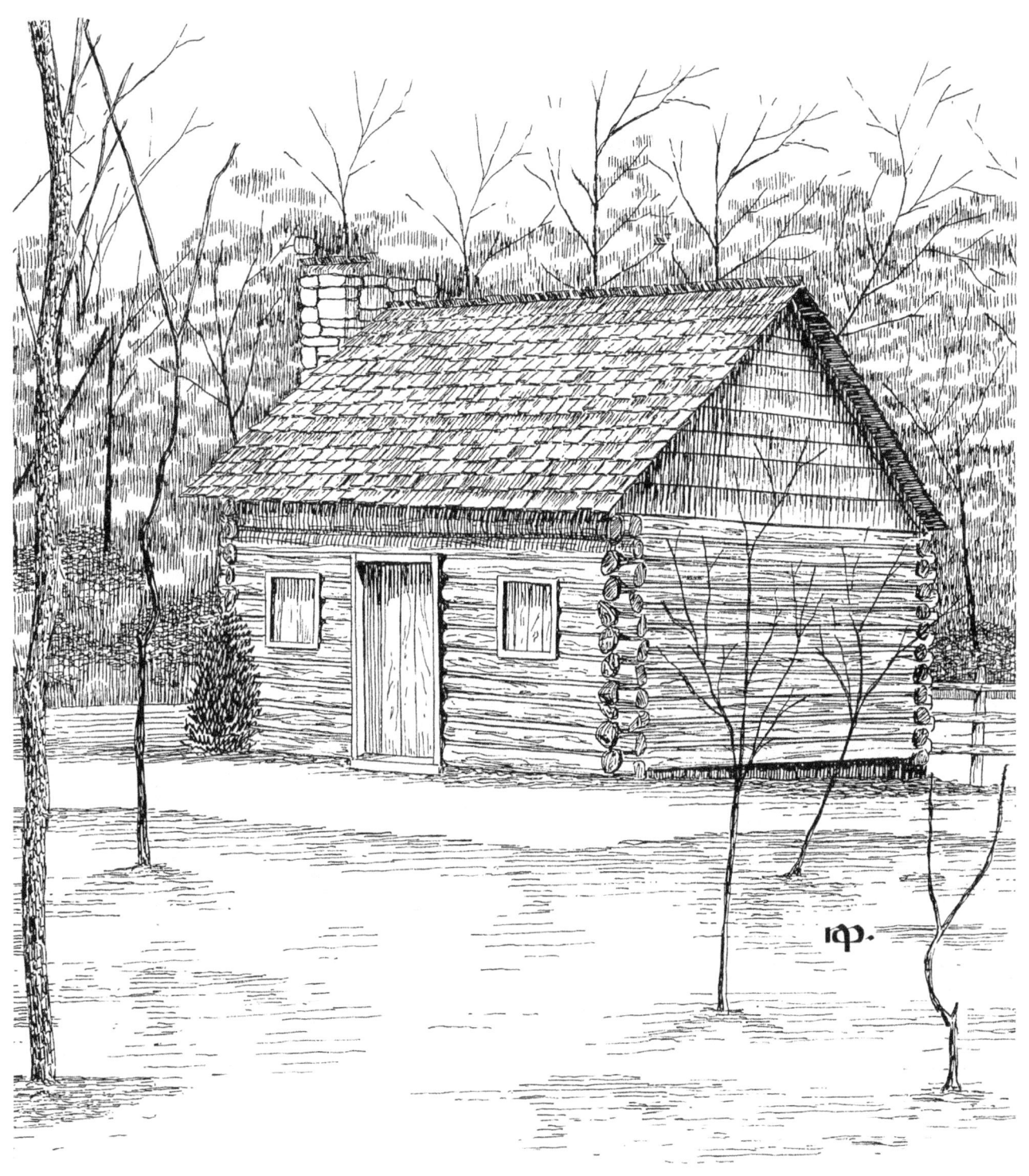

Claude Moore Colonial Farm

Coal Monument

Baxter, Kentucky

The Coal Monument at Baxter in Harlan County was erected in 1932 to publicly commemorate the coal miner and the coal industry.

The marker has long served as a directional finder; at a point where U.S. 421 and Highway 119 meet. Travelers are directed to either Hyden, Harlan, or Cumberland, Kentucky.

It was built with funds donated by Charlie Cole while he was President of the Harlan Kiwanis Club. The bridge in the background has been a main thoroughfare into the county since it was constructed in 1924.

Coal has been one of Kentucky's most valuable resources since the early pioneers ventured into the wilderness paradise that was literally filled with an abundance of natural resources.

Coal has played a major role in the development of the Commonwealth. Coal was exported to England as early as 1851, via New Orleans. It was used for gas manufacture.

However, discovery of petroleum and the Civil War were instrumental in halting that operation.

The extended veins of coal can be found in two totally separated parts of Kentucky; in the eastern bituminous Appalachian fields and also in the coal fields in the western part of the state.

Between 1880 and 1905, "rights" buyers swarmed into eastern Kentucky to secure mineral rights from the mountain landowners.

In the early 1900s, the railroad made their way into the eastern coal fields and opened the markets to every part of the nation and world.

Using modern equipment, the coal mines of eastern Kentucky boosted the state's production to nearly 39,000,000 tons in 1920.

Three railroads - The Louisville & Nashville, Chesapeake & Ohio and Norfolk & Western - combined efforts to lay tracks throughout the entire Appalachian coal producing region.

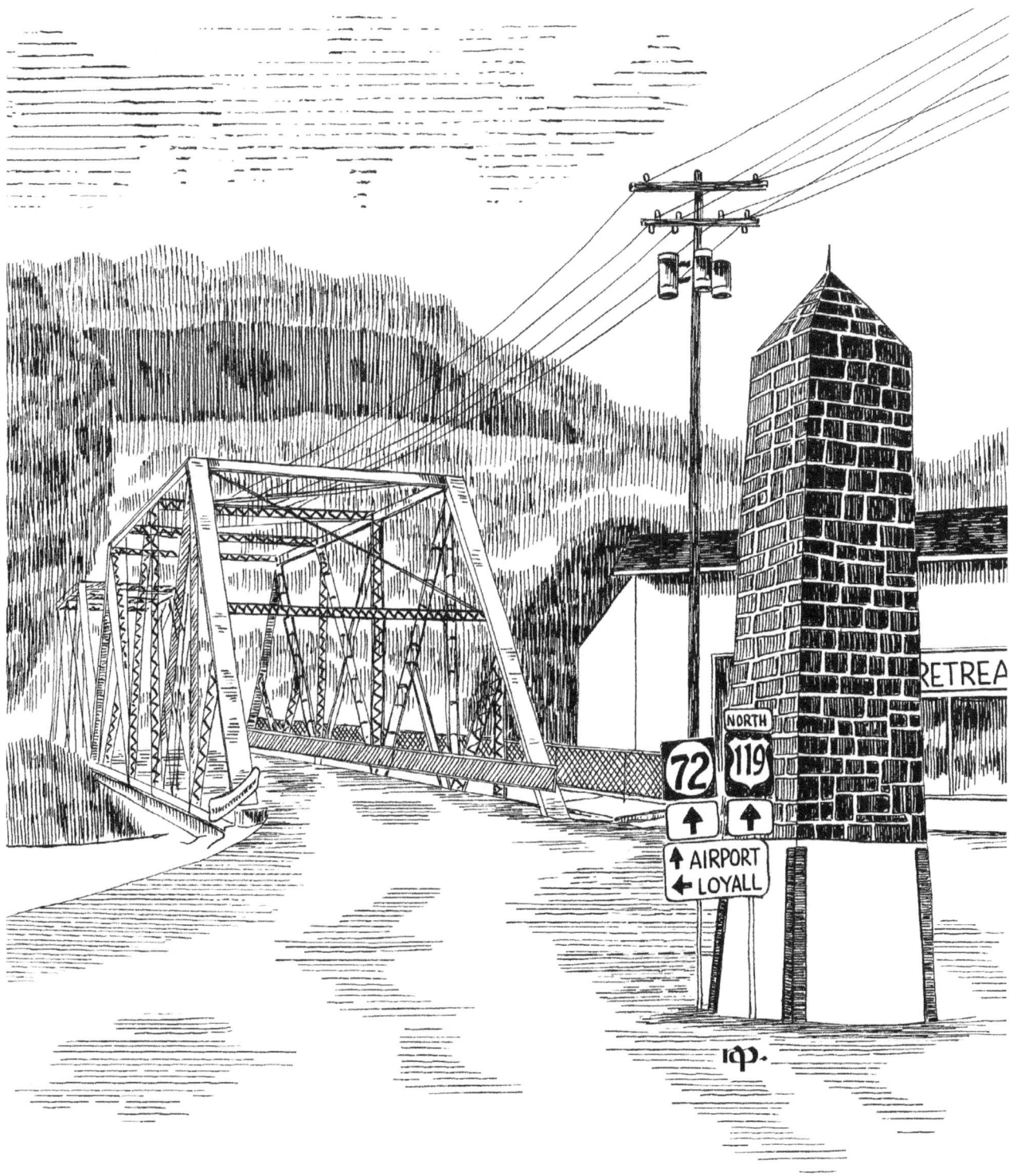

Coal Monument

Columbus-Belmont Battlefield

Columbus, Kentucky

Columbus-Belmont State Park, on the shores of the Mississippi River near Columbus, Kentucky, is the site of a Confederate fortification built during the American Civil War.

The site was considered by both North and South to be strategically significant in gaining and keeping control of the Mississippi River.

Confederate General Leonidas Polk fortified the area now occupied by the park beginning in September of 1861. The fort at Columbus was built upon a bluff along the huge river, and was christened Fort DeRussey, but Polk referred it as "Gibraltar of the West."

Polk equipped the bluff with a massive chain that was stretched across the Mississippi River to Belmont, Missouri, to block the passage of Union gunboats and supply vessels to and from Southern destinations via the mighty Mississippi.

Equipped also with 143 cannons, Columbus was the Northern-most Confederate base along the Mississippi River, protecting Memphis, Vicksburg and other key Southern holdings.

As the northern terminus of the Mobile and Ohio Railroad, Columbus was logistically tied to all Confederate supply lines.

Many of the earthen fortifications, buildings and artillery pieces were lost to erosion of the bluff during heavy flooding in the 1920s.

When the flooding receded in 1925, the giant chain was exposed, and the people of Columbus decided to save it for future generations.

The town of Columbus was moved after the floods of 1927; land for a park was deeded to the city in exchange for home sites for the relocation. The area containing the park was purchased by the state of Kentucky in 1934.

The purchase of Louisiana from France in 1803 and the burning of the national Capitol at Washington, D.C. caused great concern.

Speculation that this approximate new center of the United States would be the best possible location for a new seat of government, away from the sea.

Columbus was designed, and a military post was formed here in 1804. A settlement quickly sprang up and a courthouse and jail were built.

Engineers promptly laid out plans for the city of Columbus as the new capital. However, promoters were not successful in relocating the capital, but the name remained.

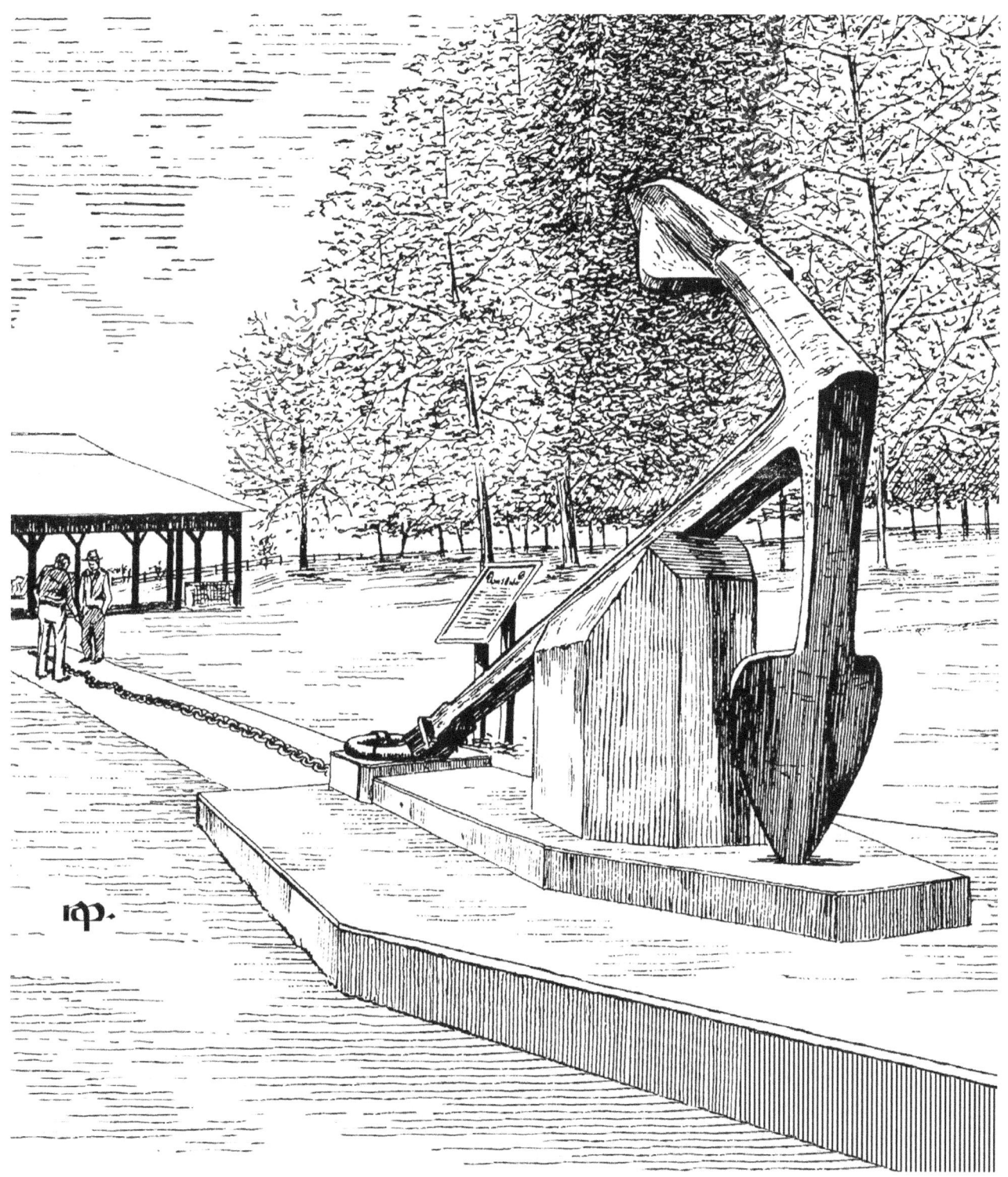

Columbus-Belmont Battlefield

Cumberland Falls

Corbin, Kentucky

Perhaps the most famous natural landmark in all of Kentucky is located on the Cumberland River in the rugged hills near Corbin, where the river cuts its way over a rocky course.

When the possibility of building a hydroelectric power plant on the Cumberland River above the falls surfaced in 1927, Kentucky native T. Coleman du Pont offered to buy the falls and surrounding acreage in order to create a state park.

He died before the state agreed to develop a park, but his wife purchased the falls and the 593 acres surrounding it for $400,000 on March 10, 1930. The Kentucky General Assembly did approve the creation of the state park, and Cumberland Falls was dedicated as a state park on August 21, 1931.

Cumberland Falls itself is 68 feet high and 125 feet across; it has an average flow of 3,600 cubic feet of water per second.

Immediately behind the curtain of water is a recess in the rock wall which makes it possible for one to go almost completely across the river through an arch formed of rock on one side and flashing water on the other.

In the river immediately below the falls are many whirlpools and rapids, as it flows for seven miles through a boulder-strewn gorge. The park is also the home of 44-foot Eagle Falls.

The steep slopes and ravines contain a great variety of forest growth: hemlock, tulip, magnolia, sweetgum, oak, dogwood, yellow pine and large holly trees. St. John's-wort, blueberry, rhododendron, Stewartia, spicebush, azalea, and strawberry bush are among the many plants found in the area.

The most phenomenal and famous feature of Cumberland Falls is the magnificent double moonbow. In the full moon, a spectrum formed in the midst of the falls is more beautiful than a rainbow. It is the only one to be seen in the Western Hemisphere.

The 900,000-acre Daniel Boone National Forest encircles Cumberland Falls State Park.

The Cumberland River was named in honor of the Duke of Cumberland, son of King George II, and the forest was called Cumberland National Forest until it was renamed in 1966 to honor frontiersman Daniel Boone.

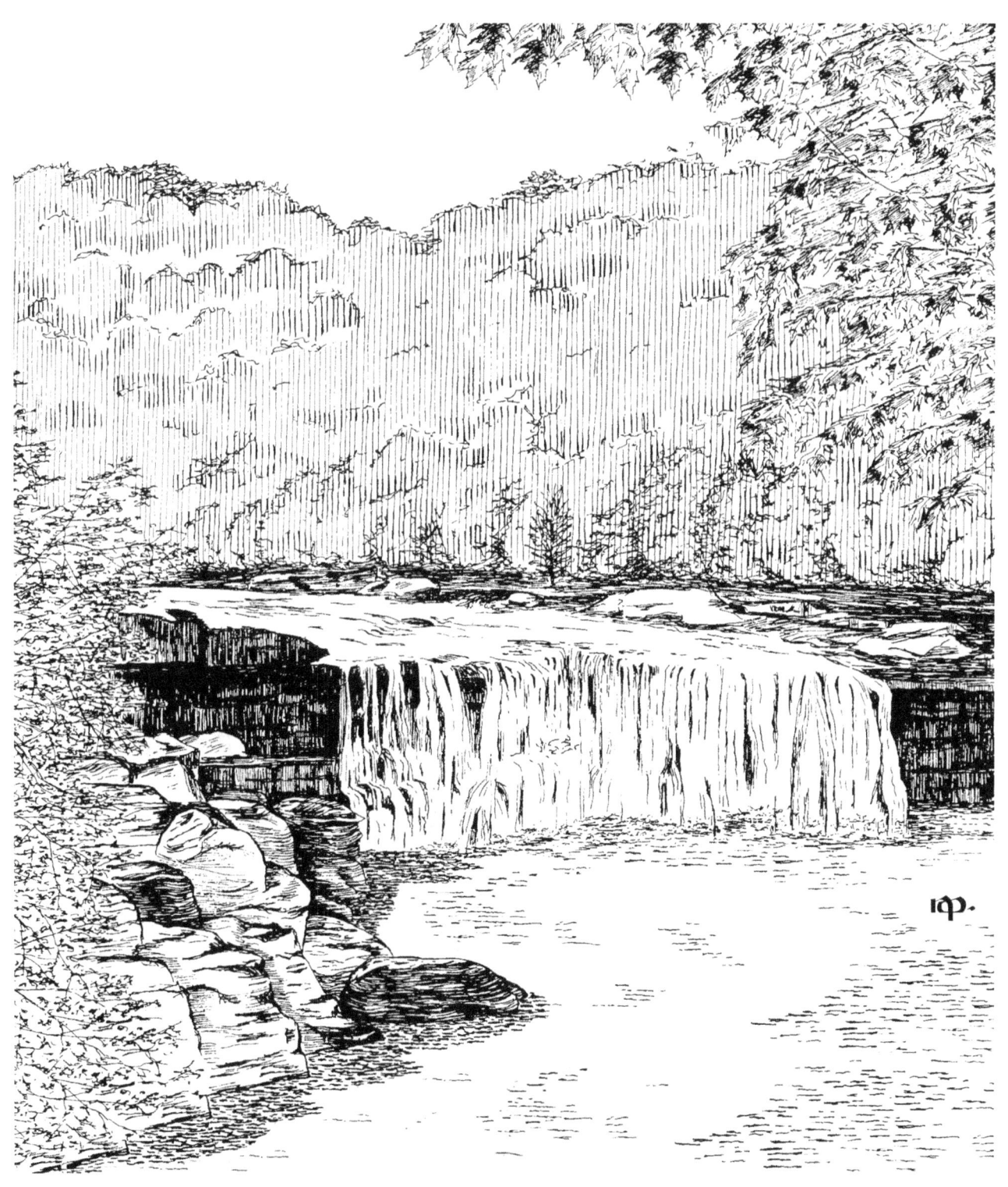

Cumberland Falls

Cumberland Gap Furnace

Cumberland Gap, Tennessee

A vast number of Iron furnaces dotted the countryside throughout the 1800s and had a great impact on the development of our nation. As the pioneers moved west, time and travel to the eastern seacoast created a need to supply the essentials for daily living.

Frontiersmen needed such items as rifles, broad axes, and utensils for cooking, which were all made of iron.

Built in 1819 at a great financial investment, this particular iron furnace proved to be one of the cornerstones in frontier development. It employed up to 300 men, and provided jobs and a lifestyle in this passageway into the Kentucky wilderness and beyond.

All that remains is the lower part of the original 30-foot-high blast furnace. It is actually a very small part of what was originally an entire complex known as the Newlee Iron Furnace.

The furnace was located here not by chance but because of the vast resources mentioned by Dr. Thomas Walker in his 1750 expedition.

The furnace itself was built 30 feet high with a hearth or a crucible where the molten iron was collected, perhaps a foot or two deep and three to four feet wide. Just above the hearth, the opening flared outward and was termed the "bosh." The bosh was about eight feet in diameter at its widest and narrowed as it converged to the top.

The outside of the furnace was built of sandstone with a liner of durable firebrick. Furnaces were usually built with an incline just behind to ease charging and loading.

The trestle leading to the charging point was usually built of heavy planks with a track on it. Men would roll the wheelbarrows of raw materials over this trestle and dump them into the top of the furnace.

The furnace required 200 bushels of charcoal, 2 tons of iron ore, and 500 pounds of limestone. These were all joined inside the furnace to produce approximately one ton of iron.

Waterwheel-powered bellows kept the fires hot. It took 4 to 6 hours to produce molten iron, with a layer of slag floating on top. The slag would be drained off through the "cinder hole," and then the molten iron would be drained through the "tap hole" below.

The daily product of the Newlee Iron Furnace was 3 and 1/4 tons of pig iron in the 1800s. The iron made at this Cumberland Gap facility was then shipped down the Powell River to Chattanooga.

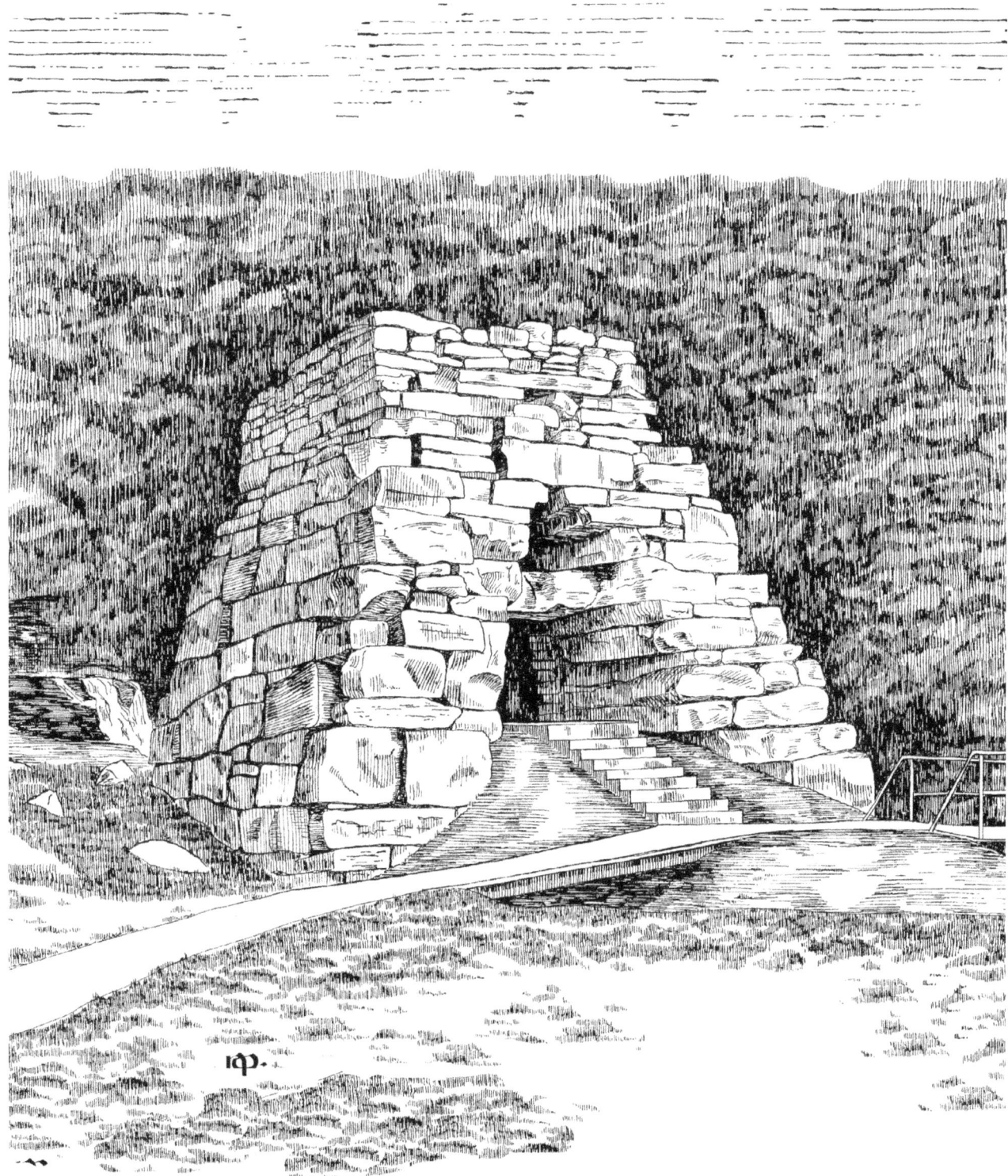

Cumberland Gap Furnace

Cumberland Gap Tunnels

Kentucky - Tennessee

Technology for the future was utilized to preserve one of the most famous and historic routes in America.

In this unique section of the vast Appalachian mountains, where the three states of Kentucky, Tennessee and Virginia meet, the trailblazers and pioneers ventured westward through a notch in the mountains known as the Cumberland Gap.

Two 4600-feet long tunnels were cut through solid rock with very little environmental impact. Seventeen years in the making, these twin vehicular tunnels, nearly a mile in length, join the state of Kentucky with Tennessee and Virginia. The tunnels allow travelers a safe and convenient journey through the extremely rough terrain.

A joint venture of the Federal Highway Administration and the National Park System, this challenging project rerouted a major highway to enable restoration of the area to resemble the path used by the pioneers heading westward from the Atlantic coast in the late 1700s.

Cumberland Gap National Park proudly serves nearly 2 million visitors each year. It is a memorial to those dedicated pioneers and trailblazers who ventured westward into the frontier of Kentucky and onward.

Even in the late 1970s, road traffic through the park had increased to the point of being unmanageable, and the project to replace the surface road began in 1980. However, construction did not begin until 1991.

It was decided that widening the existing road to four lanes would have an adverse affect on the historically sensitive areas in the park, making a tunnel the only viable choice.

As a part of the plan, the existing road through Cumberland Gap was then removed and restored as a wagon path similar to that used by early 19th-century travelers.

Kentucky and Tennessee both widened their portions of U.S. 25E leading to the Cumberland Gap tunnels to accommodate four lanes of traffic.

Construction of the actual tubes began on June 21, 1991. Excavation continued simultaneously from both sides, and the tunnels were joined on July 9, 1992. The tunnels opened to traffic on October 18, 1996.

The tunnel replaced a 2.3-mile stretch of U.S. 25E from Middlesboro, through historic Cumberland Gap into Tennessee. It was known as "Massacre Mountain" due to the large number of travelers killed on the twisting section of mountain road over the pass.

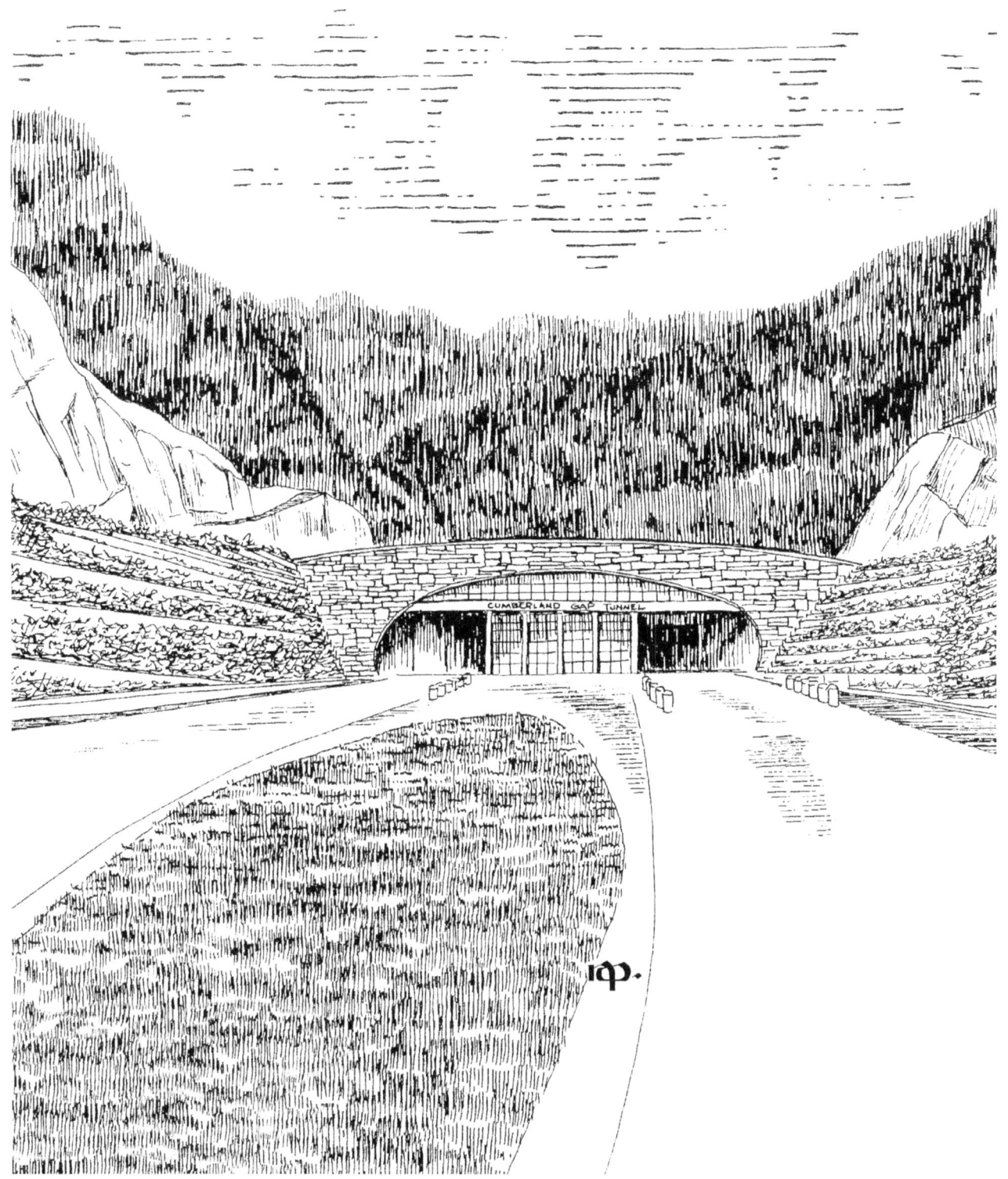

Cumberland Gap Tunnels

Farmington

Louisville, Kentucky

At the end of a long, narrow tree-lined lane near the intersection of the Watterson Expressway and Bardstown Road in Louisville, stands a prominent edifice known as Farmington.

This 18-acre historic site was once the center of a hemp plantation owned by John & Lucy Speed. The 14-room, Federal-style brick home was built in 1810. It is based on plans drawn by Thomas Jefferson, which are now in the Coolidge Library in Massachusetts Historical Society.

The property was part of a military land grant given to Captain James Speed in 1780. His son, John Speed, built the house for his wife, Lucy Gilmer Fry, daughter of Joshua Fry and granddaughter of Dr. Thomas Walker, guardian of Thomas Jefferson. Lucy's aunt and uncle had a home in Charlottesville, Virginia that was called Farmington. It had an addition that was designed by Thomas Jefferson.

A notable feature of the first floor are two 24-foot wide octagonal rooms, a rather distinctive feature of the Jeffersonian architecture.

The deed to the property was signed by Gov. Patrick Henry of Virginia in 1780, twelve years before Kentucky became a state.

Judge John Speed and Lucy Fry were married in 1808 and shortly thereafter work was begun on this large house, which stands saliently on a high basement, allowing for a magnificent stair-stepped entrance.

Their son, Joshua Fry Speed, met Abraham Lincoln when the two lived in Springfield, Illinois. They became close friends, and while Lincoln was courting Mary Todd, he spent three weeks at Farmington in the summer of 1841.

Throughout Lincoln's presidency, Joshua Speed was summoned often to the White House as an adviser. James Speed, his older brother, served as U.S. Attorney General in Lincoln's cabinet and he was with the President when he died.

The Historic Homes Foundation acquired the Speed House in 1957 and restored it to its original condition as a tourist attraction and a re-creation of a 19th-century plantation.

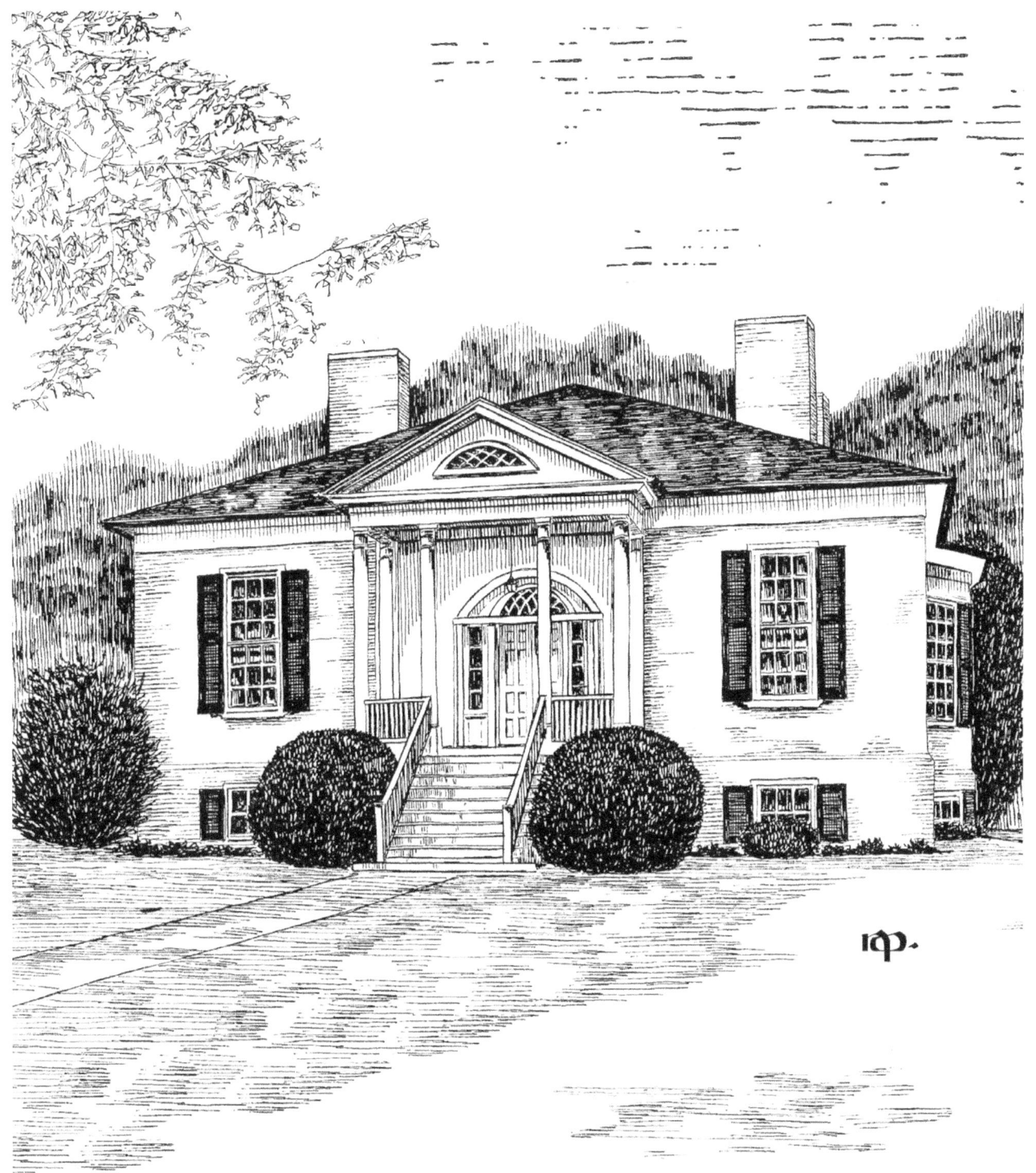

Farmington

Fort Jefferson

Garden Key, Florida

Fort Jefferson is located on Garden Key, the central island of the Dry Tortugas Islands, 68 miles west of Key West, Florida. It was constructed to help protect the Florida Straits.

The massive coastal fortress is the largest masonry structure in all the Americas. It is composed of over 16 million bricks; the largest all-masonry fortification in the Western world. The Fort Jefferson Light is still operational.

In late December 1824 and early January 1825, about five years after Spain sold Florida to the United States; U.S. Navy Commodore David Porter inspected the Dry Tortugas Islands. He was looking for a site for a naval station that would help suppress piracy in the Caribbean. Porter was not impressed; he notified the Secretary of the Navy the Dry Tortugas were unfit for any naval establishment.

However, the government thought the islands were a good location for a lighthouse to guide ships around the area's reefs and islands.

A small island called Bush Key, later named Garden Key, was selected as the site for the lighthouse, which became known as Garden Key Light.

Construction began in 1825 and was completed in 1826. The 65-foot lighthouse was constructed of brick with a whitewashed exterior.

Several others disagreed with Porter's assessment of the area for a fort. The construction of Fort Jefferson (named for the third President, Thomas Jefferson) was begun on Garden Key in 1846. The new fort was built so that the existing Garden Key lighthouse and the lighthouse keeper's cottage were contained within the walls of the fort.

The lighthouse continued to serve a vital function in guiding ships through the waters of the Dry Tortugas Islands until it was eventually replaced in 1877.

President Franklin D. Roosevelt designated the area as Fort Jefferson National Monument in 1935, and it was listed on the National Register in 1970.

In 1992 the Dry Tortugas, with Fort Jefferson, was established as a National Park. The islands still do not contain any fresh water, hence the name "dry". The island is accessible only by boat or sea plane.

The Dry Tortugas islands are part of Monroe County, about 70 miles west of Key West. A ferry boat runs a scheduled route between the two.

The park boasts famous bird and marine life sanctuaries as well as legends of pirates and sunken gold. It is open to the public, but visitors must bring all necessities with them, including food and water

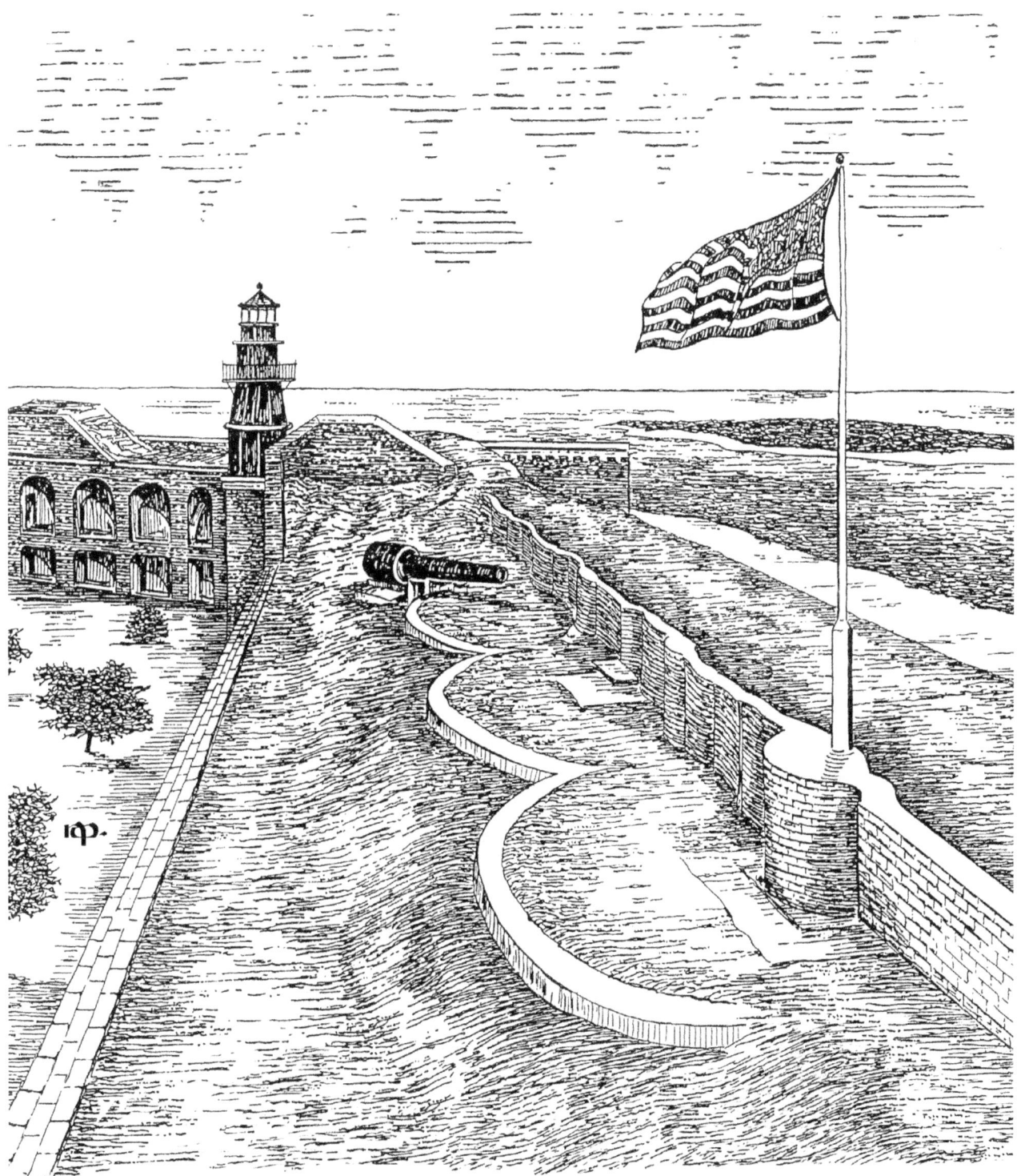

Fort Jefferson

Fort McHenry

Baltimore, Maryland

Fort McHenry National Monument and Historic Shrine is located in Baltimore, Maryland. This 18th century star-shaped fort is world famous as the birthplace of the National Anthem.

This coastal fort is best known for its role in the War of 1812, when it successfully defended the Baltimore Harbor from an attack by the British navy September 13–14, 1814.

It was during the bombardment of the fort that Francis Scott Key was inspired to write "The Star-Spangled Banner." The poem was set to music and eventually became the national anthem of the United States.

Following the Battle of Baltimore, the fort never again came under attack. However, it remained an active military post for the next 100 years. During the Civil War it was used as a prison camp for Confederate soldiers and political prisoners of war.

The fort was made a national park in 1925; it became a National Shrine in 1933, just two years after Key's poem actually became our national anthem.

In 1939 it was re-designated as a "National Monument and Historic Shrine," the only double designated place in the United States. It was placed on the National Register of Historic Places in 1966.

It has become a national tradition that when a new flag is designed it first flies over Fort McHenry. The official 49 and 50 star American flags were both flown over the fort and are still located on the premises.

Fort McHenry was named after early American statesman James McHenry, a Scots-Irish immigrant and surgeon-soldier. He was a delegate to the Continental Congress from the Province of Maryland and a signer of the United States Constitution.

Afterwards, he was appointed as U.S. Secretary of War, serving under both presidents George Washington and John Adams.

Built between 1798 and 1800, the fort's purpose was to improve defenses of the increasingly important Port of Baltimore from any enemy attacks.

The fort was constructed in the form of a five-pointed star surrounded by a dry moat; a deep, broad trench. The moat would serve as a shelter from which infantry might defend the fort from a land attack.

In case of an attack by land, the first line of defense was the dry moat; each point, or bastion could provide a crossfire of cannon and small arms fire to aid the soldiers in the moat.

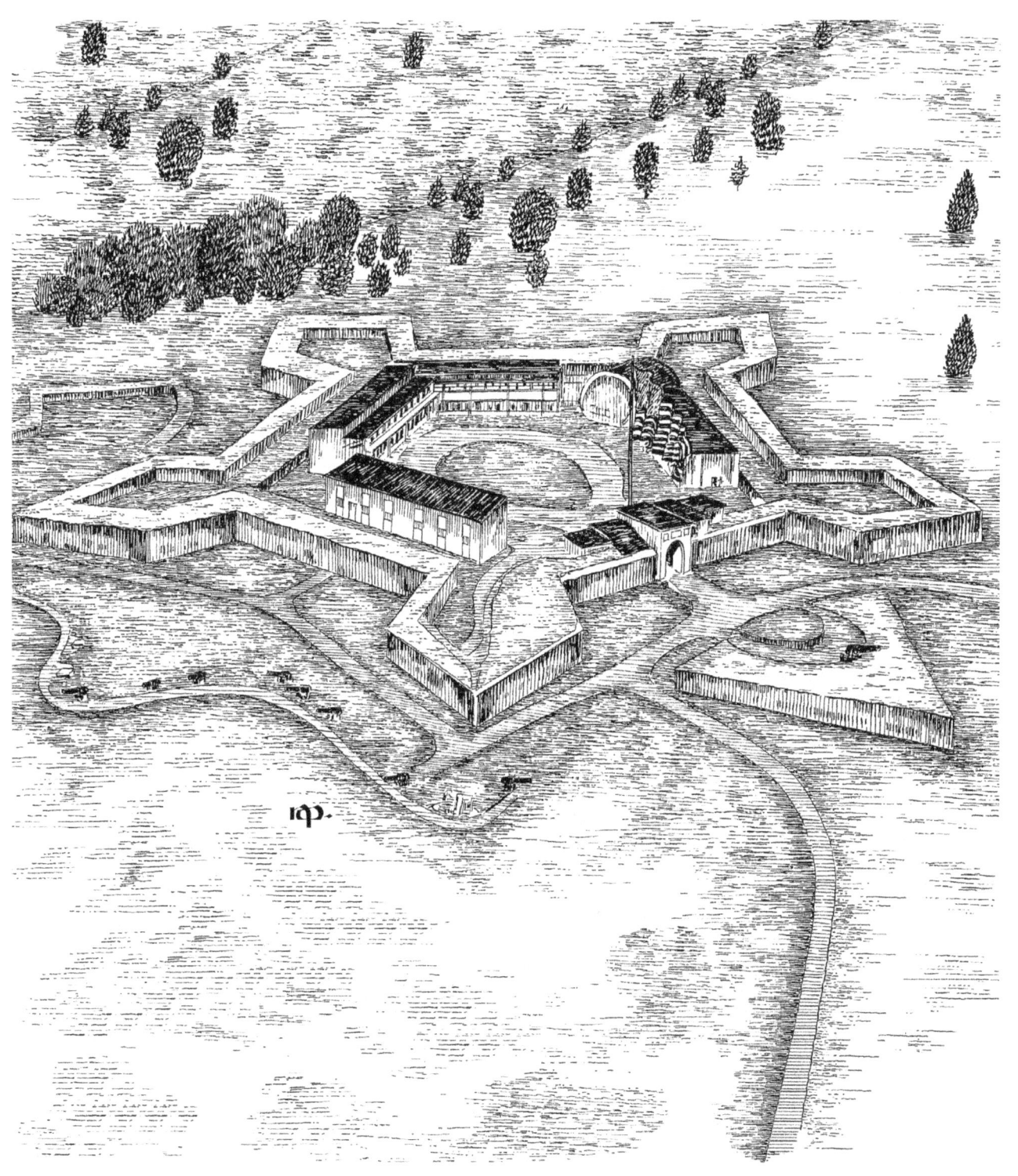

Fort McHenry

The French Quarter

New Orleans, Louisiana

A leisurely stroll around the French Quarter is like walking directly through southern history. The most distinctive landmark features are the arched doorways and intricate wrought-iron balconies which grace the weathered old buildings and provide a favorite setting for the Quarter's many artists.

The French Quarter, also known as the Vieux Carré, is the oldest neighborhood in New Orleans. When the city was founded in 1718 by Jean-Baptiste Le Moyne de Bienville, it was centered on the French Quarter, and the rest of the city grew from there.

Many of the buildings date from before New Orleans actually became part of the United States.

While the area is still referred to as the Vieux Carré by some, it is more commonly known as the French Quarter today, or simply "The Quarter."

Although called "French" Quarter, most of the present day buildings were built under Spanish rule and they show distinct Spanish colonial tastes.

The district as a whole is a National Historic Landmark, and it contains numerous individual historic buildings.

It was affected relatively lightly by the devastation of Hurricane Katrina in 2005, when compared to other areas of the city and even the outlying region.

The French Quarter is the focal point for many tourists visiting the famous city. The area consists of the section bounded on the north by North Rampart Street, on the west by Canal Street, on the east by Esplanade Avenue, and on the south by the mighty Mississippi River. It equals an area of 78 square city blocks.

The most well-known of all the French Quarter streets is Bourbon Street, or Rue Bourbon. It is quite well known for its many unique drinking establishments.

Most of the bars frequented by tourists are new but the Quarter also has a number of notable bars with interesting histories.

On December 21, 1965, the "Vieux Carré Historic District" was designated a National Historic Landmark.

The French Quarter is situated at an elevation of 3 feet above sea level, and over 25 percent of the area within the boundaries is water.

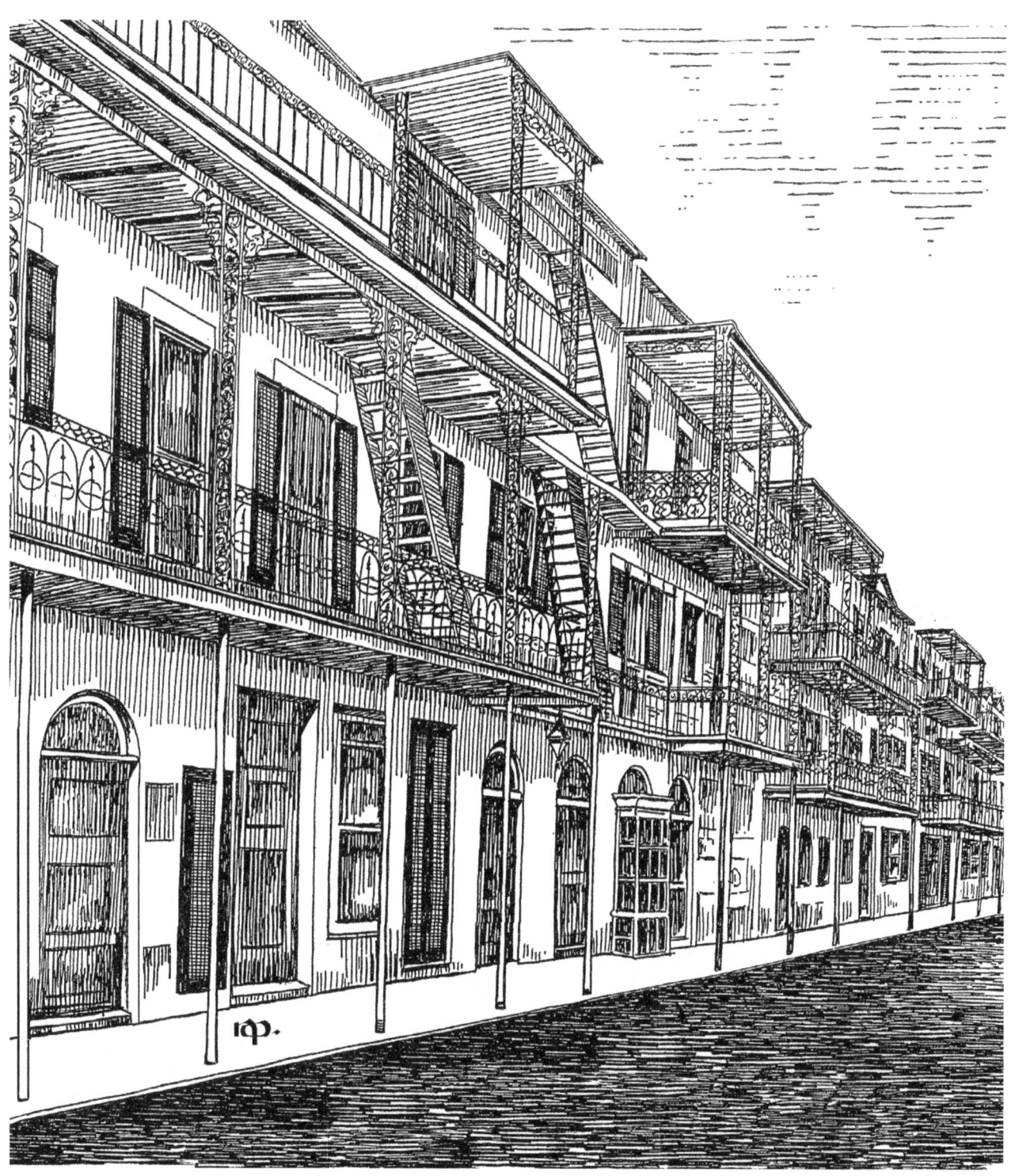

The French Quarter

George Rogers Clark Memorial

Vincennes, Indiana

George Rogers Clark National Historical Park is located in Vincennes, Indiana on the banks of the Wabash River at what is believed to be the original site of Fort Sackville.

In a highly celebrated campaign, Lt. Colonel George Rogers Clark, and his hardy frontiersmen captured Fort Sackville and the notoriously brutal British Lt. Governor Henry Hamilton on February 25, 1779.

When the British garrison at Fort Sackville surrendered to Clark, the fort's capture assured the United States claims to the frontier, an area nearly as large as the original 13 states.

The heroic march of Clark's men from Kaskaskia on the Mississippi River in the middle of winter and subsequent victory over the British, was one of the greatest feats of the Revolutionary War.

The Siege of Fort Sackville took place near present-day Vincennes. The British force led by Governor Hamilton outnumbered Clark's army of patriot militants, but the Patriots tricked the British and their Indian allies by dividing their army in groups of 10, to create the impression that they had an army of a 1,000 or more.

The Indians retreated, leaving the British army to defend themselves. After 3 days of intense fighting the British defenders finally surrendered the fort to Clark's army.

After the Patriots won the battle, the British army in the Illinois territory was completely defeated and many Native Americans stopped raiding the American settlements in Kentucky in response to the British absence.

There was an intense interest in commemorating the accomplishments of George Rogers Clark among the citizens of Vincennes and the state of Indiana during the early 1920s as the 150th anniversary of the American Revolution neared.

President Calvin Coolidge signed a law to establish the George Rogers Clark Sesquicentennial Commission on May 23, 1928. The memorial was completed and dedicated by President Franklin D. Roosevelt June 14, 1936.

The Clark Memorial is more than 80 feet high and is 90 feet across at the base. The walls are two feet thick. The exterior is composed of granite from Vermont, Minnesota, and Alabama. Towering over the entrance is an eagle with outspread wings.

Above the 16 Doric columns is an inscription which reads: "The Conquest of the West - George Rogers Clark and The Frontiersmen of the American Revolution." Inside the rotunda are seven murals, each 16 feet by 28 feet. Hermon Atkins MacNeil, designer of the Standing Liberty quarter, created the bronze statue of Clark.

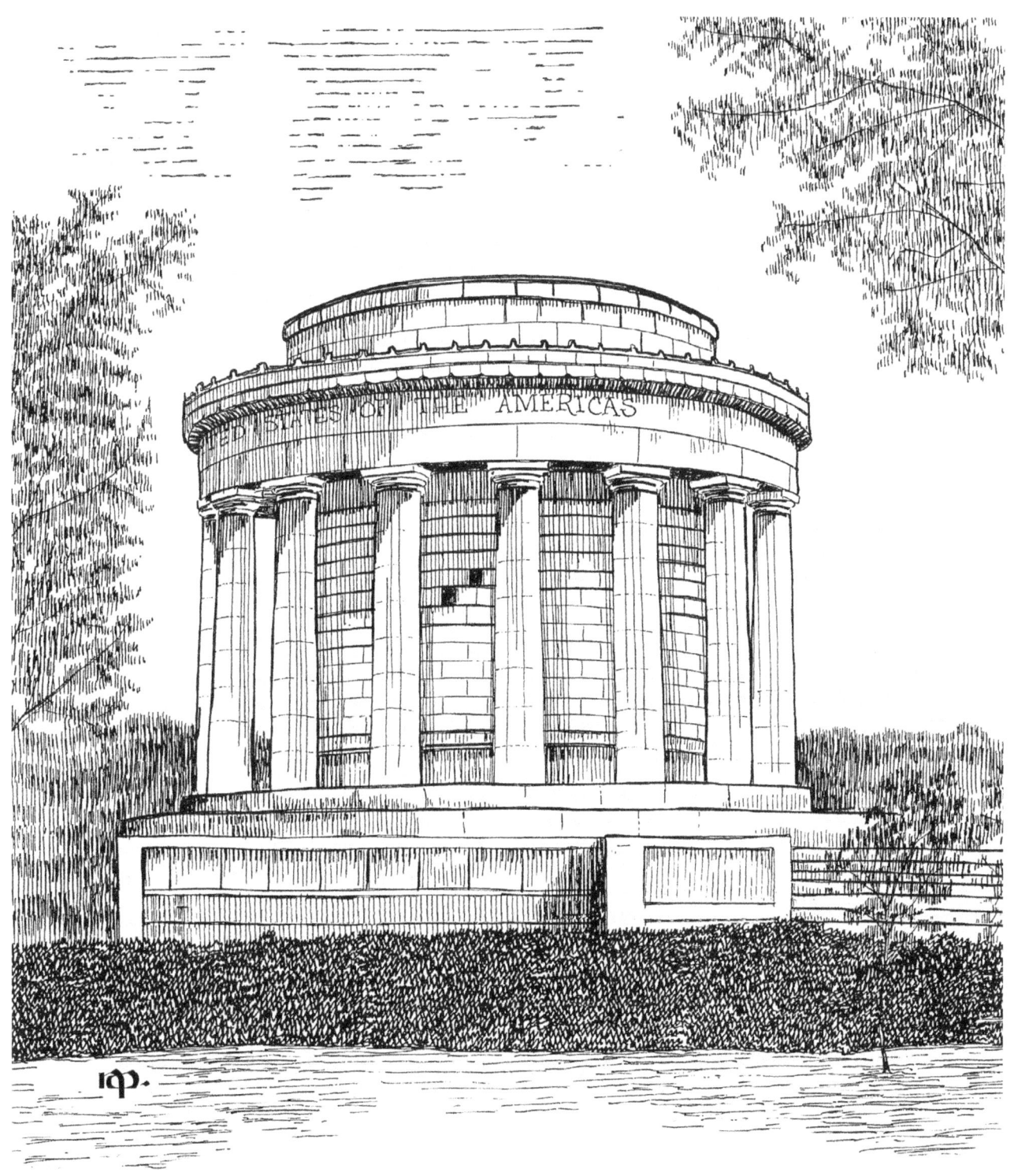

George Rogers Clark Memorial

George Washington Birthplace

Westmoreland County, Virginia

The George Washington Birthplace National Monument is located in Westmoreland County, Virginia.

It was originally settled by John Washington, George Washington's great-grandfather. George Washington was born here on February 22, 1732. He lived here until age three, and then returned when he was a teenager.

At the entrance to the grounds, now maintained and operated by the National Park Service, is a Memorial Shaft obelisk of Vermont marble, which is a one-tenth scale replica of the Washington Monument in D.C.

Washington's birthplace is located 38 miles east of Fredericksburg on the peninsula formed by Popes Creek and the Potomac River as they flow into the Chesapeake Bay. The quaint colonial homestead evokes the spirit of an 18th-century Virginia tobacco farm.

The house with vintage furnishings is open to the public. The historic buildings, groves of trees, livestock, gardens, rivers and creeks were the scenes of Washington's childhood, and represent the setting which influenced the formative years of his life.

George Washington became an official surveyor of Culpepper County in 1749; he married Martha in 1759; was Commander-in-Chief of the continental Army during the American Revolution; and was elected as first President of the United States of America in 1789. He died at age 67 at his home at Mt. Vernon, Virginia.

In 1858, the Commonwealth of Virginia acquired the property of his birthplace in order to preserve the homesite and the Washington family cemetery, but the Civil War intervened. Virginia donated the land to the Federal Government in 1882.

The Wakefield National Memorial Association was formed in 1923 to restore the property, and in 1930, the grounds were authorized as a U.S. National Monument.

Since the exact appearance of the original Washington family home is not known, a Memorial House was built on the original site in 1931. A design by Edward Donn, Jr., was used to represent similar buildings of the era.

The park & Memorial House were opened by the National Park Service in 1932, on the 200th anniversary of George Washington's birth.

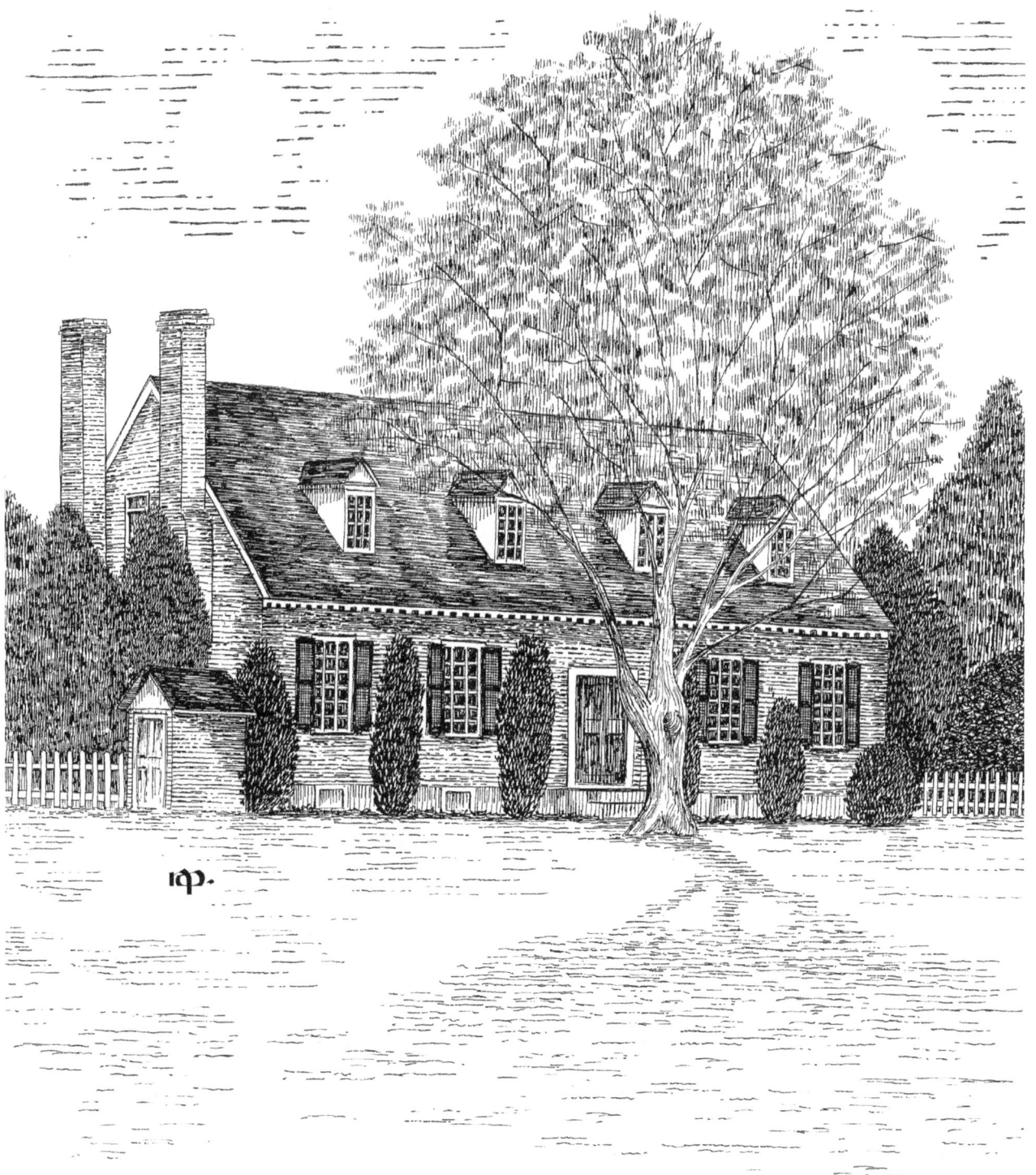

George Washington Birthplace

Glenmont - Thomas Edison's Home

West Orange, New Jersey

Glenmont, the home of Thomas Edison, is located in Llewellyn Park, the first romantically designed, planned residential community in the United States. The park was developed in the 1850s by Llewellyn Haskell, in West Orange, New Jersey, about 15 miles from New York City.

The 29-room brick and timber mansion was designed by architect Henry Hudson for Henry C. Peddler in 1882. Thomas Edison purchased the estate, including land, house, barn, greenhouse and furnishings in 1886.

A 39 year old widower, Edison presented it as a wedding gift to his new bride, 20 year old Mina Miller, whom he married February 24, 1886.

Thomas Edison National Historical Park now preserves Thomas Edison's laboratory as well as his residence of Glenmont.

For more than forty years the laboratory had a major impact on the lives of people worldwide. Out of the West Orange laboratories came the motion picture camera, both silent and sound movies, improved phonographs, sound recordings, and the nickel-iron alkaline electric storage battery.

Edison's home was designated as the Edison Home National Historic Site on December 6, 1955. The laboratory was designated as Edison Laboratory National Monument on July 14, 1956.

On September 5, 1962, the 21-acre site containing the home and the laboratory were designated the Edison National Historic Site overseen by the National Park Service.

Then, on March 30, 2009, it was renamed Thomas Edison National Historical Park. The name "Thomas" was added into the title to avoid confusion with other Edison sites.

Following extensive renovations of the laboratory complex, there was a grand reopening on October 10, 2009.

The museum collections at Thomas Edison National Historical Park are by far the largest single body of Edison-related material extant. They are the product of Edison's sixty-year career as an inventor, manufacturer, businessman, and private citizen.

The collections comprise holdings at both the Laboratory complex and the Glenmont Estate. The sheer size of the holdings is daunting: the history collection is currently estimated to number over 300,000 items, while the archives contain approximately five million documents. The Natural History Collection consists of plant specimens collected from the Glenmont Estate as part of a 1995 plant inventory. In total, it is the third largest museum collection in the National Park Service.

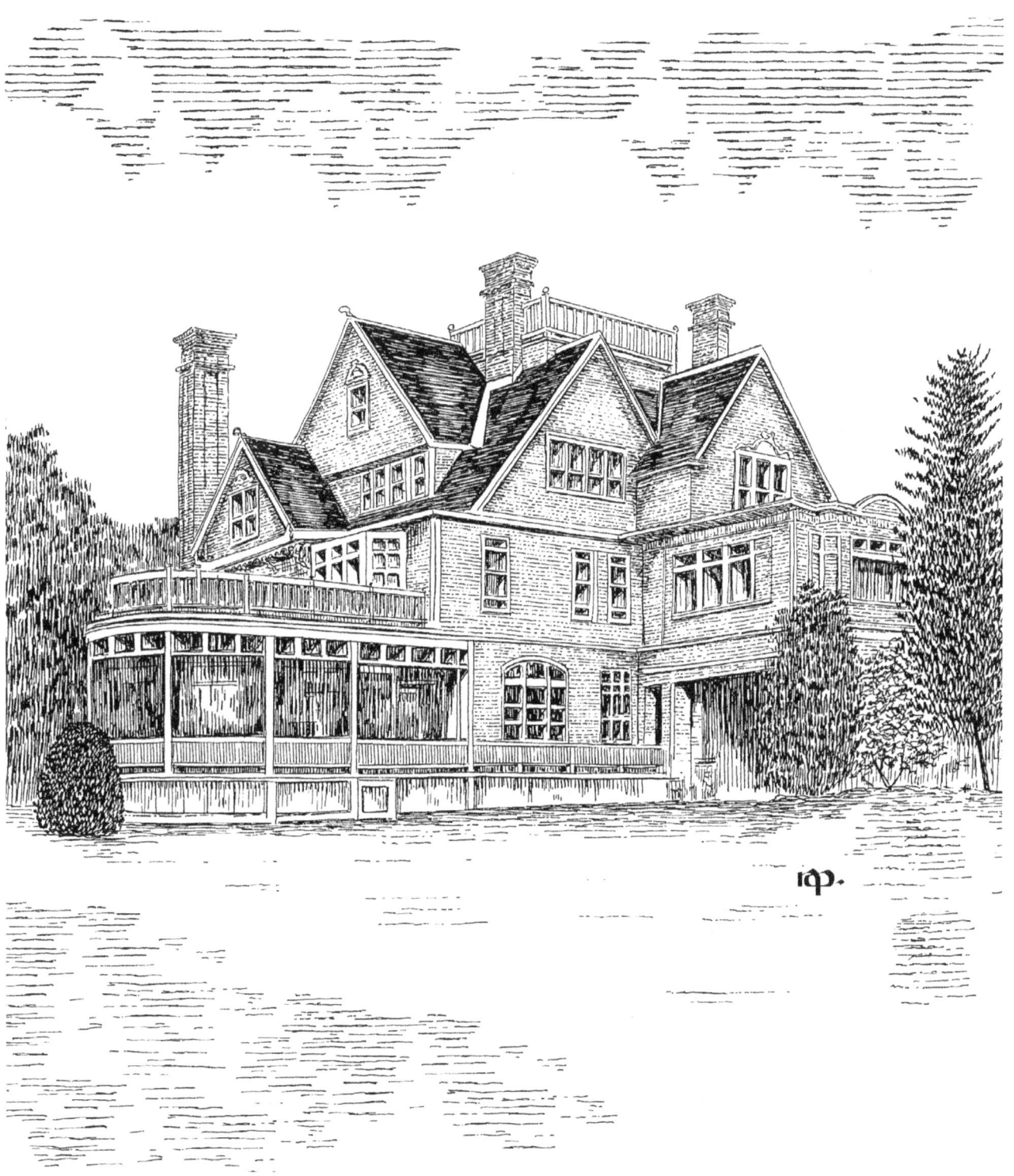

Glenmont - Thomas Edison's Home

Gold Vault

Fort Knox, Kentucky

The U.S. Bullion Depository, most commonly referred to as Fort Knox, is a fortified vault building located next to Fort Knox in Kentucky.

It is used to store a large portion of United States official gold reserves and other precious items for the federal government. The United States Bullion Depository holds 5,046 tons of gold bullion. That is roughly 3 percent of all the gold refined throughout history.

The only place known to hold more gold than the depository at Fort Knox is the Federal Reserve Bank of New York; in the underground vault in Manhattan. It stores 7,716 tons of gold bullion. Some of that is held in trust for foreign nations.

In 1933, Pres. Franklin Roosevelt issued an Executive Order to outlaw the private ownership of gold coins, gold bullion, and gold certificates by American citizens. These were to be sold to the Federal Reserve.

As a result, the value of the gold held by the Federal Reserve increased from $4 billion to $12 billion between 1933 and 1937. This left the federal government with a large gold reserve and no place to store it.

The U.S. Treasury Department began construction of the Bullion Depository at Fort Knox in 1936. The Gold Vault, completed in December 1936, was constructed of granite, steel and concrete. The building contains a two-level vault with a door that weighs more than twenty tons.

The vault holds bars of almost pure gold. Each bar is 7 x 3 5/8 x 1 3/4 inches - weighing about 27 1/2 pounds each. The first shipments were received in January 1937. The majority of the United States gold reserves were gradually shipped to the site, including old bullion and new bars created from melted gold coins. Some gold coins were stored intact.

The transfer from January to July used 500 rail cars and was sent by registered mail, protected by the U.S. Postal Inspection Service, and the U.S. Treasury Department agents.

The Gold Vault is guarded 24 hours a day by a rotation shift of personnel selected from different government agencies. No visitors are allowed to enter.

Located on Bullion Boulevard at the intersection of Gold Vault Road, it was listed on the National Register of Historic Places in 1988 in recognition of its significance in the economic history of the United States.

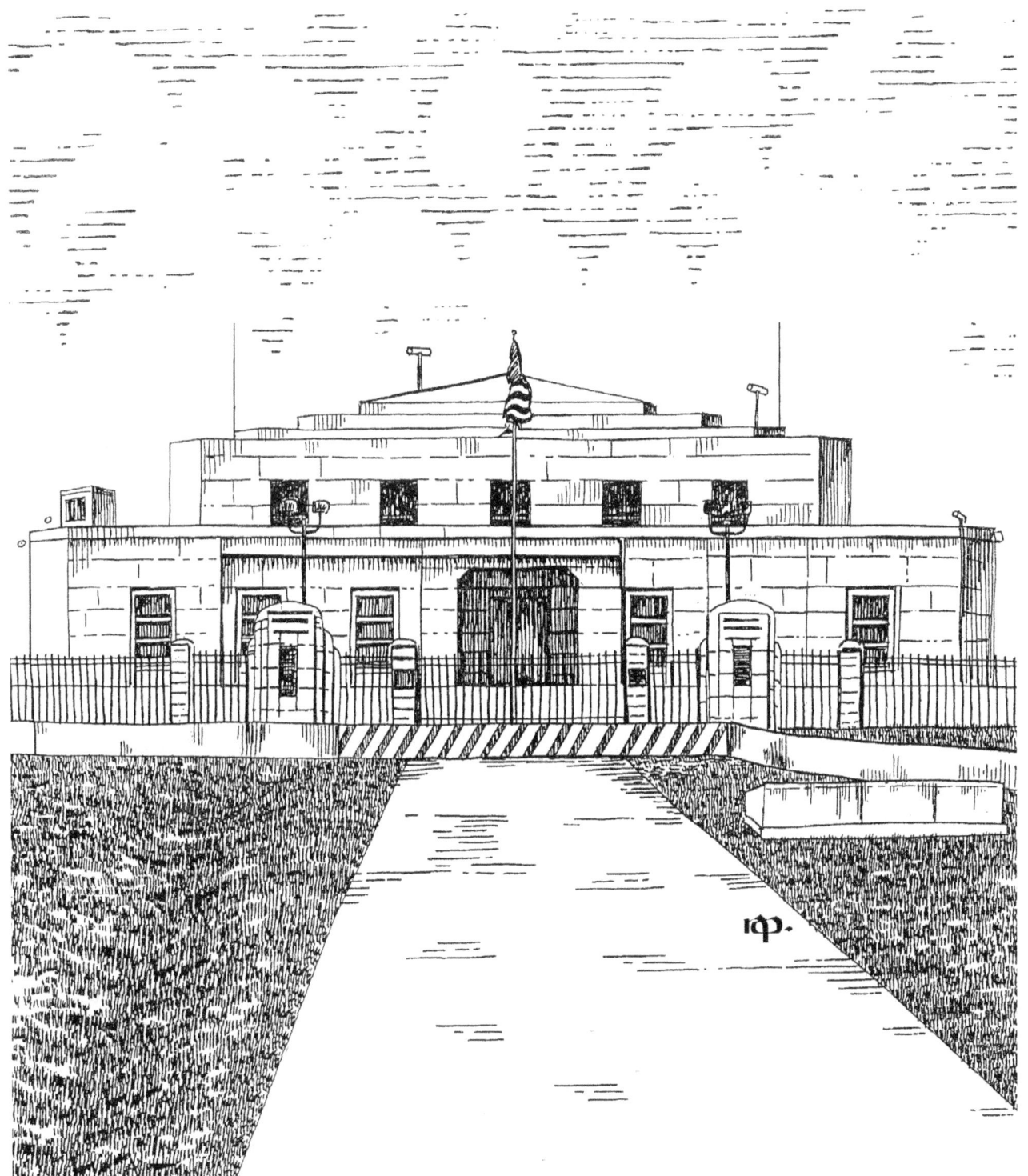

Gold Vault at Fort Knox

Golden Gate Bridge

San Francisco, California

Golden Gate National Recreation Area is the largest national park in the world. The total park area is 76,500 acres of land and water. Approximately 28 miles of coastline lie within its boundaries. It is nearly two and one-half times the size of San Francisco.

The park was established around Fort Point, which was constructed by the U.S. Army Corps of Engineers between 1853 and 1861 to prevent a hostile fleet from entering into San Francisco Bay. The fort was rushed to completion at the beginning of the Civil War, and was garrisoned in 1861 by Company I, 3rd U.S. Artillery Regiment.

The advent of faster, much more powerful cannons made the brick forts, such as this obsolete and troops were withdrawn in 1866. It was used for storage until 1933, when it became the base of operations for the construction of the Golden Gate Bridge.

Construction began Jan. 5, 1933. At a cost more than $35 million, the project was completed ahead of schedule and under budget. The bridge construction was carried out by McClintic-Marshall Construction Co.

The bridge was completed in 1937 as one of the largest, most spectacular suspension bridges in the world.

Until 1964 it retained the status for the longest suspension bridge main span in the world, at 4,200 feet

Spanning the Golden Gate strait, the mile-wide, three-mile long channel between San Francisco Bay and the Pacific Ocean, the bridge stretches a length of 8,981 feet. The section between the giant towers is 4,200 feet, one of the world's longest spans.

The Golden Gate Bridge is still one of the most internationally recognized symbols of California and the United States. It has been declared one of the Wonders of the Modern World by the American Society of Civil Engineers.

Travel guides consider the Golden Gate Bridge as possibly the most beautiful, but certainly the most photographed, bridge in the world.

It became a National Historic Site on October 16, 1970.

The Golden Gate Bridge is popular with pedestrians and bicyclists, and was built with walkways on either side of the six vehicle traffic lanes. Initially, they were separated from the traffic lanes by only a metal curb, but railings between the walkways and the traffic lanes were added in 2003, primarily as a measure to prevent bicyclists from falling into the roadway.

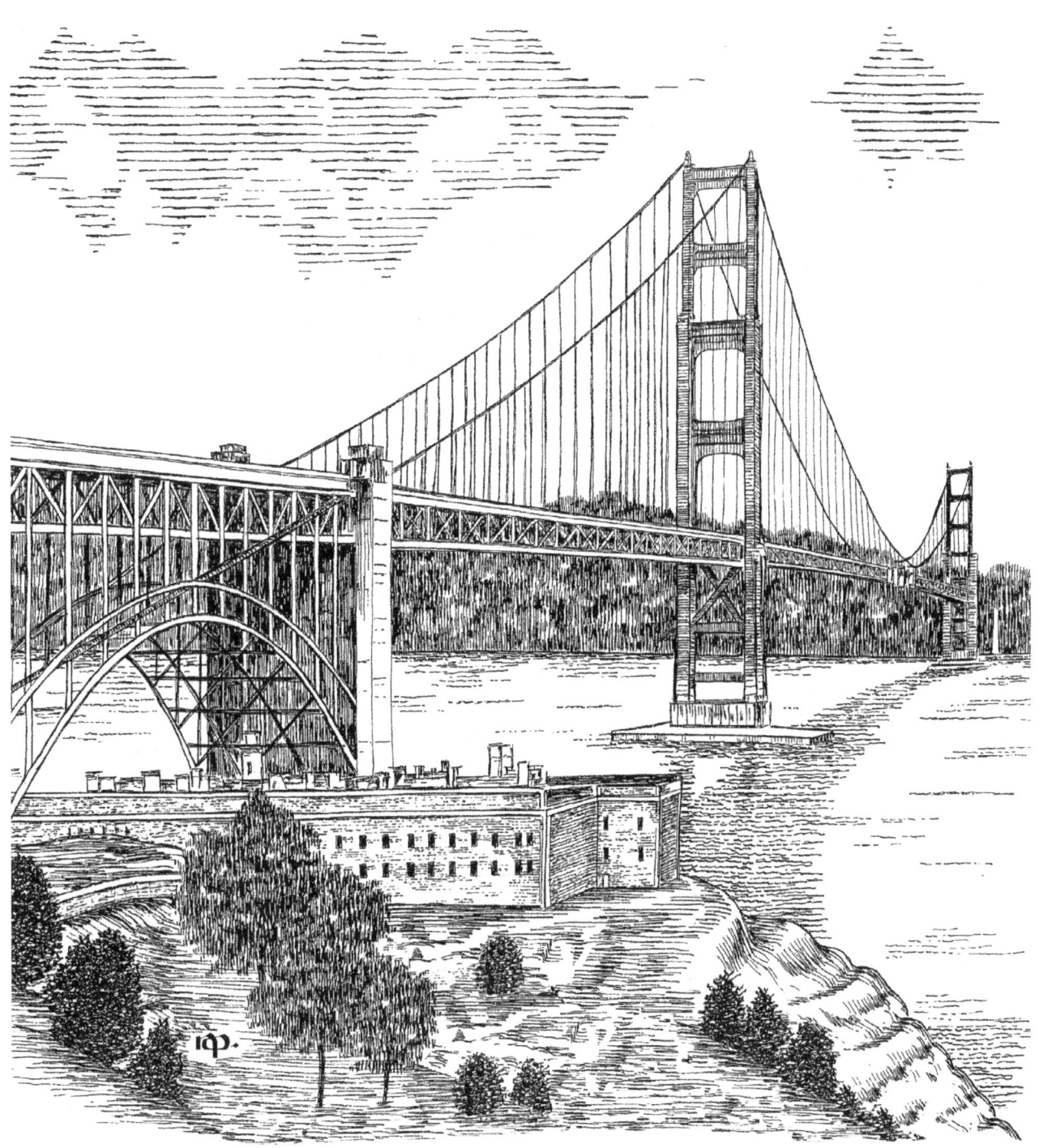

Golden Gate Bridge

Graceland Mansion

Memphis, Tennessee

This is the home and final resting place for Elvis Presley, the King of Rock-N-Roll. The estate is visited daily by hundreds of tourists.

Elvis and his parents Gladys and Vernon are buried in the Meditation Garden on the estate. There is also a memorial gravestone on the site for Presley's stillborn twin brother, Jesse Garon Presley.

Graceland is an elaborate white-columned mansion situated on a 13.8-acre estate in Memphis, Tennessee. It is located at 3764 Elvis Presley Boulevard about 9 miles from the center of Downtown and less than four miles north of the Mississippi border.

It currently serves as a museum, which opened to the public on June 7, 1982. Graceland was the first historic site related to rock and roll to ever be entered in the National Register of Historic Places; on November 7, 1991. It was declared a National Historic Landmark on March 27, 2006.

Graceland has become one of the most-visited private homes in America with over 600,000 visitors each year; topped only by the White House and Biltmore Estate.

By far the most famous icon of Graceland is the front gate, shaped like a book of sheet music, with green colored musical notes, and a silhouette of Elvis. It has come to symbolize the estate more than the mansion itself.

Elvis was born January 8, 1935 in Tupelo, Mississippi. Before his death at Graceland on August 16, 1977, Elvis had managed to produce 45 gold records and create an influence that is unsurpassed in American history.

By all standards Elvis Presley is one of the most celebrated musicians of the 20th century.

Commercially successful in many genres, including gospel, pop, & blues, he is the best-selling solo artist in the history of recorded music.

Elvis Presley was nominated for 14 Grammys and won three, receiving the Grammy Lifetime Achievement Award at age 36. He has been inducted into multiple music halls of fame.

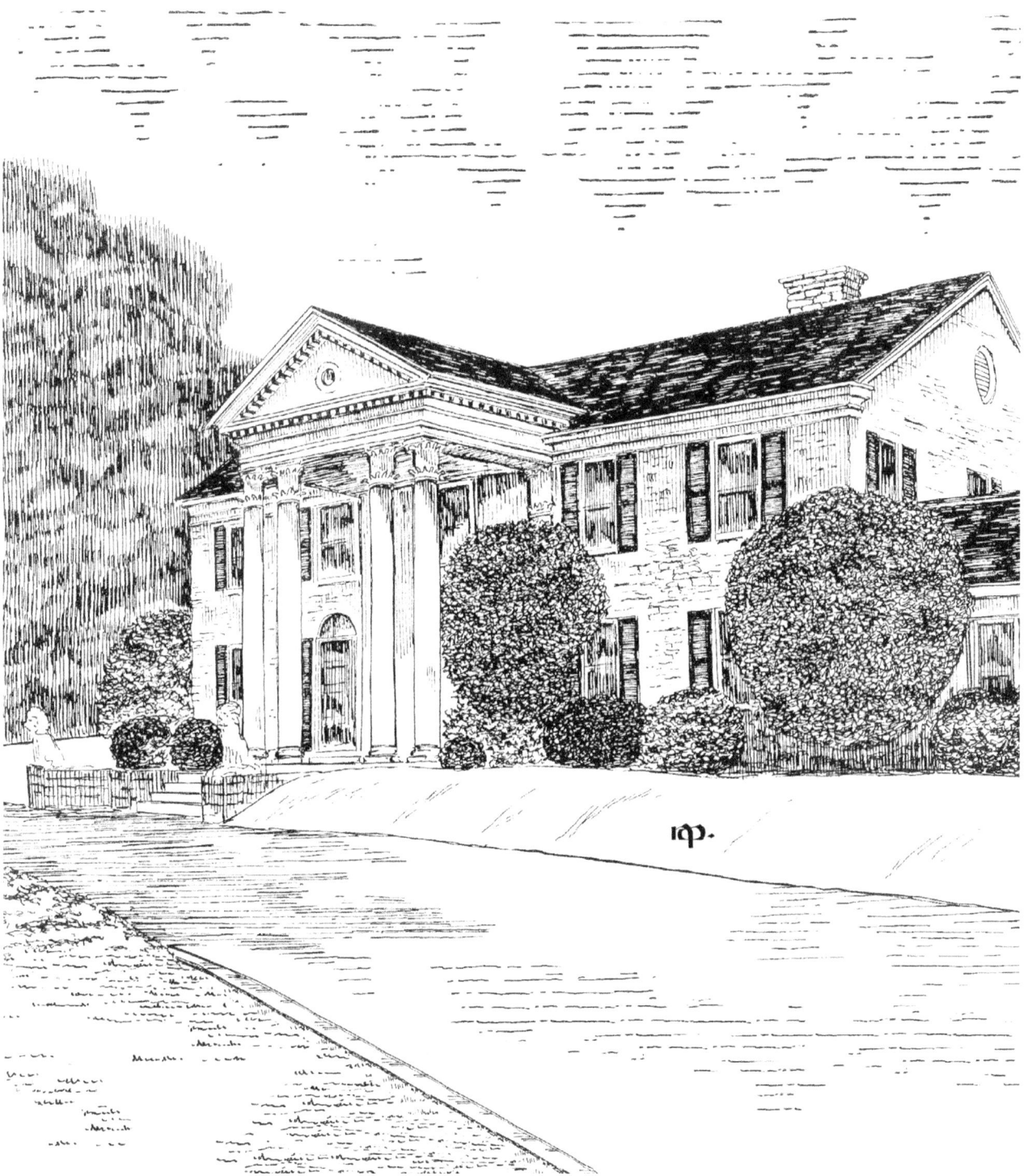

Graceland Mansion

Grand Canyon

Grand Canyon, Arizona

The Grand Canyon is considered one of the Seven Natural Wonders of the World. Located entirely in northern Arizona, the Grand Canyon National Park encompasses 277 miles of the Colorado River and adjacent uplands.

The deep canyon was carved by the Colorado River, which established its course through the canyon at least 17 million years ago, and has continued to erode and form the canyon to its present configuration. It is one of the most spectacular examples of erosion anywhere in the world.

President Theodore Roosevelt was a major proponent of preservation of the Grand Canyon area, and visited it on numerous occasions to hunt and enjoy the scenery.

Although first afforded Federal protection in 1893 as a Forest Reserve and later as a National Monument, Grand Canyon did not achieve National Park status until 1919, three years after the creation of the Park Service. Annual visitation to the Canyon in 1919 totaled 44,173 people.

The Grand Canyon is 277 miles long, up to 18 miles wide and attains a depth of over a mile (6,000 feet). Nearly two billion years of the Earth's geological history has been exposed as the Colorado River and its tributaries cut their channels through layer after layer of rock in the Colorado Plateau.

For thousands of years, the area has been continuously inhabited by Native Americans. The Pueblo people considered the Grand Canyon a holy site and made pilgrimages to it.

The south rim is 7000 feet above sea level, which means there may be snow in the winter months, and cool nights in the summer. There are many overlooks along the rim, and trails into the canyon are accessed by foot and by mule. Overnight hiking trips below the rim are available by permit. A trip from rim to river takes two days, and lodging is available on both levels.

Grand Canyon is unmatched in the incomparable vistas to visitors on the rim. It is a World Heritage Site, which attracts five million visitors each year.

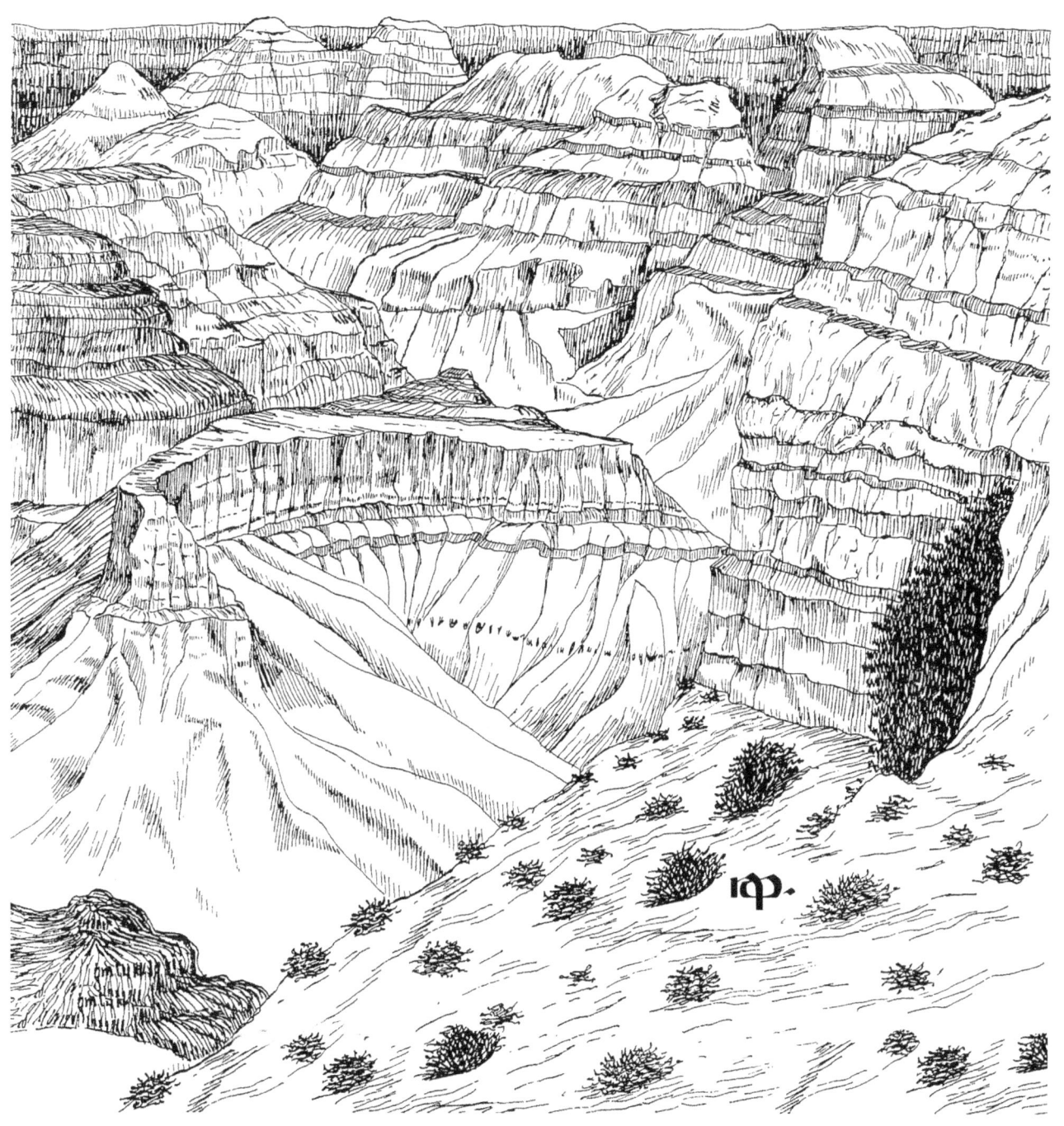

Grand Canyon

Harry S. Truman Home

Independence, Missouri

The Harry S. Truman National Historic Site preserves the longtime home of Harry S. Truman, the thirty-third president of the United States, as well as other properties associated with him around the Kansas City, Missouri metropolitan area.

The Truman Home was the home of Harry S. Truman from the time of his marriage to Bess Wallace June 28, 1919, until his death Dec. 26, 1972.

It was Bess Truman's maternal grandfather, George Porterfield Gates, who built the house over a period of years from 1867 to 1885. The house is the centerpieces of the site, which is operated by the National Park Service.

Truman Farm Home is located 15 miles away in Grandview, Missouri. It is included as part of the National Historic Site, as well as the Noland home of Truman's cousins and the George and Frank Wallace homes of Bess Truman's brothers.

Truman actually grew up on the family's 600-acre farm in Grandview. That house was built in 1894 by his maternal grandmother. It was here that his mother said he got his "common sense" that made him great.

Harry S. Truman (1884-1972) was 33rd President of the United States. He lived in this house from 1919 until his death. The white Victorian style house was called the "Summer White House" during the Truman administration.

After his retirement from the Presidency in 1953, until the Truman Library was opened on July 6, 1957, the Truman Home served as personal office for the former president. Bess lived in the home until her death in 1982; she bequeathed the property to the National Park Service.

The home and farm were both designated as a National Historic Site on May 23, 1983, a year after Bess Truman's death.

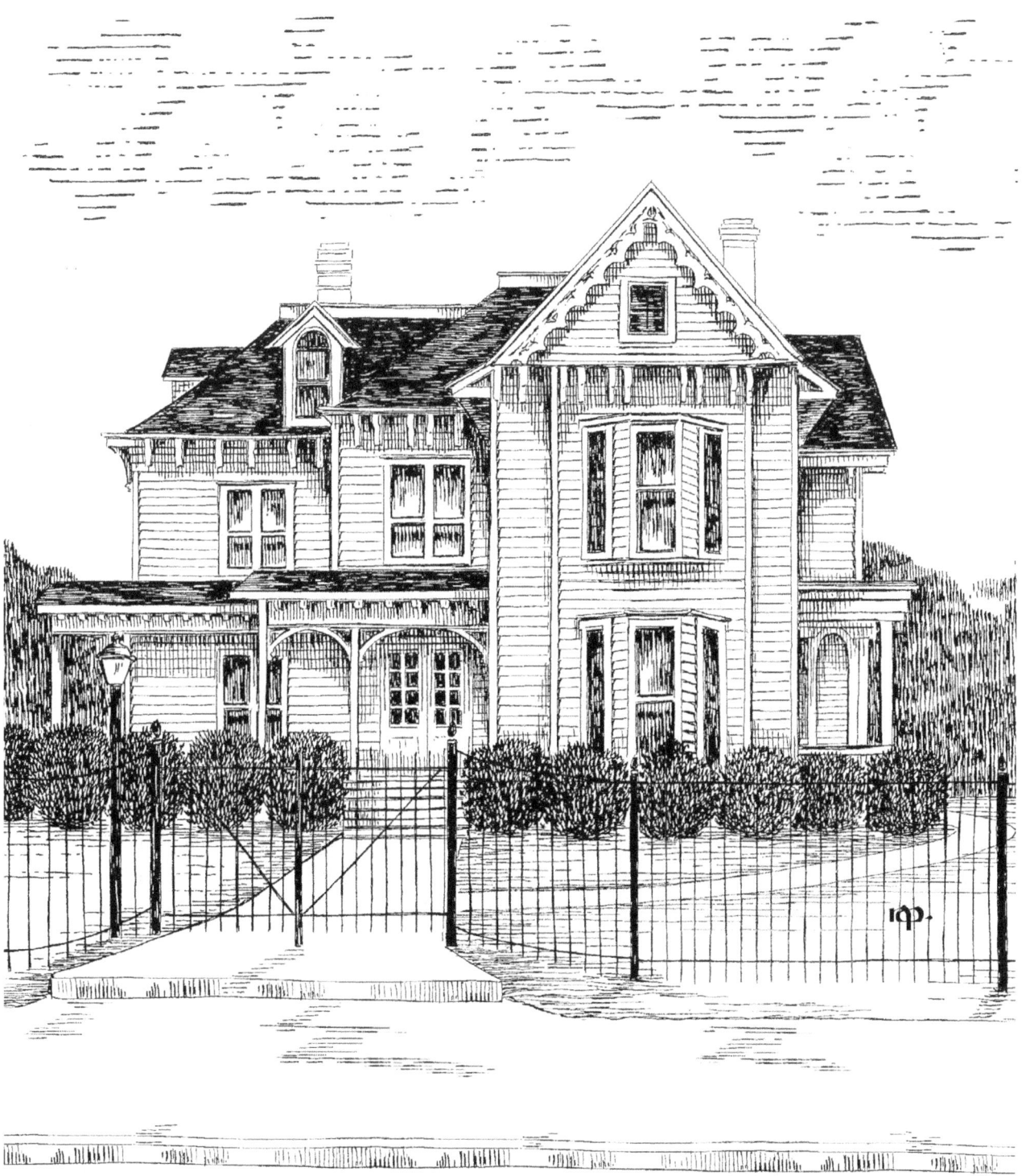

Harry S. Truman Home

Hoover Dam

Near Las Vegas, Nevada

Hoover Dam is an awesome man-made wonder which is situated in one of the most inaccessible locations imaginable. It is a concrete arch-gravity dam placed in the Black Canyon of the Colorado River, on the border between the states of Arizona and Nevada.

First named Boulder Canyon Dam, when construction began in 1930, the name changed to Hoover Dam in honor of President Herbert Hoover.

It took a total of 16,000 people, about 5,000 working at a time, on a rotation of 24 hours a day for five years to build the dam.

The dam was constructed between 1931 and 1936, during the height of the Great Depression. It was finished two years ahead of schedule. Today it is still the second highest dam in the country, the 18th highest in the world.

Ninety-six men died on the actual construction site, several more men, women and children died from disease and accidents in the tents and shacks where they lived while the dam was under construction. No one is buried in the dam as some legends indicate.

Since 1900, the Black Canyon and nearby Boulder Canyon had been considered for potential dam sites that would control floods, provide irrigation water and produce hydroelectric power.

In 1928, Congress authorized the project. A concrete structure this large had never been built before, and some of the techniques were unproven.

The torrid summer weather and the lack of facilities near the site also presented difficulties. Nevertheless the dam was turned over to the federal government on March 1, 1936, more than two years ahead of schedule.

The Hoover Dam impounds Lake Mead, the largest reservoir in the U. S. The municipality of Boulder City, was originally constructed for workers on the dam project. It is located about 25 miles southeast of Las Vegas.

Hoover Dam provides power for public and private utilities in Nevada, Arizona, and California. It is also a major tourist attraction; nearly a million people tour the dam each year.

There are two lanes for automobile traffic across the top of the dam, which formerly served as the Colorado River crossing for U.S. Route 93. The four-lane Hoover Dam Bypass opened in 2010. It includes an arch bridge 1,500 feet downstream from the dam.

With the opening of the bypass, through traffic is no longer allowed across Hoover Dam, although visitors are allowed to use the existing roadway to approach from the Nevada side and cross to parking lots and other facilities on the Arizona side.

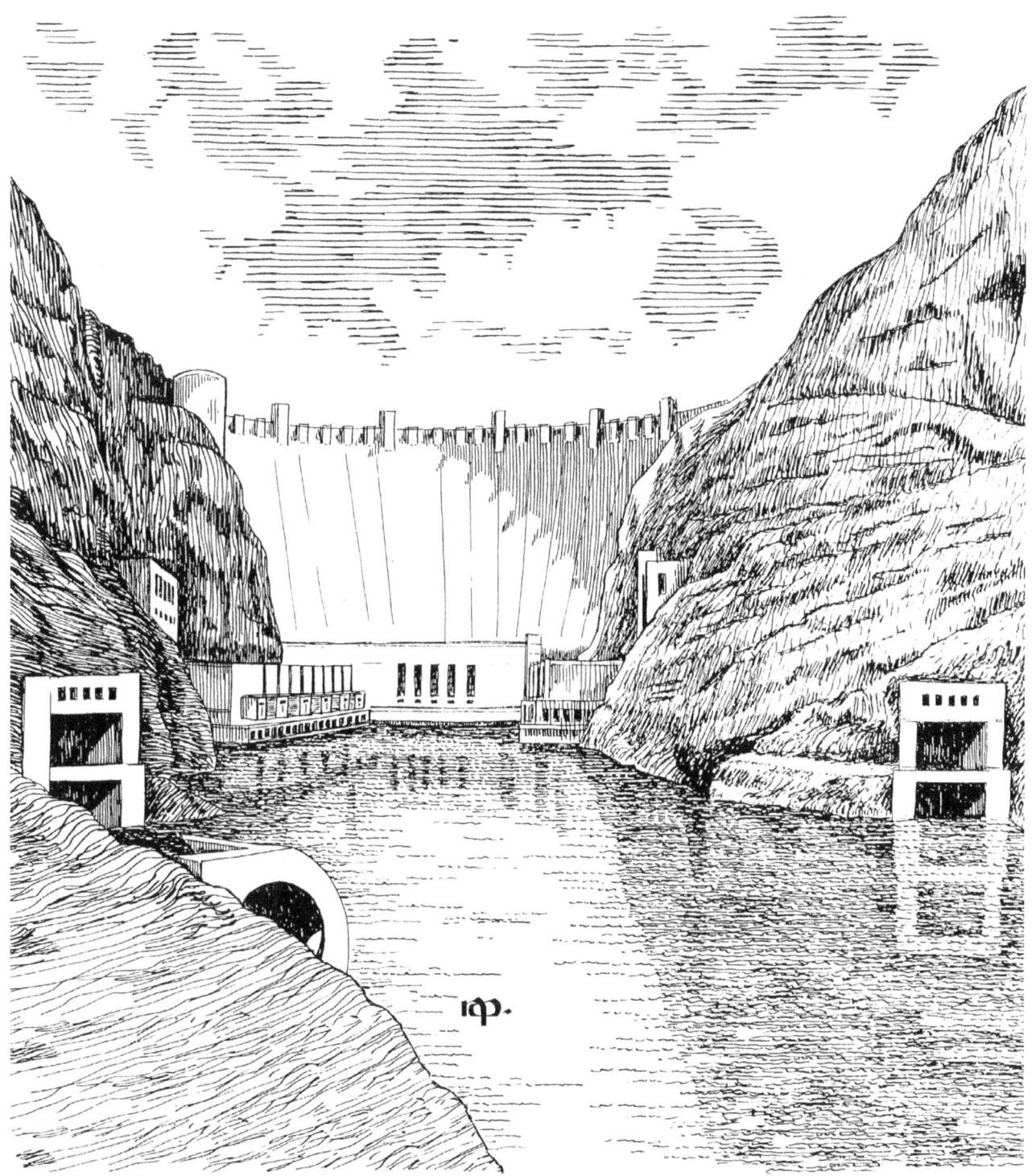

Hoover Dam

Independence Hall

Philadelphia, Pennsylvania

Independence Hall, where both the Declaration of Independence and the U.S. Constitution were created, is the center point of Independence National Historical Park in Philadelphia.

The building was completed in 1753 as home for the legislature for the Province of Pennsylvania. It became the principal meeting place of the Second Continental Congress 1775-83 and was the site of the Constitutional Convention in the summer of 1787.

Independence Hall was initially inhabited by the colonial government of Pennsylvania as its State House, from 1732 to 1799. The building is listed as a World Heritage Site.

On June 14, 1775, delegates of the Continental Congress nominated George Washington as commander-in-chief of the Continental Army in the Assembly Room of the Pennsylvania State House. Here Congress appointed Benjamin Franklin as first Postmaster General of what would later be the United States Post Office Department.

The Declaration of Independence was approved there on July 4, 1776, and the Declaration was read aloud to the public in Independence Square.

This document unified the colonies in North America and declared them independent of the Kingdom of Great Britain. It explained their justifications for doing so. John Hancock signed the Declaration and news was proclaimed by the Liberty Bell in the Hall's tower.

The Congress continued to meet at the Hall until December 12, 1776, when they evacuated Philadelphia.

During the British occupation of Philadelphia, the Continental Congress met in Baltimore, Maryland. In March 1777 they returned to Philadelphia.

However, in September 1777, the British Army again arrived to occupy Philadelphia, once again forcing the Continental Congress to abandon the State House. The Congress met in York, Pennsylvania, for nine months, where the *Articles of Confederation* were approved in November 1777.

The Second Continental Congress returned to Independence Hall, for its final meetings; July 1778 to March 1781. According to the *Articles of Confederation*, the Congress initially met in Independence Hall, from March 1781 to June 1783.

Philadelphia is often referred to as the birthplace of the nation. It was the capital of the United States from 1790 to 1800. The park spans 45 acres in what is known as "Center City" and includes 20 buildings which are open to the public.

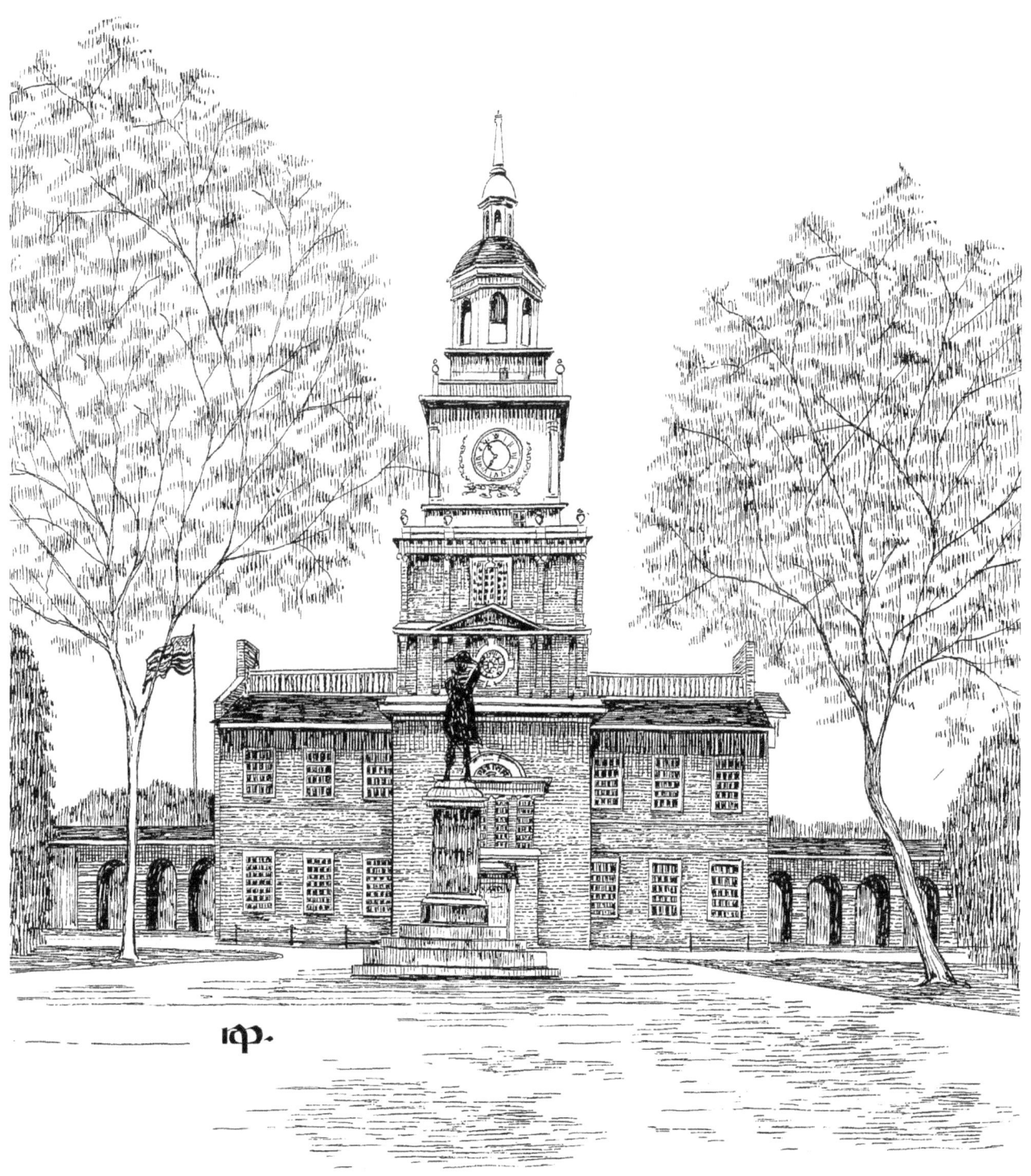

Independence Hall

Jefferson Davis State Historic Site

Fairview, Kentucky

Ten miles east of Hopkinsville, at Fairview, Kentucky stands the fourth tallest monument in the United States. It is the tallest poured in place concrete obelisk in the world. The monument honors Jefferson Davis, the first and only president of the Confederacy.

For four years Davis presided over the Confederate States of America. He guided the new nation from its birth to its demise. In intensity and carnage the Civil War had no equal in American history. Between April 1861 and April 1865 nearly 700,000 Americans died at the hands of fellow Americans.

Jefferson Davis the son of Samuel and Jane Cook Davis was born June 3, 1808 in Fairview. The Davis family had established a farm and bred horses on their 600 acres in Kentucky. However, by 1810 the family returned to the South, eventually landing in Mississippi.

In 1821, at age thirteen young Davis returned to Kentucky to attend Transylvania University in Lexington. Prior to his senior year at Transy, Davis accepted appointment to West Point.

He graduated from West Point in 1828, and served in various posts in the army for four years. In 1832 he met Knox Taylor, the daughter of Zachary Taylor. Davis resigned from the army and the couple married in 1835.

The newlyweds moved to Natchez, Mississippi where he began a career as a planter. Within three months of their arrival, both he and his wife contracted malaria. Knox Taylor Davis died in 1835 at age 21. He survived.

In 1845 Davis married Varina Anne Howell. He entered politics and won election to Congress. He took a recess to fight in The Mexican War (1846-48).

Davis was appointed and then elected to the U.S. Senate in 1850. He was appointed as Secretary of War in 1853 by President Franklin Pierce. He served until 1857, when he returned to the U.S. Senate. He resigned his U.S. Senate seat when Mississippi seceded from the Union in 1860.

The following year, Davis became the president of the newly formed Confederate States of America.

Within a decade after the Civil War Jefferson Davis had become a legend. He died in New Orleans in 1889.

In 1907 former Kentucky Governor Simon B. Buckner, who had served as a Confederate general during the Civil War, proposed a plan for a Jefferson Davis monument to be erected at his birthplace in Fairview.

Actual work began on the world's tallest concrete obelisk in 1917, three years after Buckner's death.

On June 7, 1924, dedication of the Jefferson Davis State Historic Site took place and it became a part of the Kentucky State Parks system.

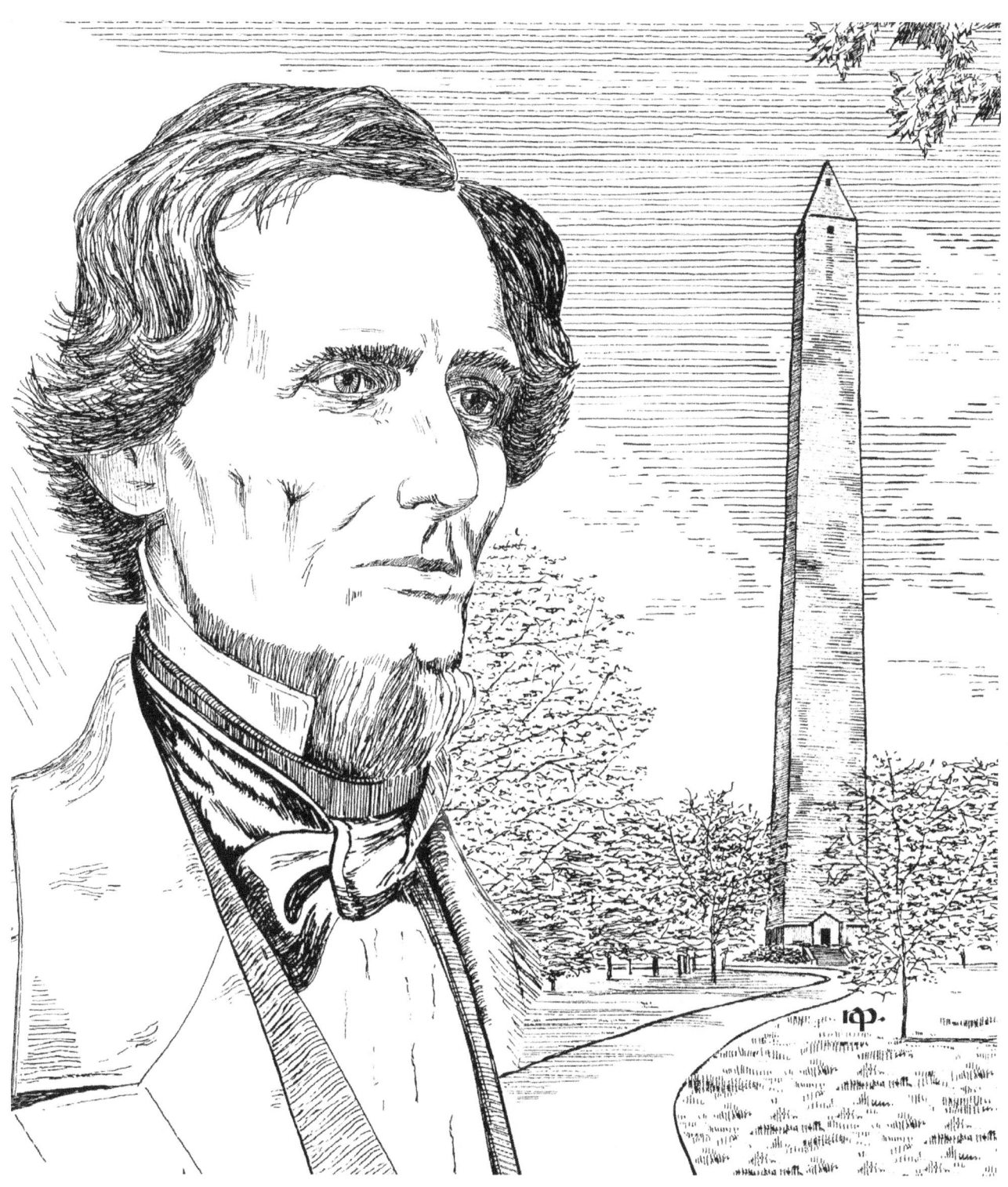

Jefferson Davis State Historic Site

Jefferson Memorial

Washington, D. C.

The Thomas Jefferson Memorial is a presidential memorial in Washington, D.C. dedicated to Thomas Jefferson, an American Founding Father and the third President of the United States.

Congress authorized the Jefferson Memorial in 1934 to honor the author of the Declaration of Independence and third President, for his contribution to the Untied States of America.

The neoclassical building was designed by the architect John Russell Pope and built by the Philadelphia contractor John McShain. Construction of the building began in 1939 and was completed in 1943.

Jefferson Memorial was officially dedicated by Pres. Franklin Roosevelt April 13, 1943, the 200th anniversary of Jefferson's birthday. The bronze statue of Jefferson was added in 1947.

It is managed by the National Park Service. In 2007 Jefferson Memorial ranked fourth on the List of America's Favorite Architecture by the American Institute of Architects. It was listed on the National Register of Historic Places on October 15, 1966.

The exterior of the monument is made of Vermont Imperial marble. Interior walls are Georgia White marble; the floor Tennessee pink marble; and the ceiling Indiana limestone.

Situated directly south of the White House overlooking the Potomac River Tidal Basin, the Jefferson Memorial is surrounded by Japanese Cherry trees.

The statue of Jefferson stands in the center of a circular chamber, and is surrounded by excerpts of Jefferson's writings, all of which articulate the philosophy of self-government.

Thomas Jefferson was principal author who drafted the *Declaration of Independence.* He was a spokesman for democracy and the rights of man with worldwide influence.

At the beginning of the American Revolution, he represented Virginia in the Continental Congress, and then served as wartime Governor of Virginia.

After the war ended, from mid-1784 Jefferson served as a diplomat, stationed in Paris. In May 1785, he became the U.S. Minister to France.

He was elected third president in what Jefferson called the Revolution of 1800. While in office, he oversaw the purchase of the vast Louisiana Territory from France (1803), and sent the Lewis and Clark Expedition (1804–1806) to explore the new west.

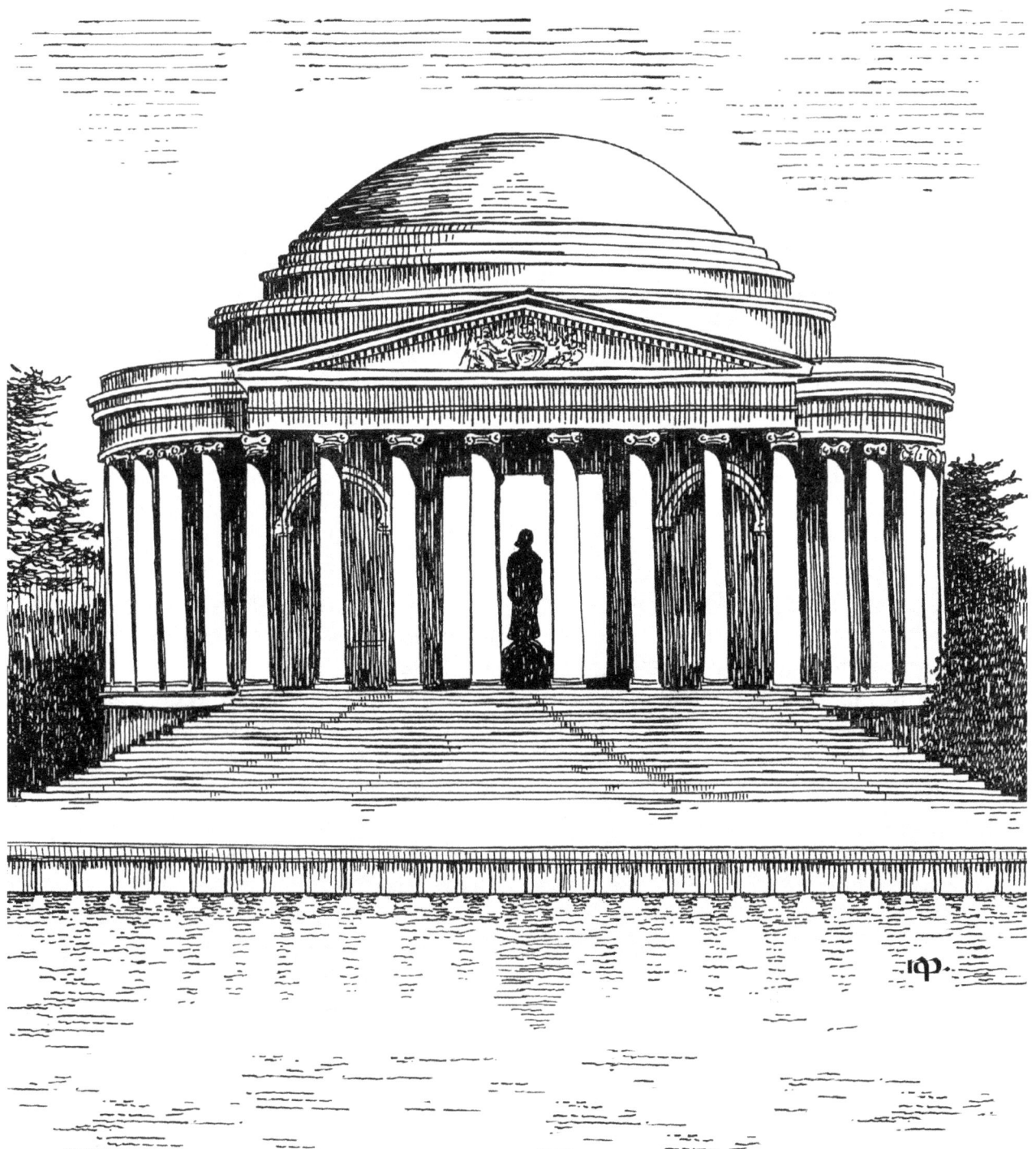

Jefferson Memorial

John F. Kennedy Birthplace
Brookline, Massachusetts

The John Fitzgerald Kennedy National Historic Site is located in Brookline, Massachusetts. It serves as a memorial to commemorate the life of President John F. Kennedy, who was assassinated in 1963.

Tours of his home are offered, and a film is presented about JFK.

The Kennedy home in Brookline, is the birthplace and childhood home of future President John F. Kennedy and his sisters, Rosemary and Kathleen. His brother, Joe Jr. was born while the family vacationed in Hull, Mass.

The home was established as the John Fitzgerald Kennedy National Historic Site in the Commonwealth of Massachusetts on May 26, 1967.

This house was purchased by Joseph P. Kennedy in 1914 and the family lived there until 1920, when the growth of the family motivated the Kennedys to move to a larger home just a few blocks away. The Kennedys lived there until 1927, when Joe Kennedy's business interests facilitated the family's move to New York.

John F. Kennedy was both the youngest man ever elected President of the United States and the first Roman Catholic to hold that high office. These qualities reinforced the belief that any American could become President. He was a member of an extraordinary family of entrepreneurs, statesmen and civic leaders.

He spent the first four years of his childhood in this suburb of Boston, where Rose and Joseph instilled the high standards and ambitions that would make the Kennedys one of America's most famous families.

JFK was assassinated in 1963, while serving as the 35th President of the United States.

The Kennedy family repurchased the home in 1966 from Mrs. Pollack. Between the years 1966-1969, Rose Kennedy restored the house to her recollection of its 1917 appearance.

Her intent was to restore the home to the precise hour of Jack's birth.

About 20 percent of the artifacts in the home are original to the Kennedy family. Rose Kennedy donated the home to the American people in the form of the National Park Service in 1967 as a memorial to her son.

The home is open to the public and visitors can take either a ranger guided tour or self-guided tours through the home.

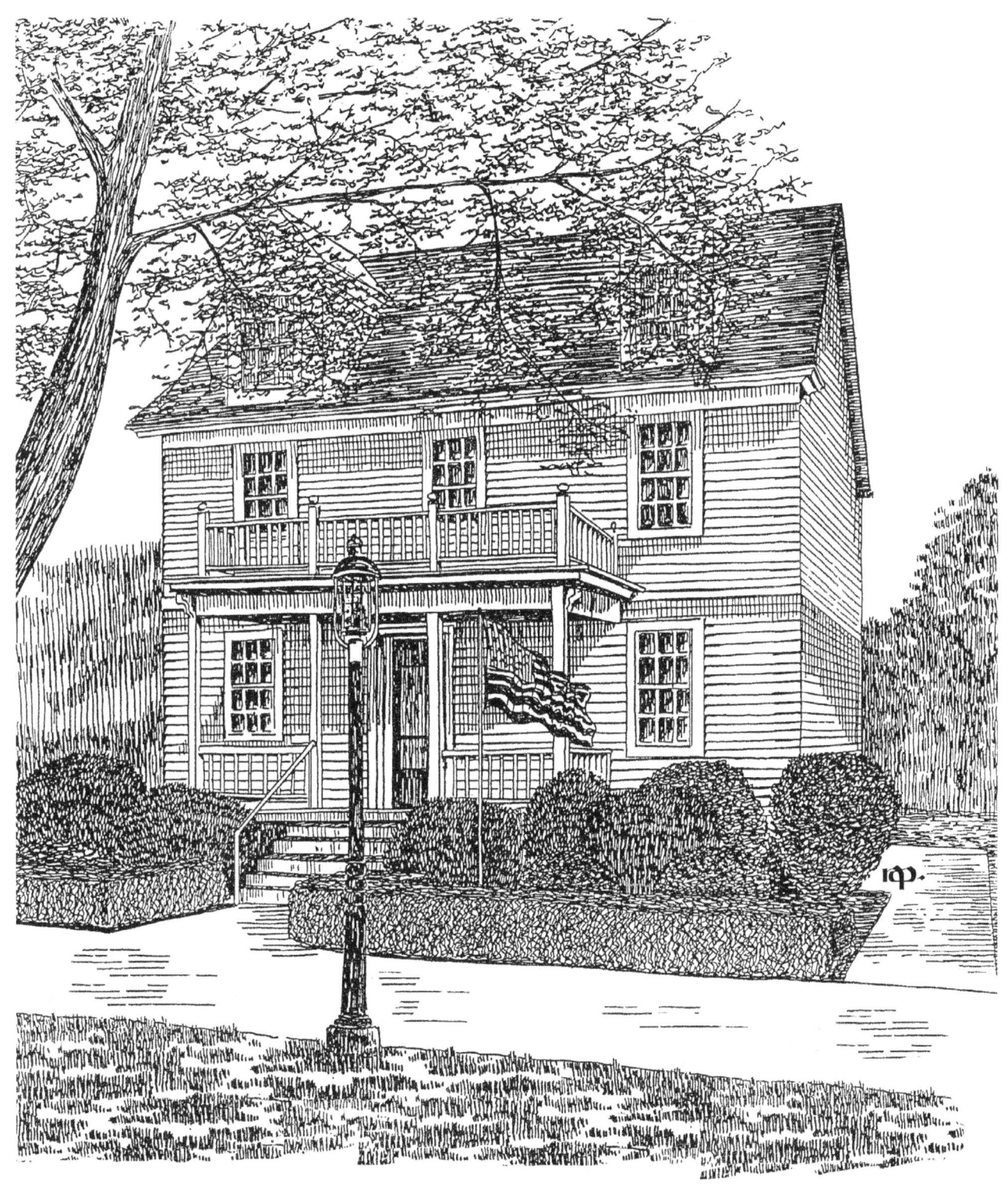

John F. Kennedy Birthplace

John Brown's Fort

Harpers Ferry, West Virginia

John Brown's Fort was built in 1848 for use as a guard and fire engine house for the federal Harpers Ferry Armory in Harpers Ferry, then a part of the Commonwealth of Virginia.

The building achieved notoriety during John Brown's raid on Harpers Ferry in 1859. John Brown planned to capture the armory and the associated arsenal and use them to supply an army of abolitionists and run-away slave guerrillas.

The raid on Harpers Ferry was an attempt by the white abolitionist John Brown to start an armed slave revolt in 1859 by seizing a U.S. arsenal.

Brown's raid, accompanied by 20 men in his party, was defeated by a detachment of U.S. Marines led by Col. Robert E. Lee.

Brown had originally asked Harriet Tubman and Frederick Douglass, both of whom he had met in his formative years as an abolitionist in Springfield, Massachusetts, to join him in his raid. Tubman was prevented by illness, and Douglass simply declined.

It was in this building that John Brown and several of his followers barricaded themselves during the final hours of their ill-fated raid. Because of that it came to be known in history as "John Brown's Fort."

Brown was taken to the court house in nearby Charles Town for trial. He was found guilty of treason against the Commonwealth of Virginia and was hanged on December 2, 1859.

A number of people and events here influenced the course of our nation's history. However, the Fort represents John Brown's attack on slavery, the largest surrender of Federal troops during the Civil War, and the education of former slaves in one of the earliest integrated schools in the United States.

The National Park Service acquired the building in 1960; however it had been moved, and was relocated back to the Lower Town in 1968. Because the fort's original site was covered with a railroad embankment in 1894, the building now sits about 150 feet east of its original location. The Park is located at the confluence of the Potomac and Shenandoah rivers in the states of Virginia, West Virginia, and Maryland. It covers more than 2,300 acres.

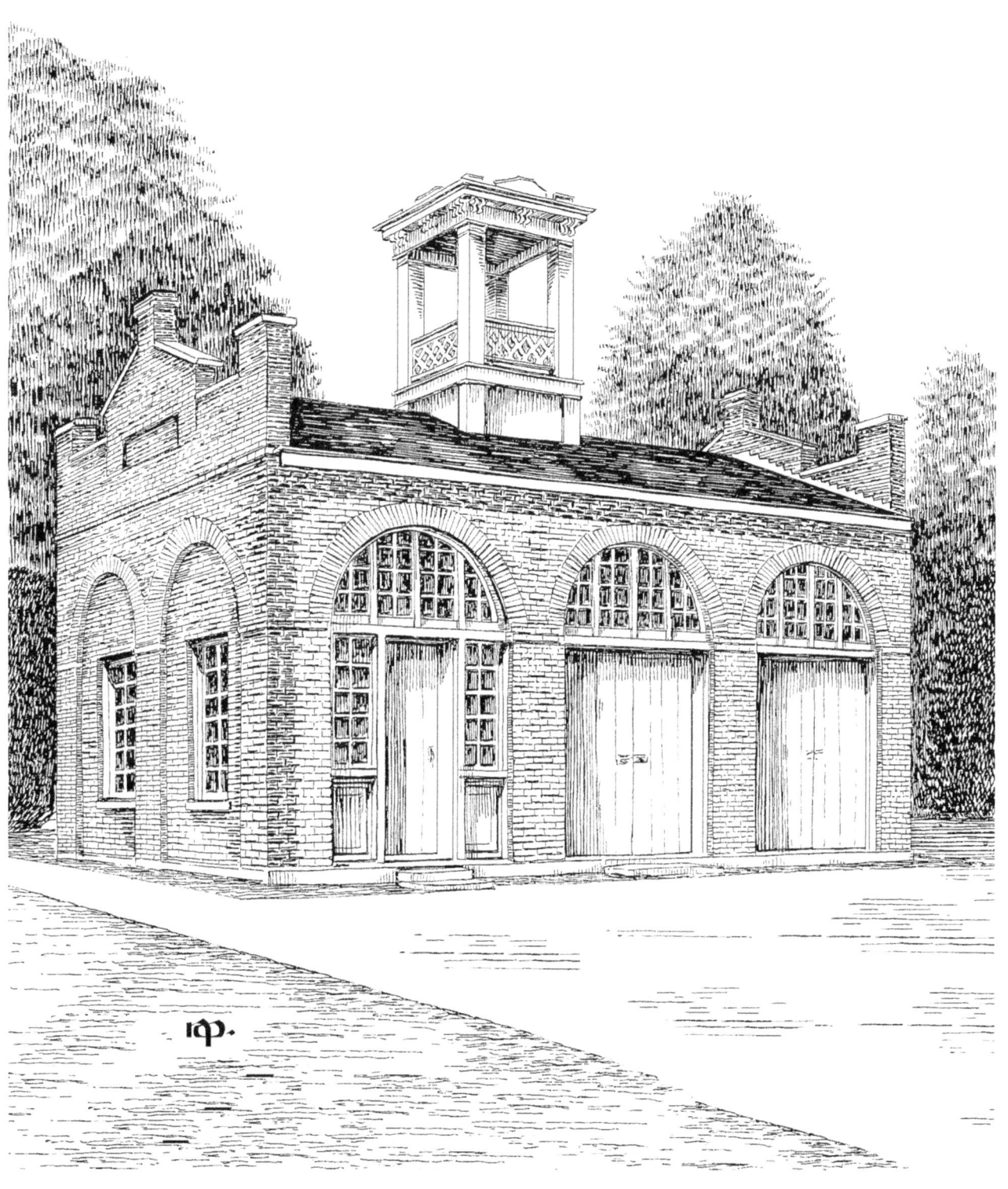

John Brown's Fort

Kentucky's Floral Clock

Frankfort, Kentucky

Kentucky's Floral Clock is unique in all the world. It sits behind the State Capitol, on the west lawn of the Capitol Annex in Frankfort.

On April 10, 1961, Governor Bert T. Combs appropriated $50,000 from the governor's contingency fund to construct the clock on the lawn of the state capitol. Combs had seen a similar clock in Edinburgh, Scotland, and believed it would be a colorful addition to the capitol grounds.

When construction was completed on the clock, some ridiculed it as "Big Bert" (an allusion to London's Big Ben). Combs' political foe, A. B. "Happy" Chandler, was particularly critical.

However, the clock quickly became one of the most talked-about and visited tourist attractions in the state that is well known for an extraordinary amount of attractions; and the most visited place in Frankfort.

The face of the clock is 34 feet across, the planter that holds it weighs 100 tons. The pedestal is faced with Kentucky field stone. It takes as many as 20,000 plants to fill the clock; all are grown in a state-owned greenhouse.

The clock is an unusual timepiece. The hands actually rest for more than 22 hours of the day. They move once every sixty seconds. The 20-foot minute hand makes a sudden, broad sweep, and the 15-foot hour hand budges perceptibly to keep pace with it. It measures off the minutes a foot and a half at a time.

The works contain a control mechanism that makes corrections every hour and even resets the clock in case of power failure. The decor of the clock changes with each of the seasons as well as special occasions.

Sometimes the numbers are replaced with letters spelling out the proud name of KENTUCKY, or PEACE ON EARTH for the Christmas season. Each letter weighs 200 pounds.

Instead of sitting on a bank of earth as most similar floral clocks do, the Frankfort clock is suspended above a pool of water. The pool is 36 feet in diameter and 4.5 feet deep. Visitors use the pool as a wishing well. The coins are collected from the pool every three weeks. In the first three years following the clock's dedication, $6,000 in coins was collected from the pool. The coins are given to educational charities.

The face of the clock slopes at an angle of 26 degrees, so that it is easily observed from the roadway that circles the capitol and runs between the capitol building and the annex; directly in front of the clock.

In the tourist season, some 4,000 cars a day from 32 different states have been recorded at the parking area in front of the clock.

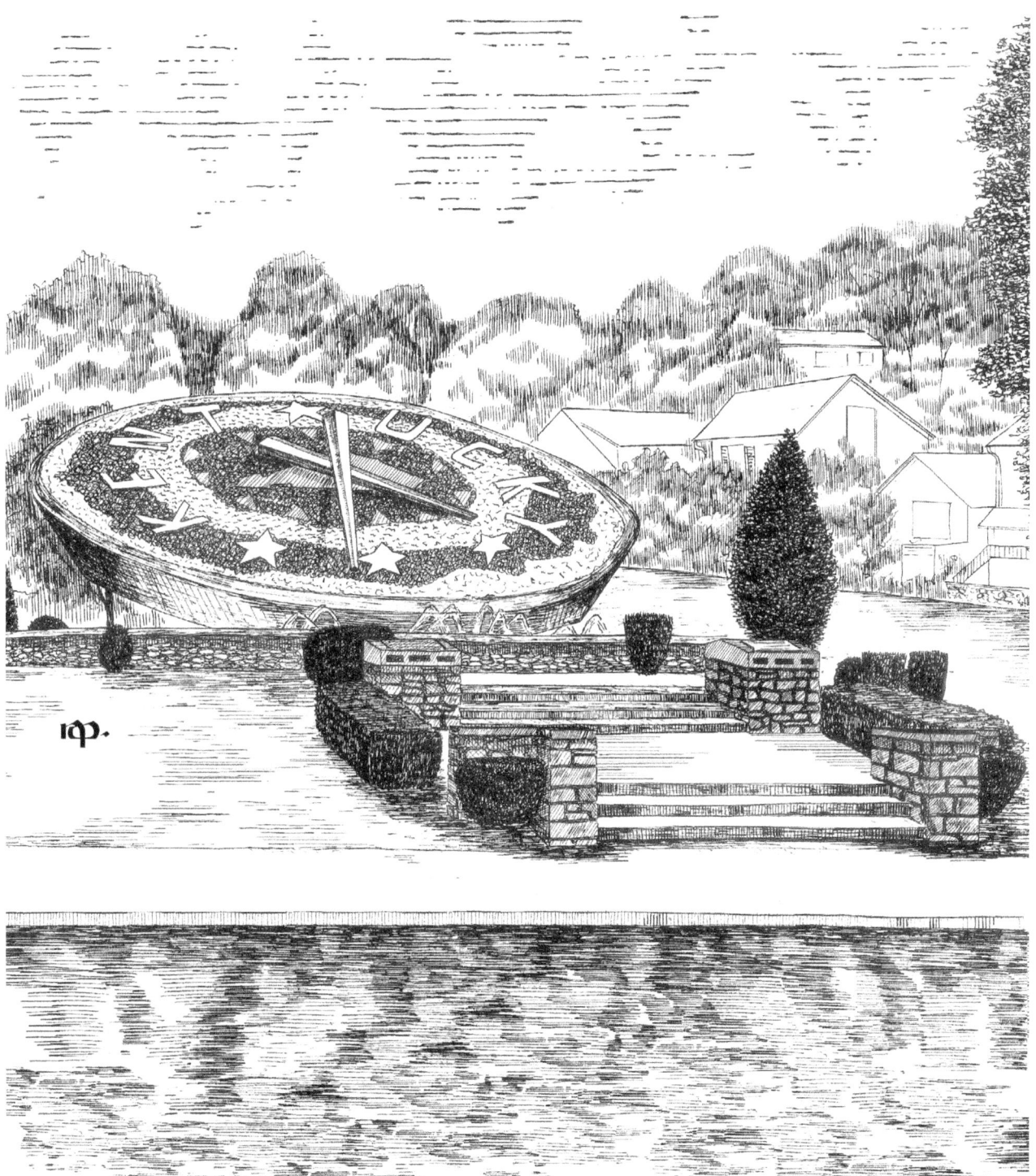

Kentucky's Floral Clock

Kingdom Come Gazebo

Cumberland, Kentucky

The Stone Gazebo is one of the most popular features at the Kingdom Come State Park near Cumberland in Harlan County.

This circular stone landmark is situated at the entrance to the park, and offers a spectacular view of Black Mountain and the town of Cumberland in the valley below.

Located on top of Pine Mountain, Kingdom Come State Park has the highest elevation of any park in the state. The views are spectacular. In the distance can be seen the 4,150 foot Black Mountain, the highest peak in the Commonwealth of Kentucky.

Between 1933 and 1937, the CCC (Civilian Conservation Corps) forged 17 miles of trails. The Kentucky Division of Forestry added 21 miles of new trail during the early 1960s.

The trail was extended over the years until the system covered the crest of Pine Mountain, providing a means for travelers to observe some of the most spectacular scenery in the state.

Originally known as Raven Rock Park, the park was developed and then renamed in 1961 to honor the inspiration of John Fox, whose novel, *The Little Shepherd of Kingdom Come* popularized the area. This was the first American novel to sell more than a million copies.

The park is located midway along the Little Shepherd Trail, which runs 38 miles along the crest of Pine Mountain from Harlan to Whitesburg.

The park proudly claims some of the most extraordinary rock formations in the state that is known for its natural wonders

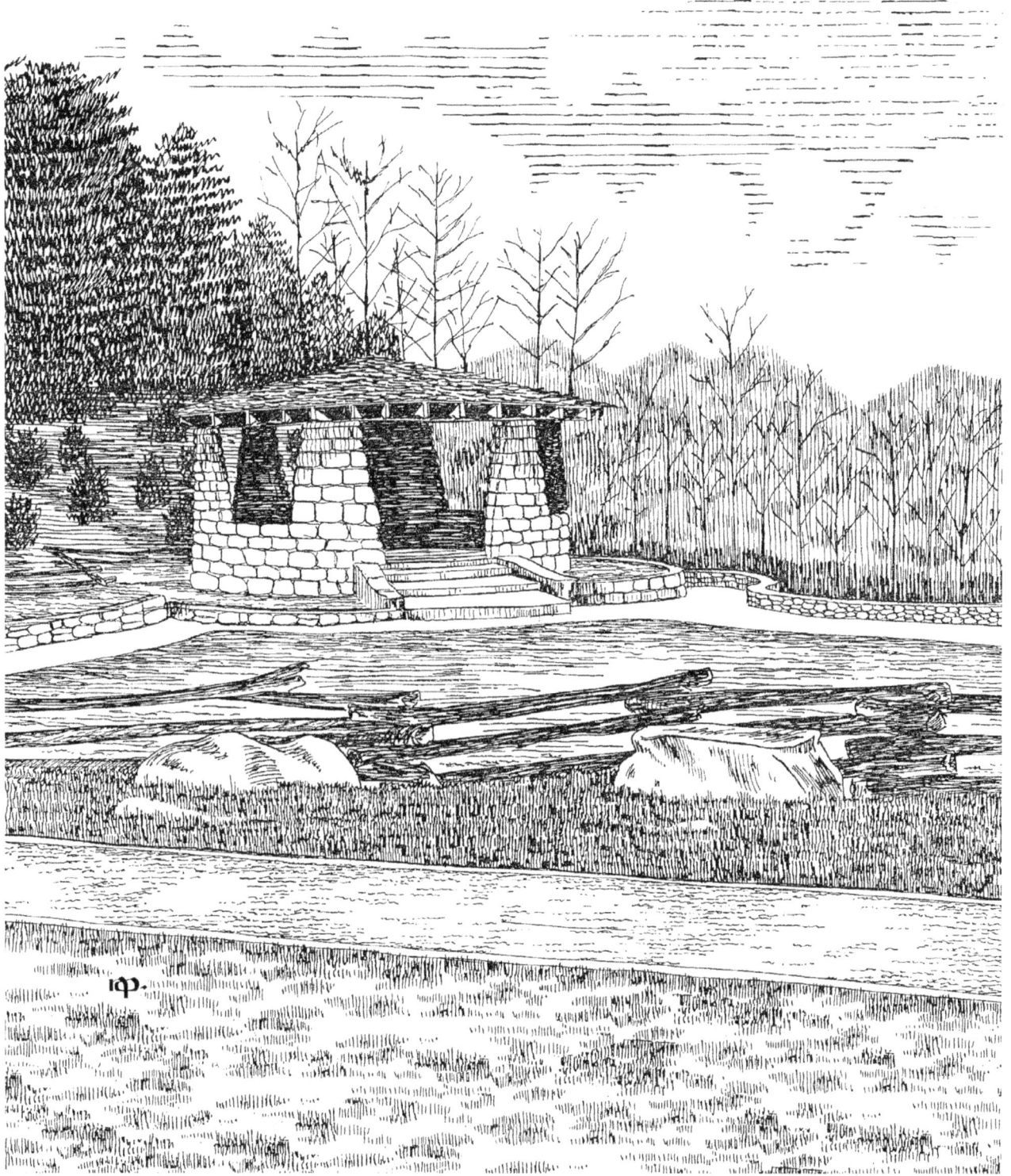

Kingdom Come Gazebo

Lincoln Memorial

Hodgenville, Kentucky

This stately structure celebrates the birthplace of Abraham Lincoln 16th President of the United States. It is located 3 miles south of Hodgenville on the site of Lincoln's birth.

Thomas Lincoln purchased the Sinking Spring Farm in 1808 and Abraham was born there February 12, 1809. The Lincoln Memorial was constructed in 1909, through funds raised by popular subscription.

It was designed by John Russell Pope and built of fine Connecticut pink granite & Tennessee marble.

The cornerstone for the memorial was laid by Pres. Theodore Roosevelt Feb. 12, 1909, the 100th anniversary of Lincoln's birth. The structure was completed and dedicated by President William Taft in 1911. Pres. Woodrow Wilson accepted the property as a gift to the nation in 1916.

The Memorial Building features 16 windows, 16 rosettes on the ceiling, and 16 fence poles, to represent him being the 16th president.

Fifty-six steps, one representing each year of Lincoln's life, lead to the entrance, over which is carved "With Malice Toward None, With charity for All." The inside walls are inscribed with life stories of his parents.

The original log cabin, in which Lincoln was born, was dismantled before 1865. The rough cabin within the memorial is a replica. Lincoln led the nation through its darkest period in history, and the original Memorial to him was constructed by the Lincoln Farm Association.

In 1916, the association donated the Memorial to the U.S. government, which then established the Abraham Lincoln National Park.

The War Department administered the site until August 10, 1933, when it was transferred to the National Park Service. It was designated Abraham Lincoln National Historical Park in 1939, but was renamed and re-designated Abraham Lincoln Birthplace National Historic Site in 1959.

The site was listed on the National Register of Historic Places, effective on October 15, 1966.

The historic site was expanded to include the Knob Creek site in 1998. On March 30, 2009, the two sites were again designated a National Historical Park. The Knob Creek site features a 19th century log cabin and a historic 20th century tavern. Lincoln lived here until the age of seven, when his family moved to Indiana.

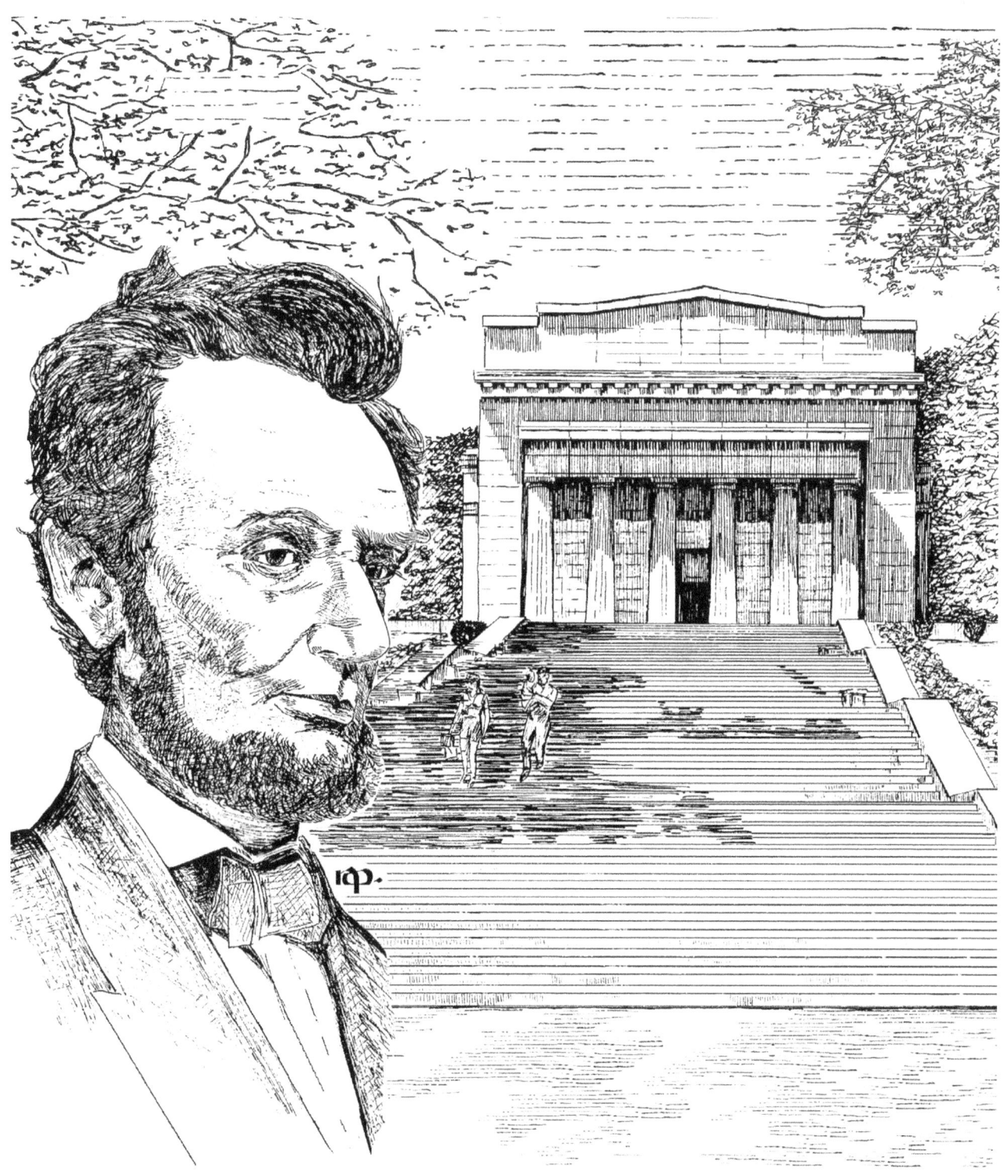

Lincoln Memorial

Longfellow Historic Site

Cambridge, Massachusetts

The Longfellow National Historic Site is located at 105 Brattle Street in Cambridge, Massachusetts. For almost fifty years (1837-1882) it was the home of the noted American poet Henry Wadsworth Longfellow.

For a time, it had previously served as the military headquarters of George Washington during the Revolution.

The house was built in 1759 for John Vassall, who fled the Cambridge area at the beginning of the American Revolutionary War due to his strong loyalty to the king of England.

George Washington used the abandoned home as his first official headquarters as commander of the Continental Army; during the Siege of Boston. He used the house as his headquarters July, 1775 to April, 1776

Andrew Craigie purchased the house in 1791. After his death in 1819 his widow Elizabeth Craigie took in boarders to help with her finances. One of her first boarders was Henry Wadsworth Longfellow.

Longfellow became its owner in 1843, when his father-in-law Nathan Appleton purchased the property as a wedding gift. Longfellow lived in the home until his death in 1882.

His daughter Alice Longfellow was the last of his children to live in the home. In 1913, the Longfellow children established the Longfellow House Trust to preserve the home as a memorial to both Longfellow and Washington.

It was designated as a National Historic Landmark in 1962. The unique collections possess a high degree of integrity and intrinsic value unequaled in most other historic house museums. The house itself is an outstanding example of mid-Georgian architecture.

In 1972, the Trust donated the property and all of its furnishings to the National Park Service. It became the Longfellow National Historic Site; open to the public as a house museum. Everything on display was owned by the Longfellow family.

The site was later renamed to The Longfellow House–Washington's Headquarters National Historic Site on December 22, 2010, to ensure that the connection to Washington was never lost in time or significance.

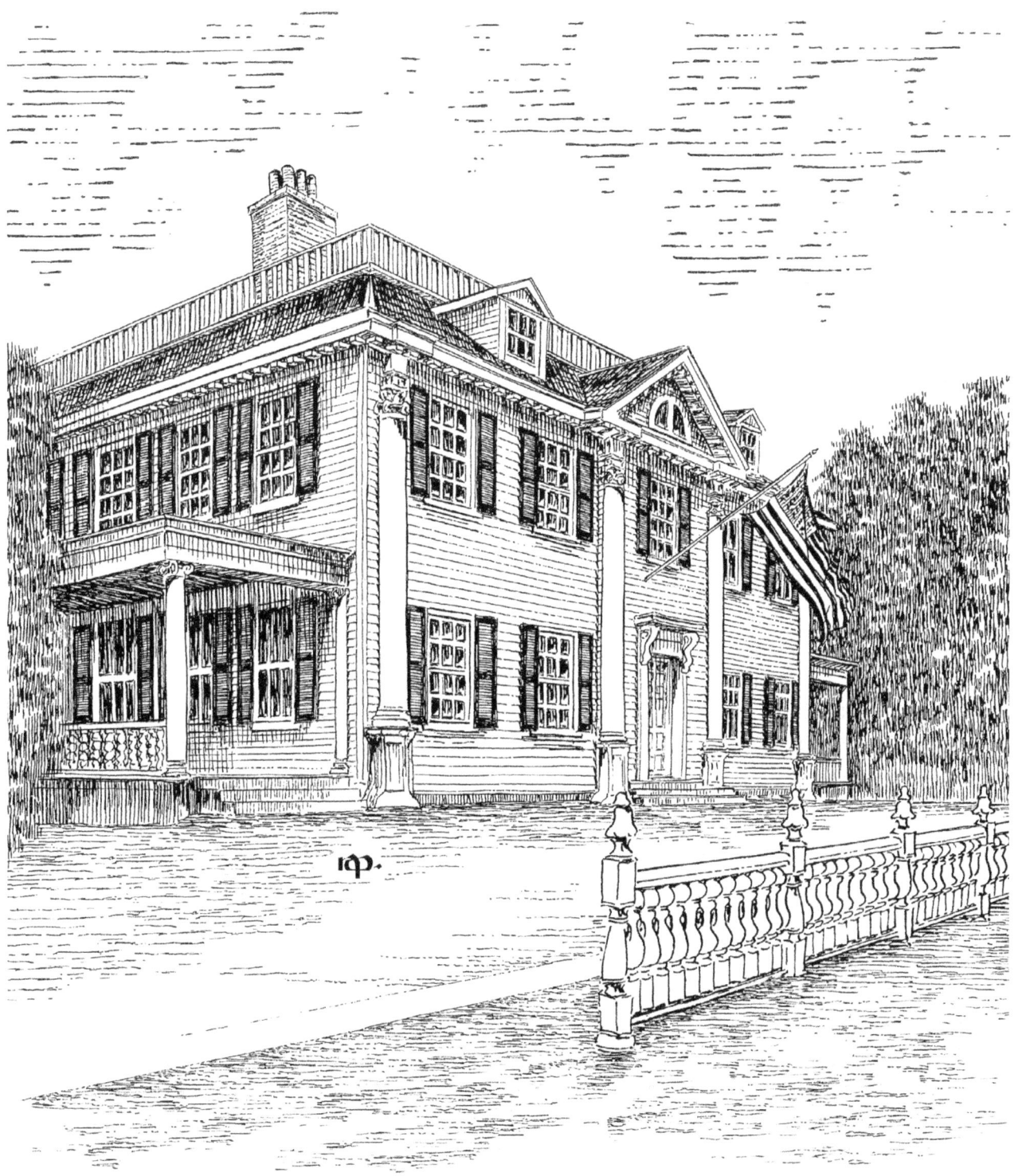

Longfellow Historic Site

Mansfield Roller Mill

Mansfield, Indiana

Located on the banks of the Big Raccoon Creek in Parke County, Indiana, Mansfield Roller Mill extends three and a half stories from a sandstone foundation.

The Mansfield Mill is a gristmill that was built by James Kelsey and Francis Dickson in 1820; it has always run on water power from Big Raccoon Creek. The original mill was a 30-foot by 30-foot log building.

Glacial stones quarried from a nearby farm were used for grinding. In the mid-19th century a sash saw mill and a carding mill were added to the gristmill. The mill is a state historic site still in operation; now run by water turbine engines.

Kelsey built a dam and a water-powered mill, anchoring the foundation deep into the rocky creek bed. This rocky bed can be seen below the dam.

The first dam was made of wood. During the great flood in 1913, the wooden dam was washed away, and a new dam was built out of concrete.

Kelsey named the new community around the mill 'New Dublin'. This name lasted only a few years until other settlers, most of them Irish, began calling the newly developed village Mansfield, believed to have been the Indian name for the area.

In pioneer times a sawmill was attached to the gristmill, and George Hansel, a veteran of the War of 1812, established a boat yard nearby and built flatboats to transport lumber, grain, and salted meats down the Big Raccoon to the Wabash River and on to destinations south.

In 1880 a new mill was built next to the original one, and in 1886 the roller process was introduced. The mill flourished until 1929.

Between 1973 and 1978 actor Tex Kelly, "The Bad Man of the movies" purchased the Mansfield Roller Mill and several other buildings and attempted to turn the town into Frontier City. His efforts failed and in 1979, Tex and wife Isabel sold out and relocated.

Owners Jack & Shirley Dalton and Frank & Sharon Hutcheson donated the mill to the Indiana Department of Natural Resources, Division of State Museums and Historic Sites in 1995. It was developed as an historic park, and the mill continues to operate as part of the exhibition.

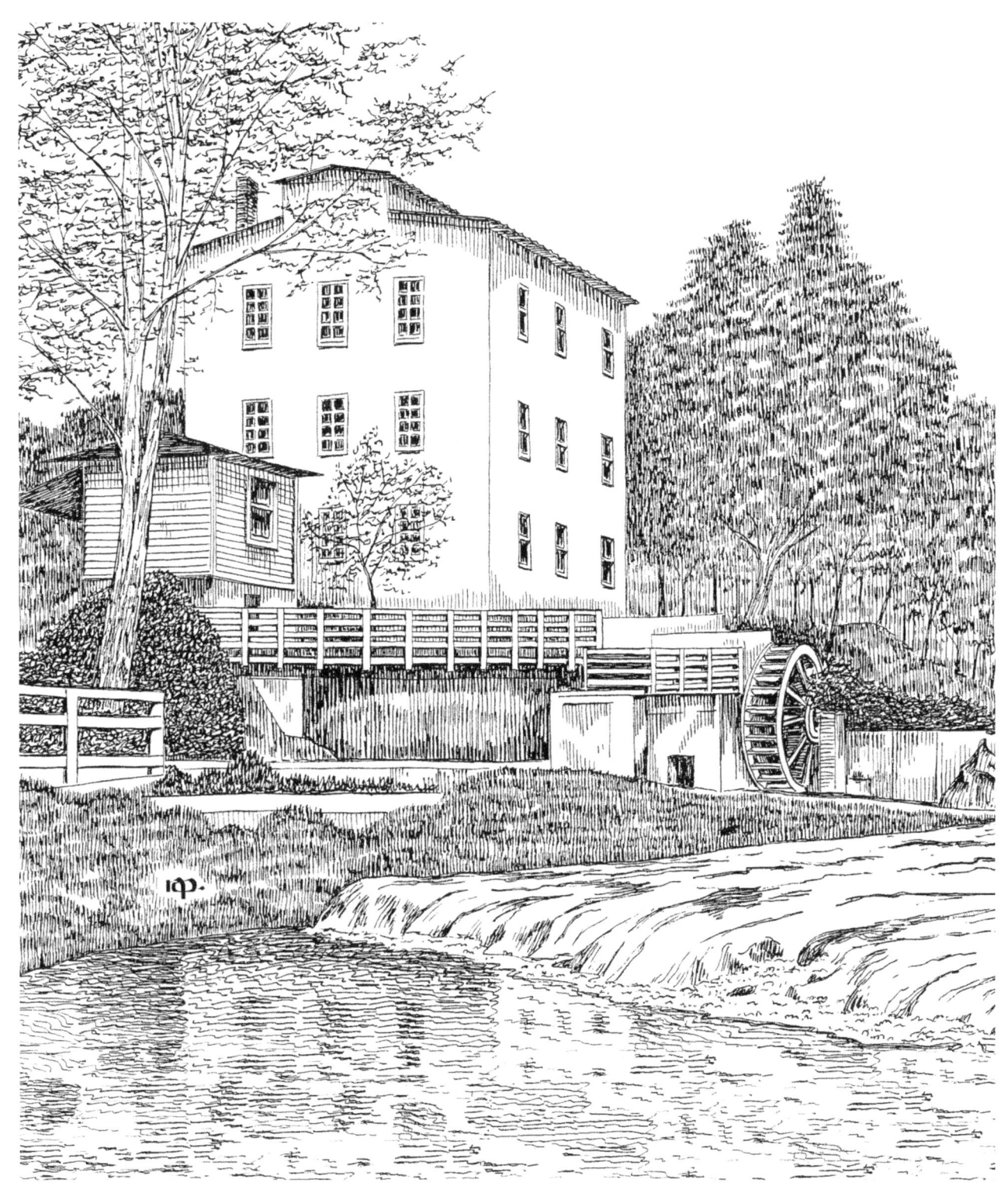

Mansfield Roller Mill

McHargue's Mill
Levi Jackson State Park • London, Kentucky

This stunning old log watermill, situated on a picturesque mill site in southeastern Kentucky, is an actual working model. Set in the stone wall about the mill and on pedestals along the walk is the largest collection of millstones in America.

These specimens of old millstones were gathered from across the state.

At one time there were thousands of these water powered mills situated on Kentucky's numerous streams. Most were built in the early 1800s, and continued until the wide scale use of electricity in the 20th century made them obsolete. The old mills were a vital part of the daily living for the early frontier settler.

The grain that farmers took to the mill was ground between a round, flint-like stone on top that turned, and a stationary stone underneath.

Water rushing over or under the large waterwheel powered the gears which turned the great grinding stone. A bushel of corn could be ground in about five minutes.

Levi Jackson Wilderness Road State Park is on the historic Wilderness Road. In 1775, Daniel Boone blazed a trail through the Cumberland Gap into Kentucky. The road was the main route used by settlers to reach Kentucky from Virginia and all points east.

The Wilderness Road was rough and steep. In spite of the conditions, thousands of people used it. Many of their descendants still live in Kentucky.

Levi Jackson was one of the first settlers in Laurel County. He arrived in 1802 with his partner, John Freeman, who claimed a large tract of land along the Wilderness Road as payment for Freeman's services in the American Revolutionary War.

Jackson built a large two-story house which he licensed as a tavern in 1803. He and John Freeman ran the Wilderness Road Tavern and Laurel River Post Office. The surrounding area became known as "Jackson's Farm" and remained in the Jackson family until 1931 when the land was donated to the state to honor the pioneers.

The land on which Levi Jackson Wilderness Road State Park sits was donated to the state, and park facilities were constructed in 1935, during the Great Depression.

The National Park Service built cabins, foot-bridges, parking areas, an auditorium, and observation tower.

The Civilian Conservation Corps restored an old log cabin and built the McHargue's Mill in 1939. Levi Jackson Wilderness Road State Park serves as both a recreational and historic park.

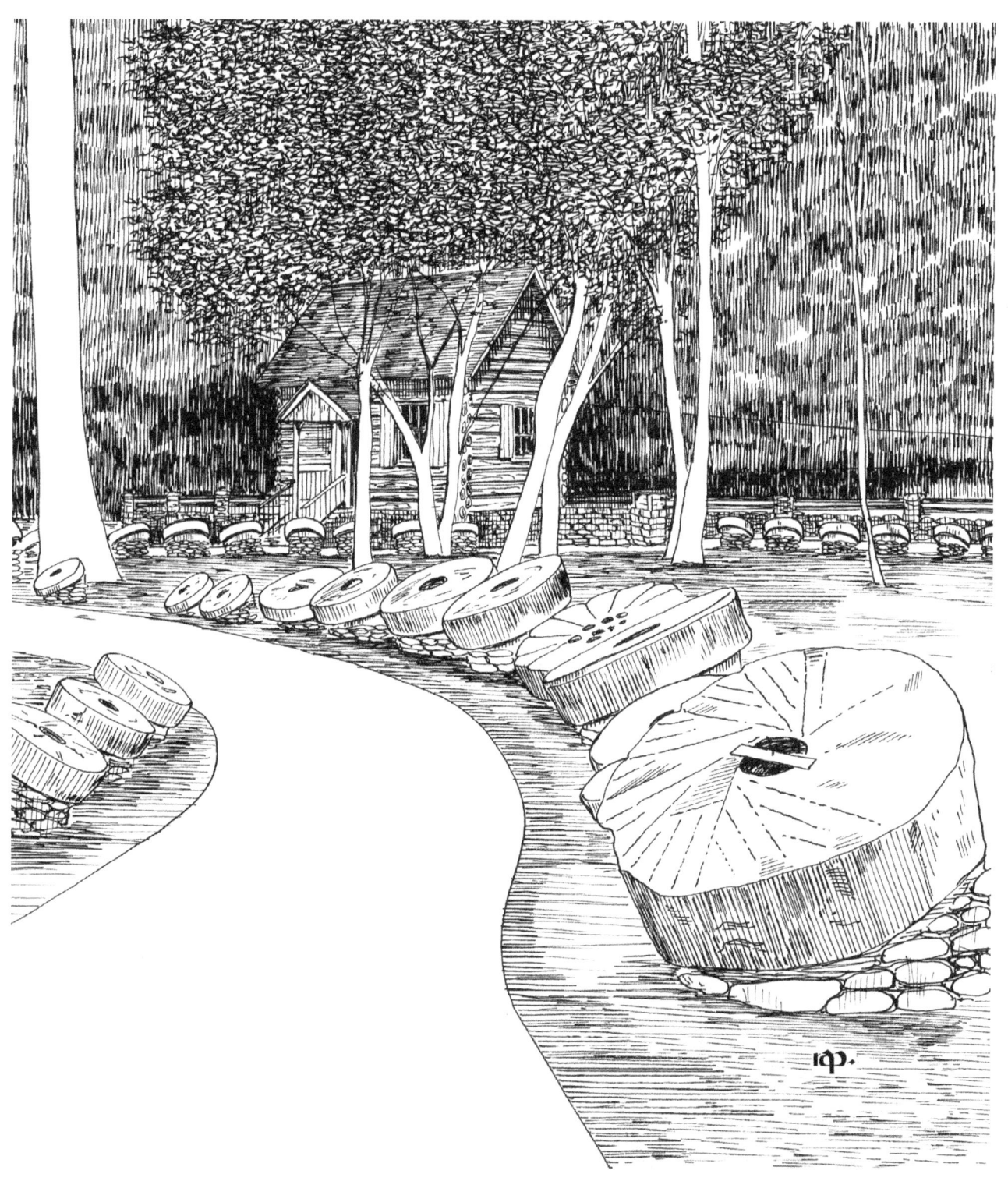

Millstones at McHargue's Mill

Martin Luther King Birthplace
Atlanta, Georgia

Martin Luther King, Jr. was born January 15, 1929 in the home of his maternal grandparents. For the next 12 years he lived here with his parents, grandparents, siblings, other family members and boarders.

His legal name at birth was Michael King. His father was also born Michael King. The father changed both names during a 1934 trip to Nazi Germany to attend the Fifth Baptist World Alliance Congress in Berlin. He decided to be called Martin Luther in honor of the great German reformer Martin Luther.

Young Martin was simply called "M.L." by the family.

Two blocks west of the house is Ebenezer Baptist Church, the pastorate of Martin's grandfather and father, and where for eight years he shared the pulpit with his father.

King became pastor of the Dexter Avenue Baptist Church in Montgomery, Alabama, in 1954, when he was twenty-five years old. In 1960 he returned to become co-pastor at the church with his father, where he would preach about his dream of love, equality and non-violence. The birth home, church, and museum are part of the Martin Luther King, Jr. National Historic Site.

Martin Luther King, Jr. was a clergyman, activist, humanitarian, and leader in the Civil Rights Movement. He is best known for the use of nonviolent civil disobedience.

In 1957 he was elected president of the Southern Christian Leadership Conference (SCLC), an organization formed to provide new leadership for the civil rights movement. As President of the SCLC, Martin Luther King, Jr., worked tirelessly to assure the passage of the Civil Rights Act of 1964 and the Voting Rights Act of 1965.

King helped to organize the 1963 March on Washington, where he gave his "I Have a Dream" speech. There, he established his reputation as one of the greatest orators in American history. On October 14, 1964, King received the Nobel Peace Prize for combating racial inequality through nonviolence.

In 1968 King was planning the campaign; Poor People's occupation of Washington, D.C. However, he was assassinated on April 4, in Memphis, Tennessee. His death was followed by riots in many U.S. cities.

King was awarded the Presidential Medal of Freedom as well as the Congressional Gold Medal after his death. Martin Luther King, Jr. Day was established as a U.S. federal holiday in 1986. Hundreds of streets across the nation have been named in his honor, and a memorial statue on the National Mall was opened to the public in 2011.

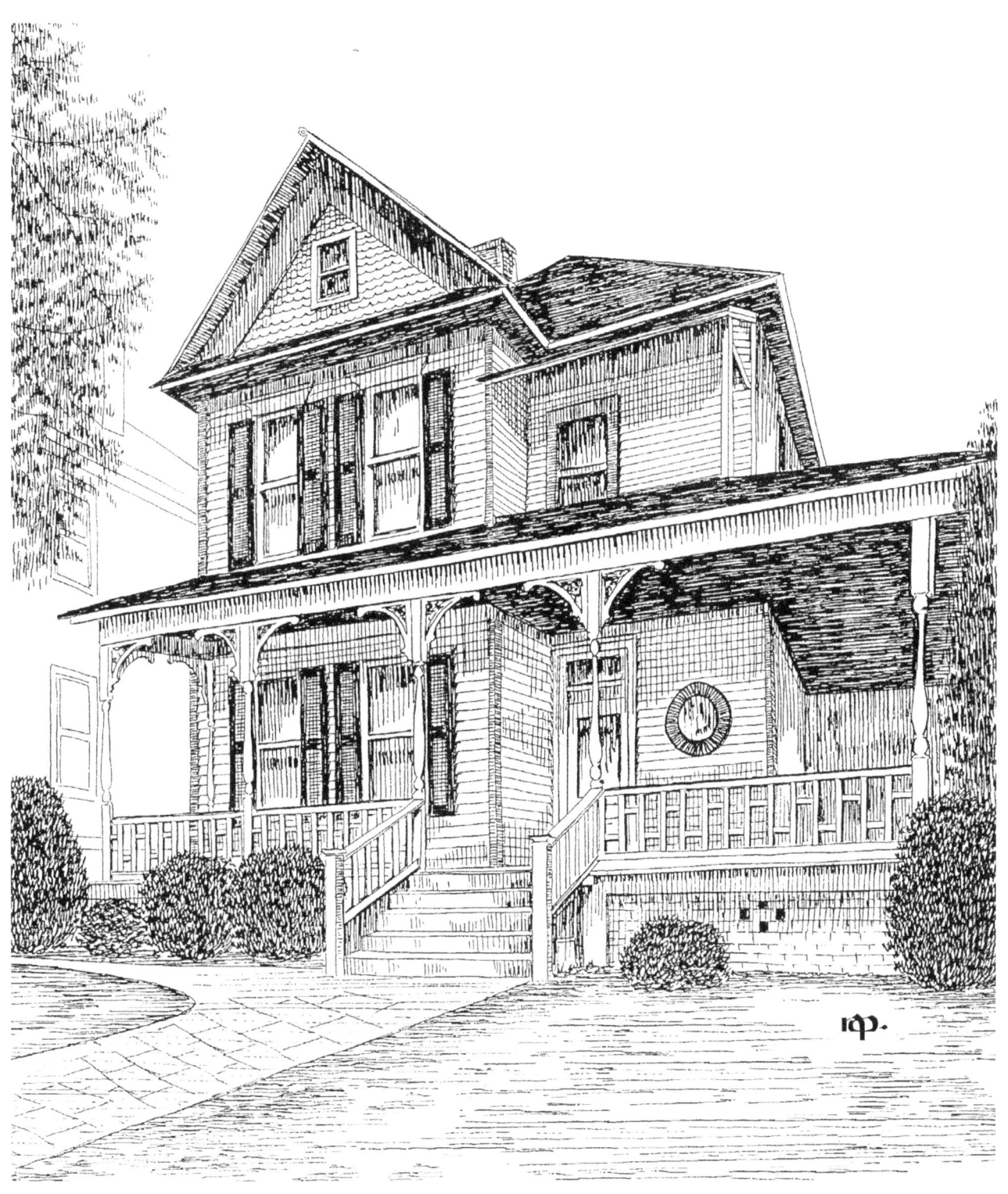

Martin Luther King Birthplace

Mount Rushmore

Keystone, South Dakota

The Mount Rushmore National Memorial represents the American character, ambitions and visions with the sculptured busts of four exalted U.S. presidents; George Washington, Thomas Jefferson, Theodore Roosevelt and Abraham Lincoln.

The Memorial is carved into the granite face of Mount Rushmore in the Black Hills at Keystone, South Dakota. It was sculpted under the direction of Danish-American Gutzon Borglum and his son, Lincoln Borglum.

Mount Rushmore features 60-foot sculptures of the heads of the four presidents; the entire memorial covers 1,278 acres and is situated 5,725 feet above sea level.

South Dakota historian Doane Robinson is credited with conceiving the idea of carving the likenesses of famous people into the Black Hills region of South Dakota. It was his idea in order to promote tourism for the region. In 1924, he persuaded sculptor Gutzon Borglum to travel to the area to ensure the carving could be done.

Borglum was involved in sculpting the Confederate Memorial Carving on Stone Mountain in Georgia.

After securing federal funding through the enthusiastic sponsorship of Mount Rushmore's great political patron, U.S. Senator Peter Norbeck, construction on the memorial began in 1927. The actual faces were completed between 1934 and 1939.

By July 4, 1934, Washington's face was dedicated. The face of Thomas Jefferson was dedicated in 1936, and the face of Abraham Lincoln was dedicated on September 17, 1937. In 1939, the face of Theodore Roosevelt was dedicated.

In 1933, the National Park Service took Mount Rushmore under its jurisdiction. Gutzon Borglum died in March 1941, and his son Lincoln took over to complete the final stages of construction.

The initial concept called for each president to be depicted as a full bust, from head to waist; however, lack of funding forced construction to end in late October 1941.

Drilling into the immense 6,200 foot mountain began in 1927, and took 14 years to complete at a mere cost of one million dollars. It is now considered to be priceless.

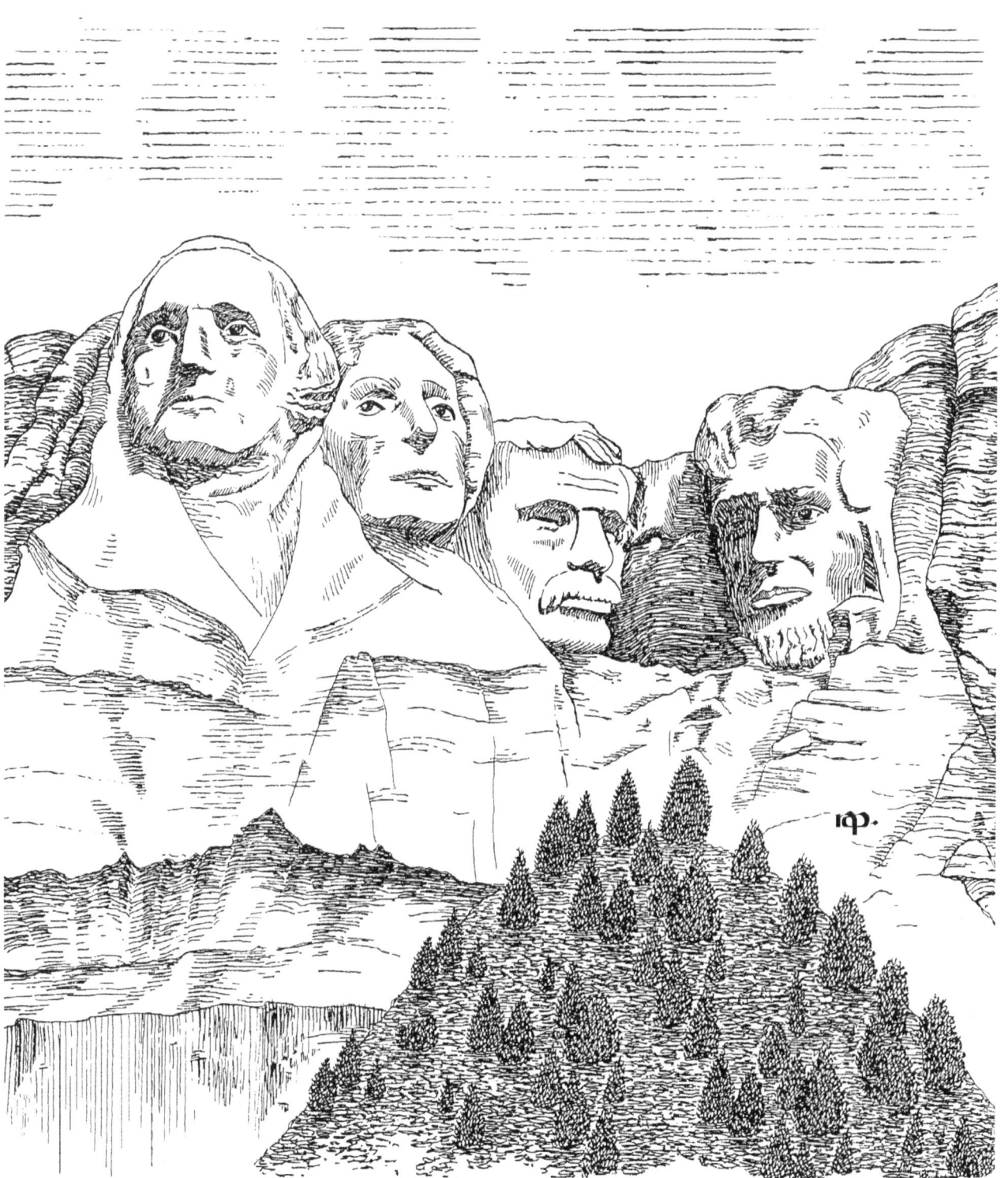

Mount Rushmore

Natural Bridge

Slade, Kentucky

Natural Bridge has exhilarated Americans long before the days of Daniel Boone. The area surrounding the bridge is full of Indian relics, shelters and burial grounds.

It has been estimated that the formation of this impressive natural arch took several million years. The ridge, of which this reddish rock of the Paleozoic era is a part, forms the line which separates the Kentucky counties of Powell and Wolfe.

The state park contains 137 acres of rugged land and natural wonders. It is located totally within Powell County.

Natural Bridge forms a giant arch with an opening 78 feet in length and 65 feet high. There are more than 15 million pounds of rock in suspension, supported by two immense abutments.

The rock at the center of the arch is 40 feet thick and 30 feet wide, and flat enough on top to actually serve as a bridge, but it is located on top of the mountain ridge, a mile from the closest roadway; available by foot traffic only.

It was not carved by steam erosion, but by the disintegrating action of wind, mist, rain and frost.

The park was founded as a tourist attraction in 1896 by the Lexington and Eastern Railroad.

When the L & E was purchased by the Louisville & Nashville Railroad in 1910, Natural Bridge was a popular excursion from the nearby Bluegrass.

It was turned over to the state with the belief that State ownership and more extensive improvements would give the park the status it deserved. It became one of Kentucky's original four state parks in 1925.

The park has 2,369 acres and is basically surrounded by the Daniel Boone National Forest. There are over 20 miles of trails over uneven terrain from moderate to strenuous difficulty. The park's half-mile original trail to the natural bridge dates from the 1890s.

Natural Bridge has several unique sandstone rock formations, including the Balanced Rock, not far from the Hemlock Lodge. In the early days it was called the Sphinx because it crudely resembles the Sphinx in Egypt.

Although it is now called Balanced Rock, it is in fact a pedestal; a single piece of stone that has weathered in such a fashion that its midsection is narrower than its cap or its base.

This formation is one of the biggest and most perfectly formed examples of a pedestal rock east of the Rocky Mountains.

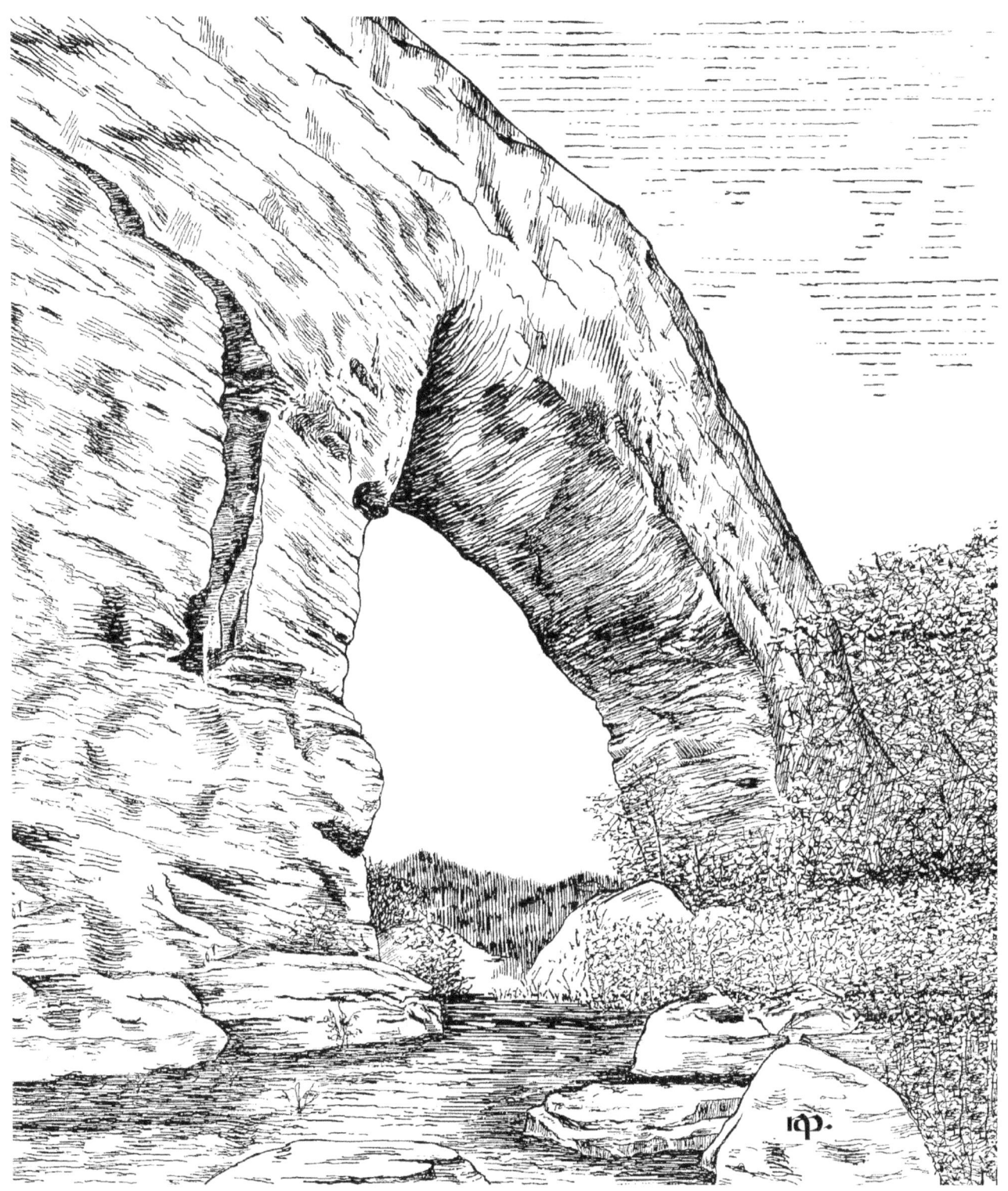

Natural Bridge

New River Rafting

Fayetteville, West Virginia

The New River, part of the Ohio River watershed, is a tributary of the Kanawha River about 320 miles long.

The river flows through the states of North Carolina, Virginia, and West Virginia. Much of the river's course through West Virginia is designated as the New River Gorge National River, and the New River itself is classified as an American Heritage River.

Much of the river's course is lined with steep cliffs and rock outcrops, particularly in its gorge in West Virginia.

The New River Gorge is not only quite scenic, but also offers numerous opportunities for white-water recreation such as rafting and kayaking.

Many open ledges along the rim of the gorge offer popular views, with favorites including Hawks Nest State Park and various overlooks on lands of the New River Gorge National River.

New River Gorge National River includes 53 miles of free-flowing New River, beginning at Bluestone Dam and ending at Hawks Nest Lake.

The New River rafting typifies West Virginia style whitewater.

It was named New River because it was not known to early Atlantic Coast explorers. Despite its name; however, the New River is the third-oldest river in the world geologically, and the only non-tidal river that crosses the vast Appalachian Mountains.

The New River is impounded by Bluestone Dam, to create Bluestone Lake in Summers County, WV. The Bluestone River tributary joins the New River in Bluestone Lake.

Just below the dam the Greenbrier River joins New River, which continues its northward course into the New River Gorge. Near the end of the gorge the river flows by the town of Fayetteville, West Virginia. A few miles northwest of Fayetteville, much of the New River's flow is diverted through the 3-mile Hawks Nest Tunnel for use in power generation. The water re-enters the river just upstream of Gauley Bridge, where the New merges with the Gauley River to form the Kanawha River.

The Kanawha is a tributary of the Ohio River, which in turn is a tributary of the Mississippi River.

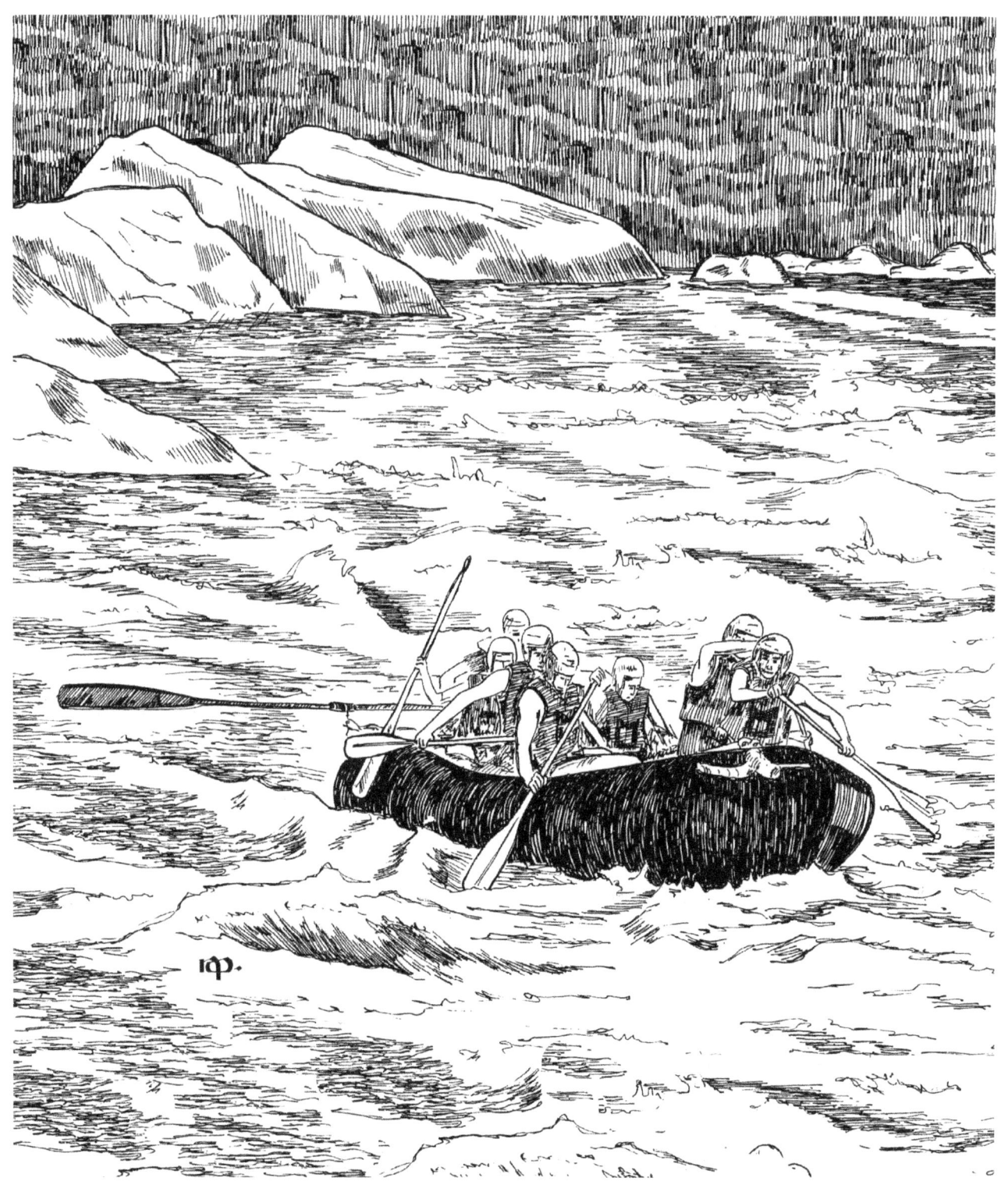

New River Rafting

Norris Dam

Tennessee

Norris Dam is part of Norris Dam State Park located in Anderson County and Campbell County, Tennessee. It was the first dam built by the TVA (Tennessee Valley Authority).

Norris Dam was the pilot project of the Tennessee Valley Authority, a Great Depression-era entity created by the United States government in 1933 to control flooding and bring electricity and economic development to the Tennessee Valley.

Construction on Lake Norris Dam began in 1933 and was completed in 1936. The Dam is a straight concrete gravity-type dam; 1860 feet long and 265 feet high.

Norris Lake is the largest reservoir on a tributary of the Tennessee River. The dam has a maximum generating capacity of 131,400 kilowatts.

Norris has the largest flood control storage of any TVA dam on a tributary of the Tennessee. Norris Lake extends 72 miles up the Clinch River and 56 miles up the Powell River. It has 809 miles of shoreline and a surface area of more than 34,000 acres.

Recreational use of the reservoir exceeds that of any other tributary lake. TVA acquired the entire shoreline of the reservoir, and it is all dedicated to public use.

Norris Dam State Park is situated along the shores of Norris Lake. It includes 4,038 acres managed by the Tennessee Department of Environment and Conservation.

The park administers the Lenoir Museum Complex, which has a mission to interpret the aboriginal, pioneer, and early 20th-century history of the area.

Along with Norris Dam State Park, there are several protected entities along Norris Lake's shores, including Big Ridge State Park, Chuck Swan State Forest, the Cove Creek Wildlife Management Area, and River Bluff Small Wild Area.

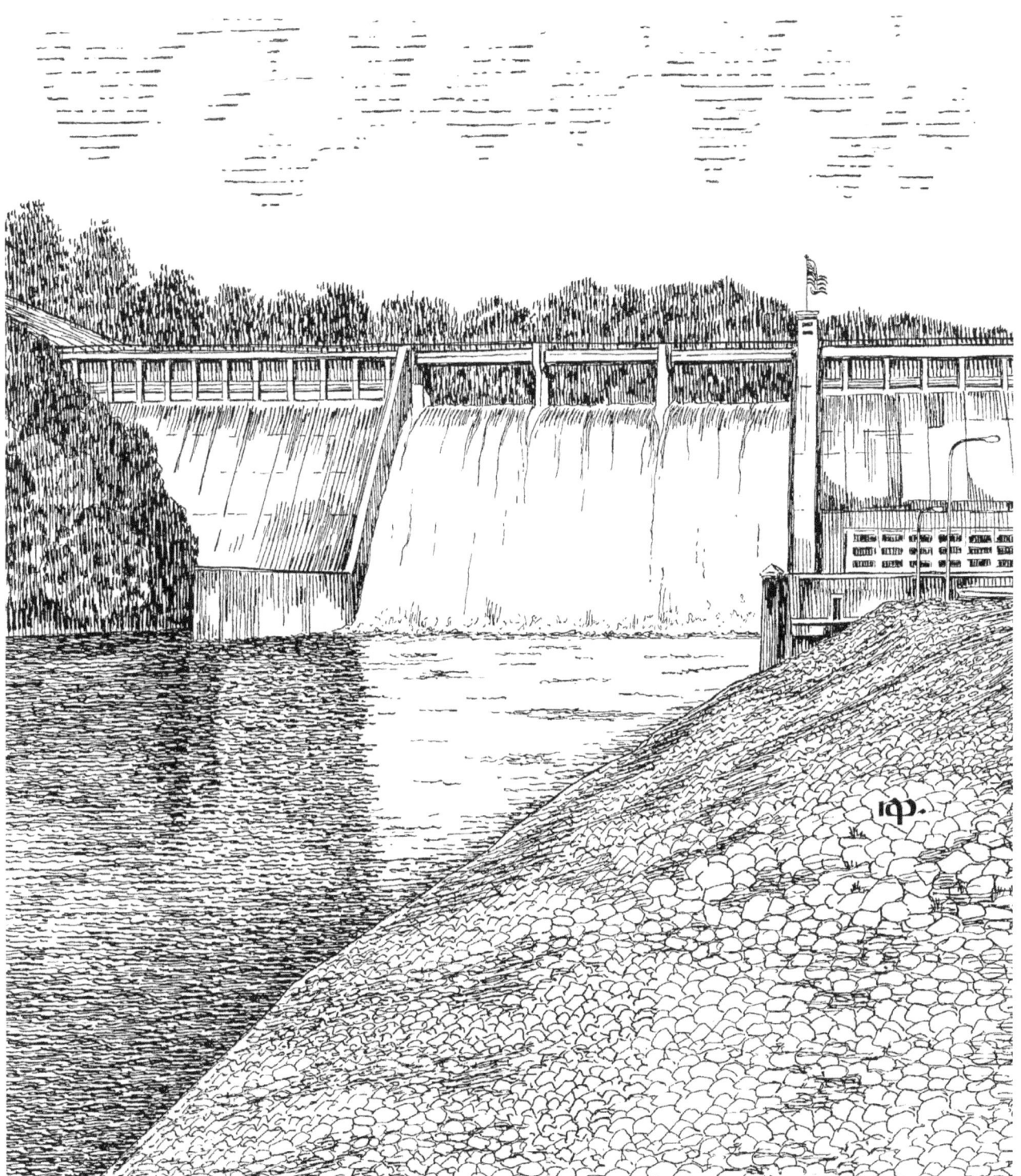

Norris Dam

Orlando Train Depot

Orlando, Florida

The Atlantic Coast Line Station in Orlando was built in 1926. The Mission style of Spanish Revival is identifiable by elements adapted from mission churches of the Southwest.

The Orlando Amtrak Station lies south of Downtown Orlando, about a mile south of the old stations at Church Street and Central Boulevard.

It was built in 1926 by M. A. Griffith and W. T. Hadlow for the Atlantic Coast Line Railroad, and used by the Seaboard Coast Line Railroad after the 1967 merger with Seaboard Air Line.

Orlando Station serves the Silver Meteor and Silver Star lines. It is a planned stop on the SunRail commuter rail system, which is proposed to be operational in 2014. Additionally it is the designated terminus for the Orange Blossom Express commuter rail project out of Lake County.

Plans to upgrade the station for SunRail service include a matching canopy for the second platform and a name change to "Orlando Health/Amtrak Station" due to its proximity to the main Orlando Health hospital campus, Orlando Regional Medical Center, the Arnold Palmer Hospital for Children and the Winnie Palmer Hospital for Women & Babies.

Perhaps the most reliable story about how this famous city got its name, concerns an American volunteer soldier. During the Seminole Wars in 1835, Orlando Reeves saw an Indian sneaking up on the camp, and gave the alarm to save his company.

Some soldiers who stayed to make this beautiful site their home, named the future town in his honor. The town was founded in 1857.

The Civil War took people and money away from the young town and caused the economy to flounder. However, the town survived on cattle and citrus farming.

Completion of the South Florida Railroad in 1880 expanded the limits of population, prosperity and architecture. The farming community that survived is what Walt Disney found in the 1960s when he quietly began buying farmland for what was to become the world's largest theme park.

Disney World opened in 1971, and is still the most popular man-made attraction in the world. The park spurred all kinds of growth and other attractions to the area. Orlando was quickly transformed into a bustling modern International city.

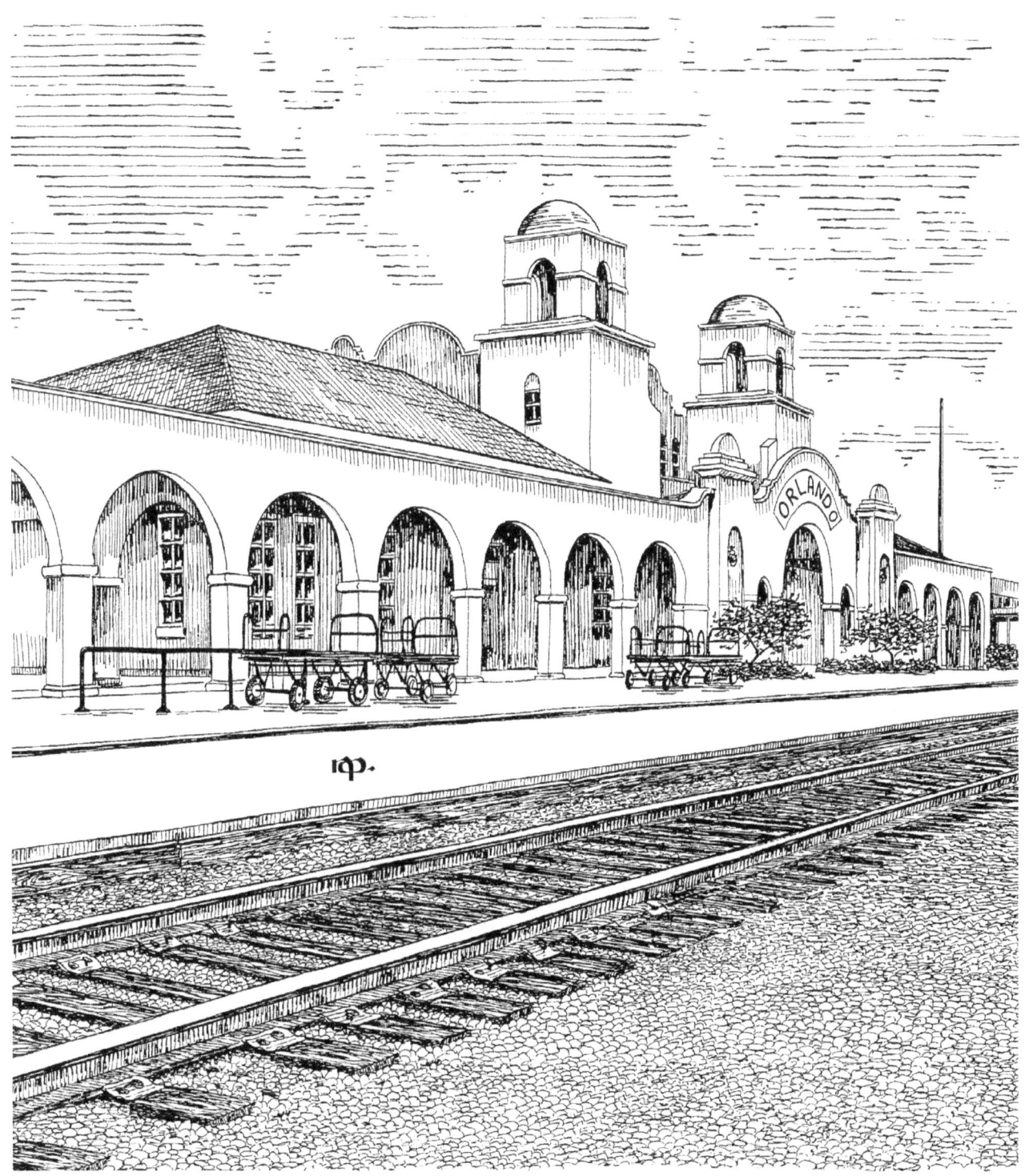

Orlando Train Depot

Paul Revere

And the Old North Church • Boston, Massachusetts

Paul Revere and the Old North Church are symbols for American Independence and Freedom. The Old North Church in the background of the statue of Revere was built in 1723.

This beautiful building is still an active Episcopal Church. It was from the steeple that the two lanterns were hung by Robert Newman, on April 18, 1775 to signal Revere and ignite the War for Independence that led to the birth of our Nation.

This statue of Paul Revere on the Freedom Trail is one of the most photographed sculptures in Boston. Not surprisingly the sculptor portrayed Revere during the famous Midnight Ride, but unlike many images where he is galloping at full speed, the motion of the bronze Revere is more dignified.

Although the statue is one of the most recognized landmarks in Boston, it is hard to imagine that it took 16 years to create and 40 years to install in its present location.

The sculptor Cyrus Edwin Dallin began working on it in 1883, more than 20 years after the name of Revere was immortalized by Henry Wadsworth Longfellow in his poem in 1860.

Dallin was at the time a teacher at the Massachusetts State Normal Art School when he received the contract. The final design was approved in 1899.

The sculptor was only 22 when he was awarded the contract. But it was not until September 22, 1940 that the statue was opened for the public. Dallin died four years later in 1944.

In the spring of 1775 Paul Revere went to warn John Hancock and Samuel Adams of the possibility of their arrest by the British and to alert the population and the militia that the British soldiers were coming to disarm them. He was asked to let them know when the British were actually on the move and how they might advance.

Revere had to figure out the fastest way to alert the Patriots that the British were on the march. On his way back to Boston he stopped in Charlestown. He met Colonel Conant and they set up a plan to place signals in the tower of the Old North Church in the North End of Boston. The tower of the Church was the highest point across the Charles River so the signal would be visible.

They would hang one lantern if the British were moving by land or two lanterns if they were crossing the Charles River by boat. The plan was all set and ready for execution.

Two days later on April 18, Revere was told that the British were preparing their boats to cross the river. Paul Revere took the horseback ride to Lexington that immortalized him.

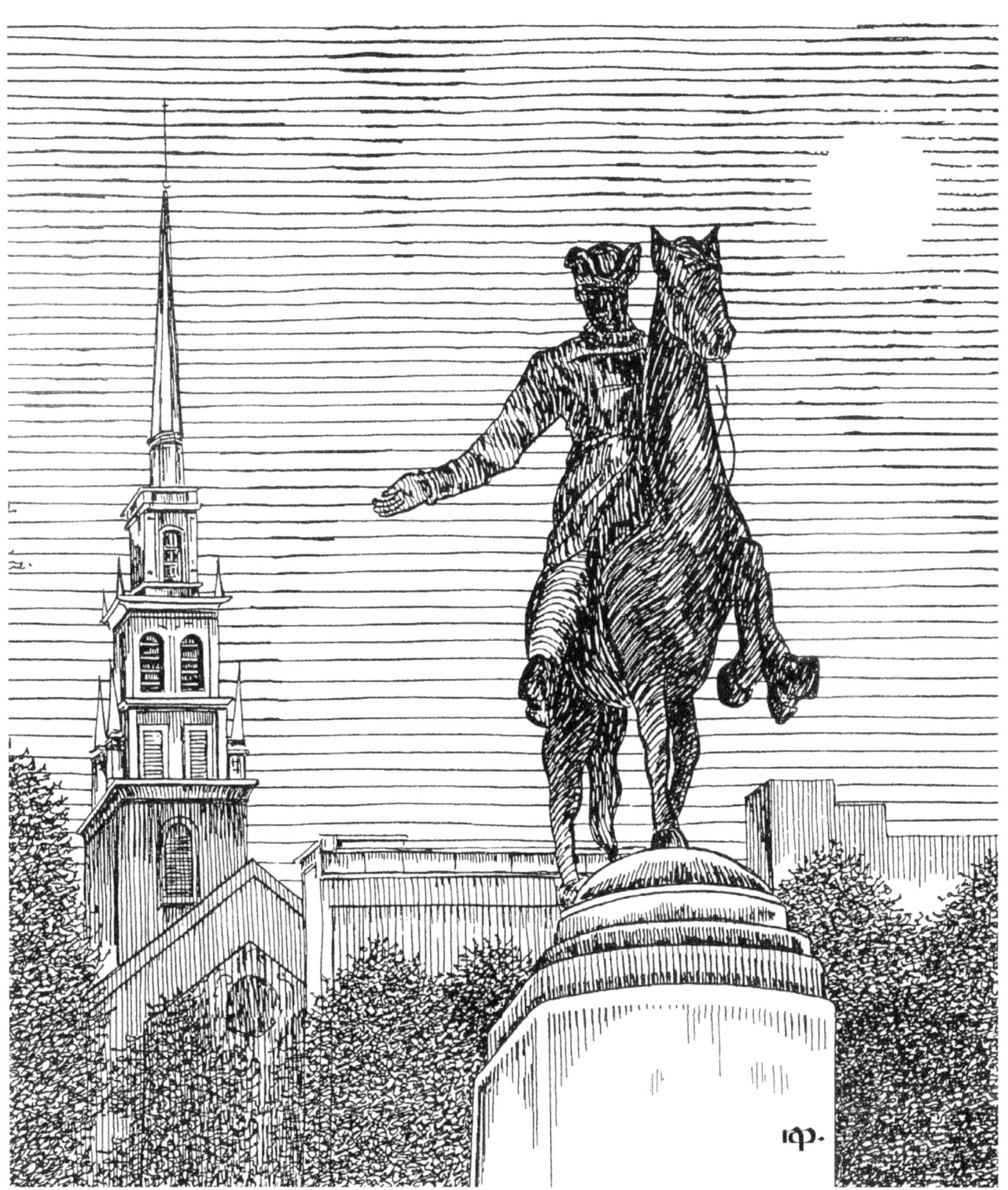

Paul Revere

Point Park

Chattanooga, Tennessee

Point Park is located atop of Lookout Mountain near Chattanooga, Tennessee. The famous Incline Railway runs straight up the steep face of the mountain to over 2,100 feet above sea level. The park, where the Civil War Battle Above the Clouds was fought in 1863, is located just a short walk from the incline railway station.

At one point the rail grade is 72.7 percent. It is the steepest passenger incline in the world.

In 1890, the U.S. Congress made provisions to establish a military park to commemorate the Civil War battles of both Chickamauga, Georgia and the nearby battle at Chattanooga.

The Point Park facility was officially dedicated in 1895.

Lookout Mountain is one of the Chattanooga area's most visited tourist attractions. Civil War-related landmarks include Point Park, which is operated by the National Park Service.

Besides the beautiful park and its monuments, many other marvelous sights are located in the immediate vicinity where the Confederate soldiers defended Lookout Mountain from Gen. Ulysses S. Grant; such as Rock City and Ruby Falls.

The Battle of Lookout Mountain was fought November 24, 1863, as part of the Chattanooga Campaign of the Civil War. Union forces under Maj. General Joseph Hooker defeated the Confederate forces commanded by Maj. General Carter L. Stevenson.

Lookout Mountain was only one engagement in the Chattanooga battles between Gen. Ulysses S. Grant's Military Division of the Mississippi and the Confederate Army of Tennessee, commanded by Gen. Braxton Bragg.

The battle lifted the siege of Union forces in Chattanooga, and opened the gateway into the Deep South.

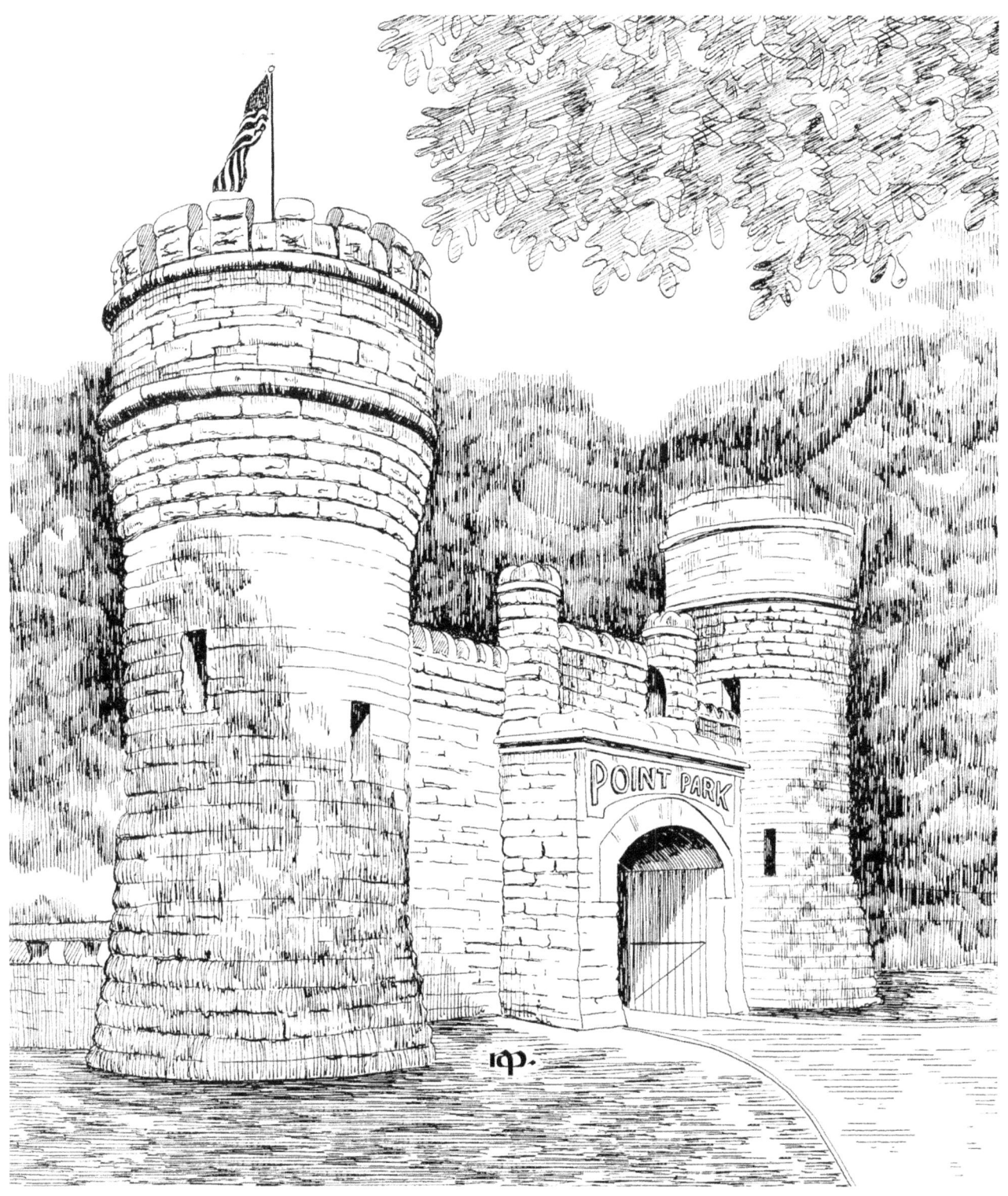

Point Park

Prickett's Fort

Fairmont, West Virginia

Prickett's Fort is perched on a small rise overlooking Prickett's Creek and the Monongahela River.

This rustic old log fort has been reconstructed on the site of the original 1774 fort, which served as a refuge from Native American war parties on the western frontier of Colonial Virginia.

The Fort was built to defend early European settlers of what today is West Virginia from raids by hostile Native Americans, a portion of whose territory the settlers appropriated following the Treaty of Fort Stanwix (1768).

A band of settlers led by Daniel Greathouse perpetrated the Yellow Creek massacre in 1774, initiating Lord Dunmore's War. After that, all settlers in the Ohio River Valley were in peril from Indian attack.

Perhaps as many as 80 families, several hundred people, gathered at Prickett's Fort during crisis periods, where they stayed for days or even weeks. Prickett's Fort was never attacked, although militiamen from the area were killed by Indians elsewhere.

The re-constructed Prickett's Fort was completed in 1976 under the direction of Prickett's Fort Memorial Foundation. The 100 by 100 foot square fort is built with 12-foot-high log walls and blockhouses at each corner.

The complex includes 16 cabins, a meeting hall and storehouse. It serves as a living history site that features costumed interpreters and authentic demonstrations of pioneer crafts.

When the threat of any uprisings occurred, all families from the area surrounding the fort would hurry inside. They crowded into the small fort as long as the threat existed - days, weeks or even months. "Forting up" was a way of life on the frontier. Cramped quarters were unpleasant, but such sacrifices were necessary for survival in the late 1700s.

Also on site is the restored home of Job Prickett. This home was built in 1859 by the great-grandson of Captain Jacob Prickett, for whom the fort is named. It accentuates development of the lifestyle in the 85-year span of time.

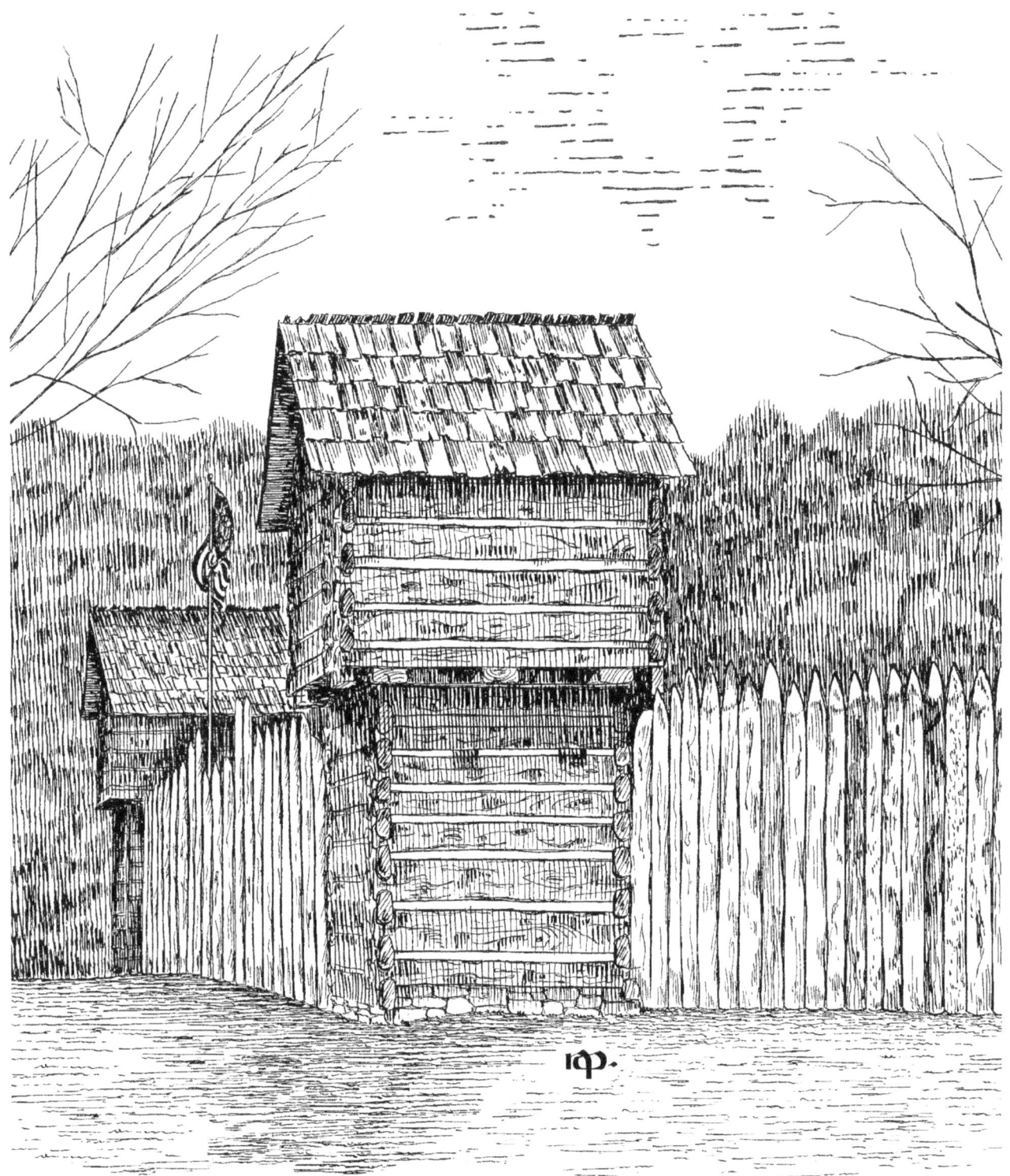

Prickett's Fort

Sponge Docks

Tarpon Springs, Florida

The Sponge Docks at Tarpon Springs embody the key focus for this unique community. The region, with a series of bayous feeding into the Gulf of Mexico, first attracted attention as a place for winter homes about 1876.

The area was known as Anclote. A. W. Ormond was standing on the shore of the bayou with his daughter Mary, who saw a tarpon (fish) jump high out of the water. "Look at that tarpon spring!" she exclaimed.

Since that time, the town has been called Tarpon Springs, and the bayou is known as Spring Bayou. Tarpon Springs was incorporated in 1887, with 46 registered voters. That year, railroad service to New York was inaugurated, and this vicinity became a popular winter resort for northern tourists.

The first Greek immigrants arrived in this city during the 1880s. They were hired to work as divers in the growing sponge harvesting industry. They brought with them their culture, food, religion and music.

In 1905, John Cocoris introduced the technique of sponge diving to Tarpon Springs. He recruited Greek sponge divers from the Dodecanese Islands of Greece.

By the 1930s, a very productive sponge industry had developed, generating millions of dollars a year.

The 1953 film *Beneath the 12-Mile Reef,* depicting sponge diving, takes place & was filmed in Tarpon Springs.

There were some 200 boats working the Gulf of Mexico from Key West to Appalachicola, harvesting 3 million dollars' worth of sponges annually in the 1930s.

When a red tide algae bloom occurred in 1947, wiping out the sponge fields in that region of the Gulf of Mexico, most of the sponge boats and divers switched to fishing and shrimping for a livelihood.

The city converted most of its sponge-related activities, especially the warehouses where they were sold, into tourist attractions.

The Sponge Docks are now mostly shops, restaurants, and museums that are dedicated to the memory of Tarpon Springs' earlier industry.

Attempts have been made in recent years to restart local sponge harvesting, and in the late 1980s the sponge industry made a comeback. In the fall of 2007 a record harvest of sponges by a single boat was made.

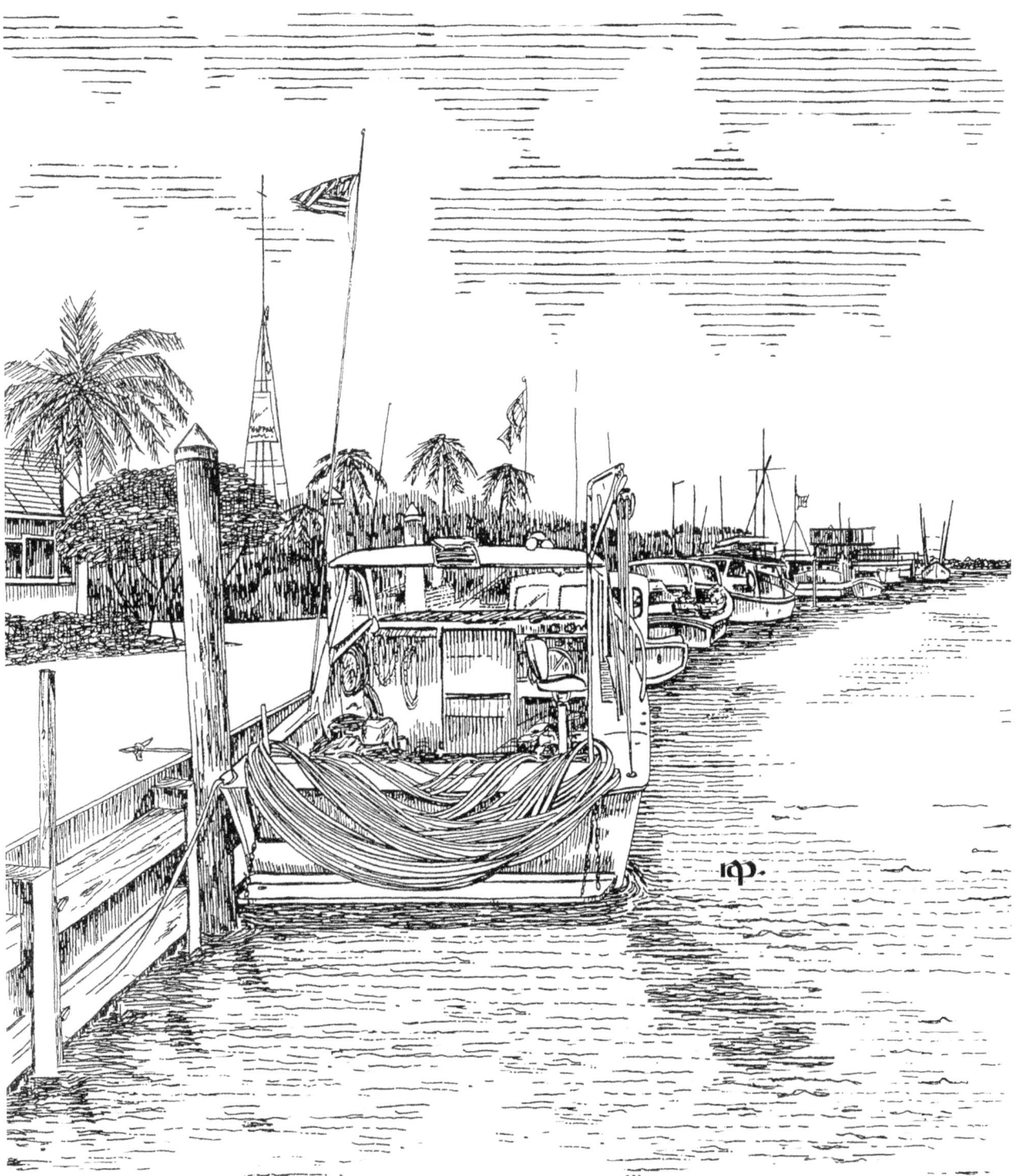

Sponge Docks

Springwood

Home of Franklin D. Roosevelt • Hyde Park, New York

Home of Franklin D. Roosevelt National Historic Site preserves the Springwood estate in Hyde Park, New York. This was the birthplace, lifelong home, and burial place of the 32nd President of the United States, Franklin D. Roosevelt. The National Historic Site was established in 1945.

The magnificent home, as well as Rose Garden and Gravesite, Ice House and Stables are maintained by the National Park Service.

The land of the Springwood estate was originally part of a land grant which covered the area between the Hudson River in the west and the border of Connecticut in the East. The estate, which comprised about one square mile of land at the time, was purchased by Franklin D. Roosevelt's father, James Roosevelt, in 1866.

At that time, a stable and a horse track were included. James Roosevelt took a great interest in horse breeding.

FDR was born in the house, and grew up here. After his marriage to Eleanor in 1905, the young couple moved in with his mother. The estate remained the center of Roosevelt's life in all stages of his career.

Roosevelt used the estate as a retreat for himself and his political associates. He delivered many of his speeches on the front terrace.

In 1943, Roosevelt donated the estate to the American people under the condition that his family maintain a life-time right to usage of the property.

Roosevelt made his last visit to Springwood in the last week of March 1945, about two weeks before his death. He died April 12, 1945, while preparing a speech for the charter conference of the United Nations.

At his own request, he was buried near the sundial in the Rose Garden. His wife was buried at his side after her death in 1962.

Between 1911 and Roosevelt's death in 1945, more than 400,000 trees were planted on the estate.

Eventually, large portions of the estate were turned into an experimental forestry station under an agreement with the Forestry Department of the Syracuse University.

On November 21, 1945, after the family had relinquished their rights, the estate was transferred to the U.S. Department of the Interior. Since then, the estate has been administered by the National Park Service as a National Historic Site and is open to the public.

The FDR Presidential Library here is the nation's first Presidential Library, and the only one ever used by a sitting President.

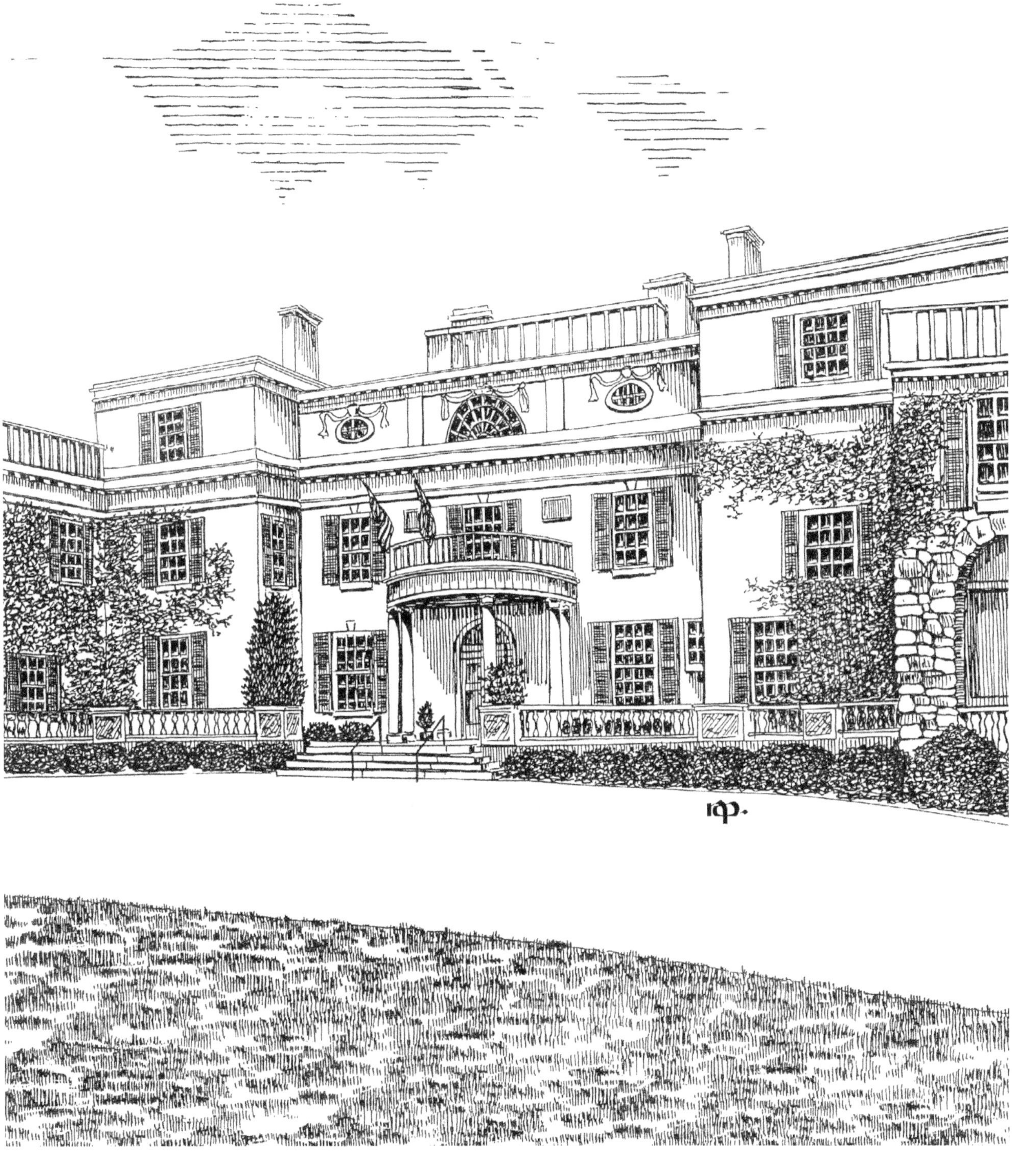

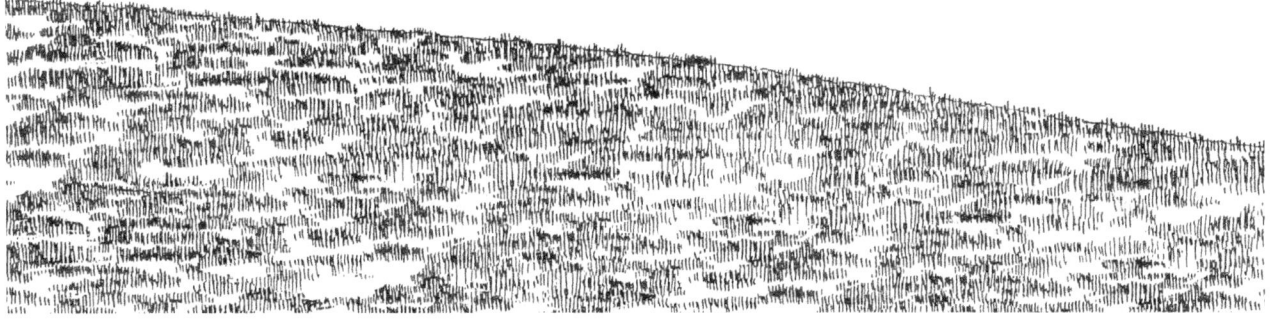

Springwood

Old Talbott Tavern

Bardstown, Kentucky

The Talbott Tavern, also known as the Old Stone Tavern, was built in 1779. It is located in the historic district of Bardstown, Kentucky, across from the historic Nelson County Courthouse.

It was placed on the National Register of Historic Places on October 30, 1973. The tavern has been in continuous operation since 1779.

The Old Talbott Tavern was built in 1779; a year before the settlement of Salem (later renamed Bardstown) began, making it the oldest western stagecoach stop still in operation.

The original facility, called Hynes Hotel, was strategically located near the end of the stagecoach road that led east to Philadelphia and Virginia.

George Rogers Clark used the tavern as a base during the end of the American Revolutionary War; Daniel Boone stayed here, and the exiled Louis-Philippe of France, stayed at the tavern in 1797. A member of his entourage painted murals that were on display until damaged by a devastating fire at the Inn in 1998.

The 19th century visitors included future presidents Andrew Jackson, William Henry Harrison, and Abraham Lincoln. Other prominent figures who visited the tavern were Henry Clay, the inventor of steamboats John Fitch, artist & environmentalist John James Audubon, songwriter Stephen Foster, and Jesse James, who is said to have been the cause of the bullet holes in the murals. He was drunk and shooting at imaginary butterflies.

George Talbott purchased the tavern in 1886. Within two years, six of his children died in the tavern; included one by falling down the stairs, and another hanging herself after being unlucky in love.

Throughout its history, the tavern has been called by different names: Hynes House, Bardstown Hotel, Chapman's House, Shady Bower Hotel, the Newman House, Talbott Hotel, Talbott Tavern, and the Old Stone Tavern. However, The Talbott Tavern has been the official name since 1885.

On March 7, 1998, a fire at the tavern severely damaged the roof and second floor. The fire also caused great damage to the Louise-Philippe murals. The Old Talbott Tavern was repaired and reopened on November 9, 1999.

The old Talbott Tavern currently serves as both a restaurant and a five-room bed and breakfast. A writer for Travel and Leisure magazine described it as having "slightly spooky charm". It was ranked the 13th most haunted inn in the United States.

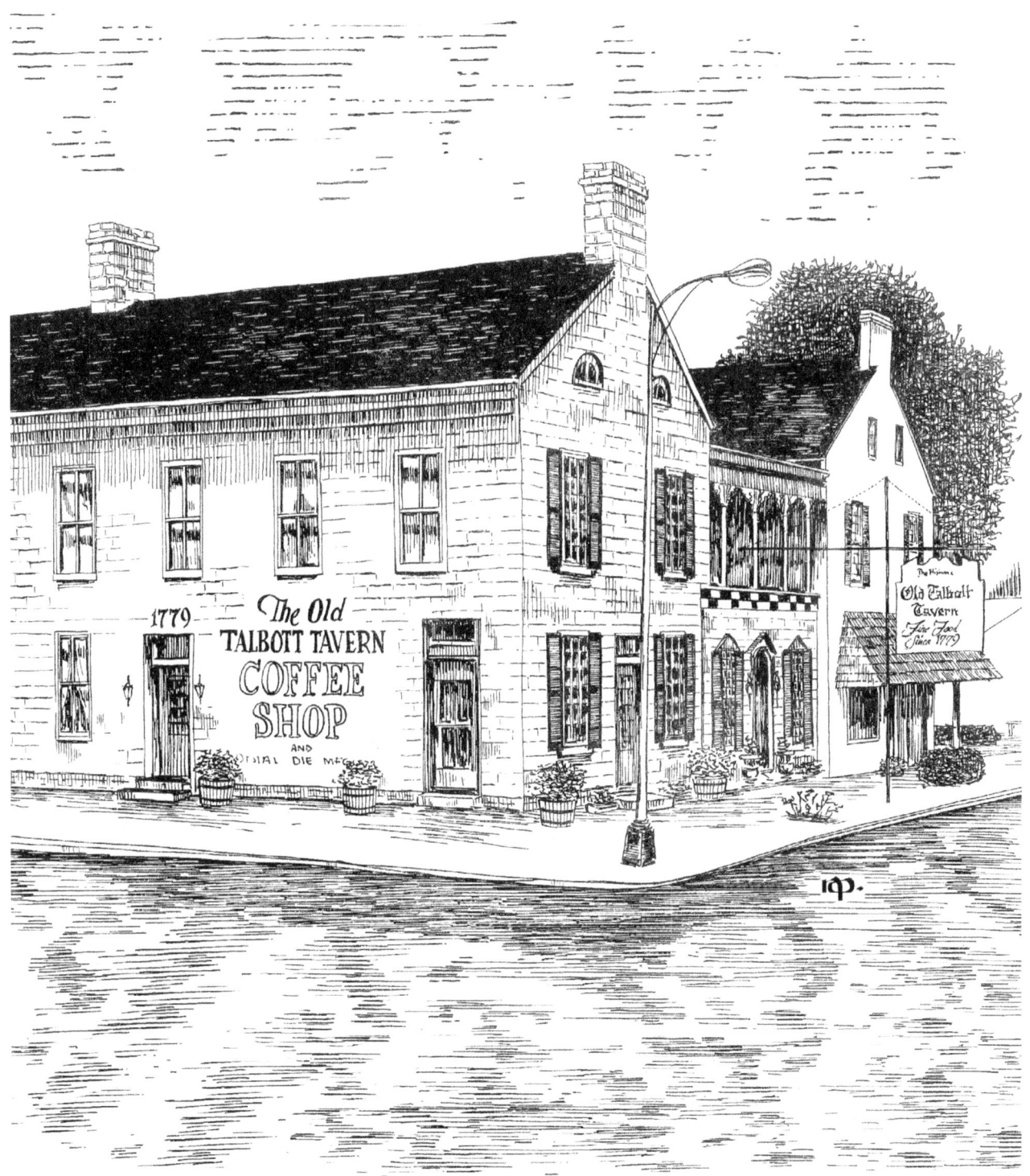

Old Talbott Tavern

Tipton-Haynes Farm

Johnson City, Tennessee

Tipton-Haynes State Historic Site, known also as Tipton-Haynes House, is a Tennessee state-owned historic site located near Johnson City, Tennessee.

The site represents several periods of Tennessee history. The grounds were frequented by both the Woodland and Cherokee Indians, but the first white resident was Col. John Tipton, a member of the Territorial Assembly.

Tipton built a log cabin here in 1784, and his career embraced early Tennessee statehood. John Tipton Jr. was also an active politician, serving as Lt. Governor & president of the senate.

In 1839, the estate was given as a wedding present to London Carter Haynes, who practiced law here and was active in state politics.

It includes a house originally built in 1784 by Colonel John Tipton, and 10 buildings, including a smokehouse, pigsty, loom house, still house, springhouse, log barn and corncrib. There is also the home of George Haynes, a Haynes family slave.

In late February 1788, the so-called "Battle of Franklin" took place when a militia led by John Sevier, who had been elected governor of the proposed state, surrounded the Tipton farm and demanded the return of several slaves Tipton had confiscated for North Carolina authorities.

When Tipton refused, gunfire was exchanged, followed by a two-day standoff. Sevier's forces were finally scattered by the Sullivan County militia. The North Carolinians won this battle which signaled the end of the battle for a State of Franklin. Both Tipton and Sevier went on to serve important roles in the State of Tennessee when it was formed in 1796.

Following Tipton's death in 1813, the farm passed to his son, John Tipton, Jr., who in turn sold it to a land speculator, David Haynes, in 1837.

In 1840, Haynes gave the farm to his son, Landon Carter Haynes, as a wedding present.

A Confederate senator during the Civil War, Landon Carter Haynes was forced to flee the region in 1865. He sold the farm to his brother-in-law, Lawson Gifford.

In 1945, Gifford's grandson, David Simmerly, sold the farm to the Tennessee Historical Commission, though he continued living there until his death.

It is maintained by the Tipton-Haynes Historical Association and was opened to the public in the 1970s as one of the 17 Tennessee Historical Commission state-owned historic sites.

In 1970 the farm was listed on the National Register of Historic Places.

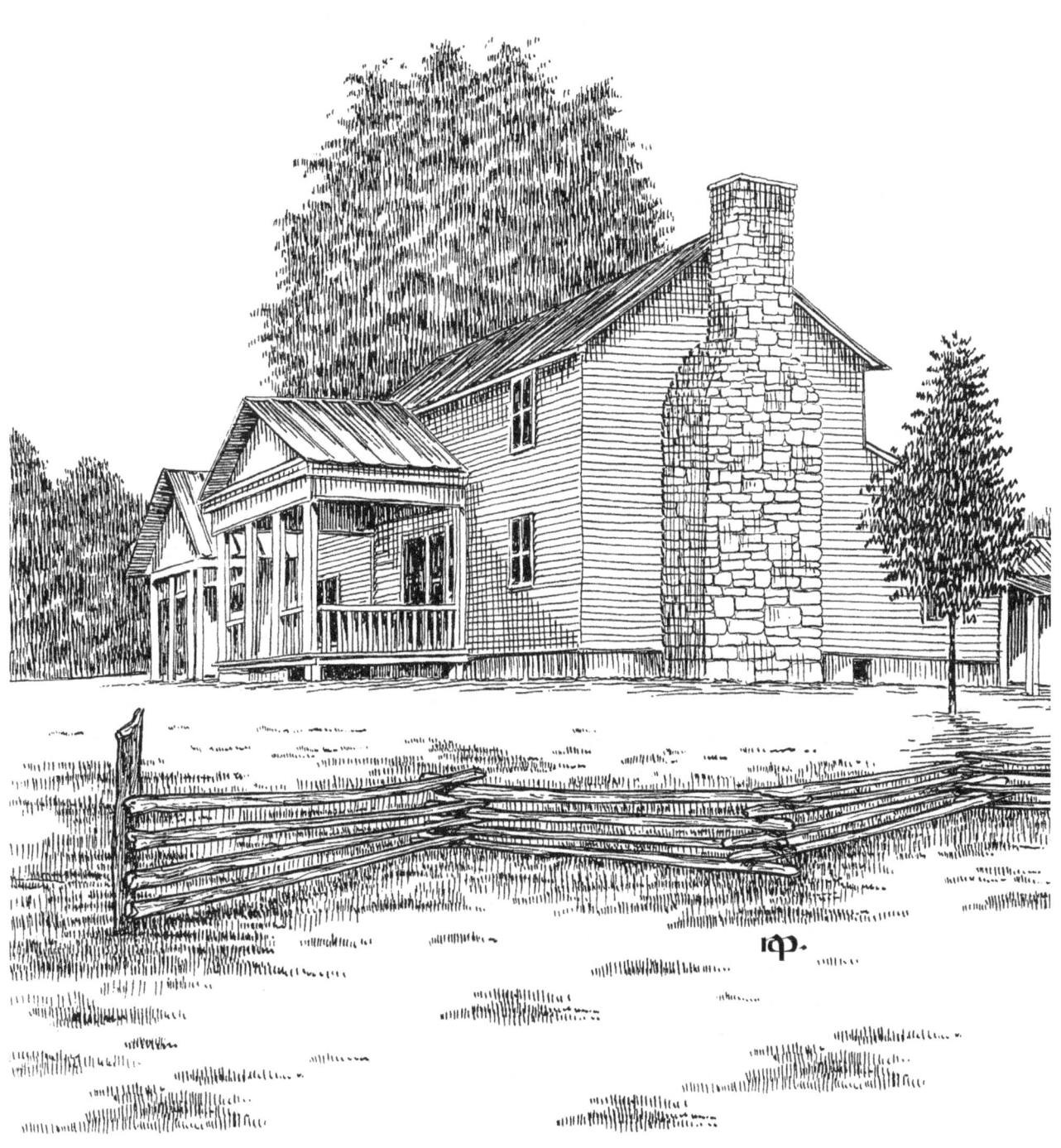

Tipton-Haynes Farm

U. S. Navy Memorial

Washington, D. C.

The United States Navy Memorial, on Pennsylvania Avenue NW between 7th Street Northwest and 9th Street Northwest in Washington, D.C., honors those who have served or are currently serving in the Navy, Marine Corps, Coast Guard, and the Merchant Marine.

The National Park Service provides technical and maintenance assistance to the foundation. The memorial is adjacent to the Archives station and the National Archives building.

Associated with the Memorial is the Naval Heritage Center. The Heritage Center is open 362 days a year, closed only on Thanksgiving, Christmas Day, and New Year's Day.

Although Pierre L. 'Enfant included a Navy Memorial in his original plans for Washington D.C. over 200 years ago, it was not until 1977 that real action was taken. At the inspiration of Admiral Arleigh A. Burke, World War II hero and three-times Chief of Naval Operations, a committee was formed to create the Memorial.

Pennsylvania Avenue, the main boulevard that links the U.S. Capitol and White House, the scene of so many parades, pageants, and national memories, was chosen as the site.

When President John F. Kennedy inspired the total redevelopment of Pennsylvania Avenue, another Navy war hero, Adm. Arleigh Burke campaigned for development of a Navy Memorial.

Congress authorized the Memorial in 1980, with a stipulation that funding come solely from private contributions. In March 1980, President Jimmy Carter signed a law which authorized the Memorial as a part of a Department of the Interior bill.

To celebrate America's enduring naval heritage, the statue of a lone sailor 7-feet tall stands on the broad granite map of the world, surrounded by fountains and pools.

In August 1987, Stanley Bleifeld completed his work on *The Lone Sailor* statue as construction of the Memorial neared completion.

The Memorial and amphitheater was dedicated on October 13, 1987, and since then has been the site of weekly summer concerts by various military bands.

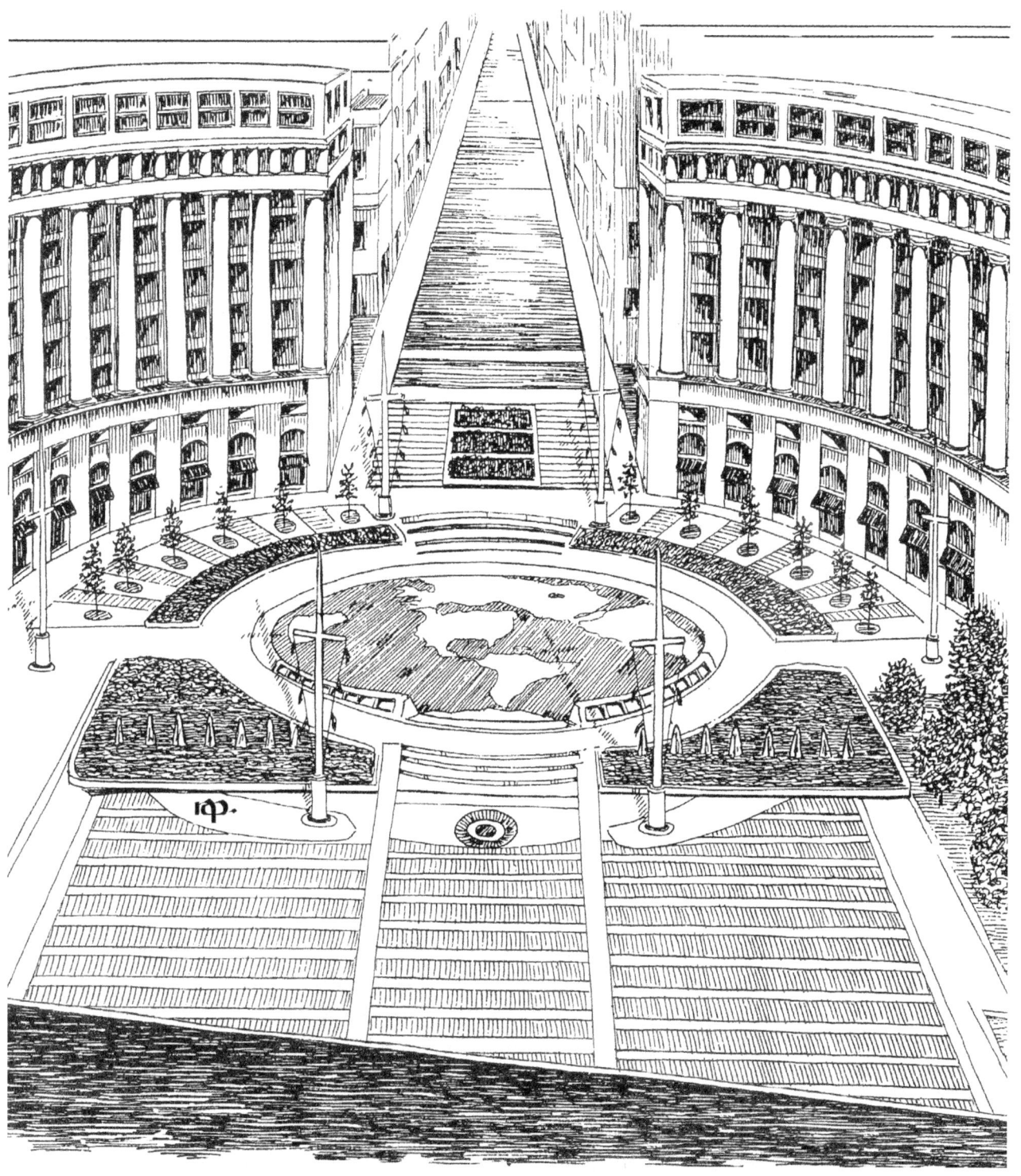

U. S. Navy Memorial

United States Capitol

Washington, D. C.

The United States Capitol is one of the most widely recognized buildings in the world. Built, burned by British troops in 1814, rebuilt, extended, and restored, it stands today as a symbol of the American people and democracy.

The Capitol is the meeting place of the U.S. Congress, the legislature of the U.S. federal government.

Located in Washington, D.C., it sits atop Capitol Hill at the eastern end of the National Mall. Though it has never been the geographic center of the federal district, the Capitol is the origin by which the quadrants of the District of Columbia are divided and the city was planned.

Like the federal buildings for the executive and judicial branches, the capitol is built in the distinctive neoclassical style with a white exterior.

Prior to establishing the nation's capital in Washington, D.C., the United States Congress and its predecessors had met in Philadelphia (Independence Hall and Congress Hall), New York City (Federal Hall), and a number of other locations (Maryland State House in Annapolis, Maryland, Nassau Hall in Princeton, New Jersey).

The United States Congress was established upon ratification of the United States Constitution and formally began on March 4, 1789. After long an arduous debate, and much wrangling, the decision was made to locate the capital along the Potomac River.

Philadelphia was chosen as a temporary capital for ten years; until the permanent capital in Washington, D.C. would be ready.

The cornerstone was laid by President George Washington on September 18, 1793, with full Masonic ceremonies. Work progressed under the direction of three architects in succession for nearly 30 years.

Although the building was not yet completed, the Capitol held its first session of United States Congress on November 17, 1800.

The legislature was moved to Washington prematurely, at the urging of President John Adams in hopes of securing enough Southern votes to be re-elected for a 2nd term as president.

A steep, metal staircase, totaling 365 steps, leads from the basement to an outdoor walkway on top of the Capitol's dome. The number of steps represents each day of the year.

In 1960, the Capitol was declared a National Historic Landmark.

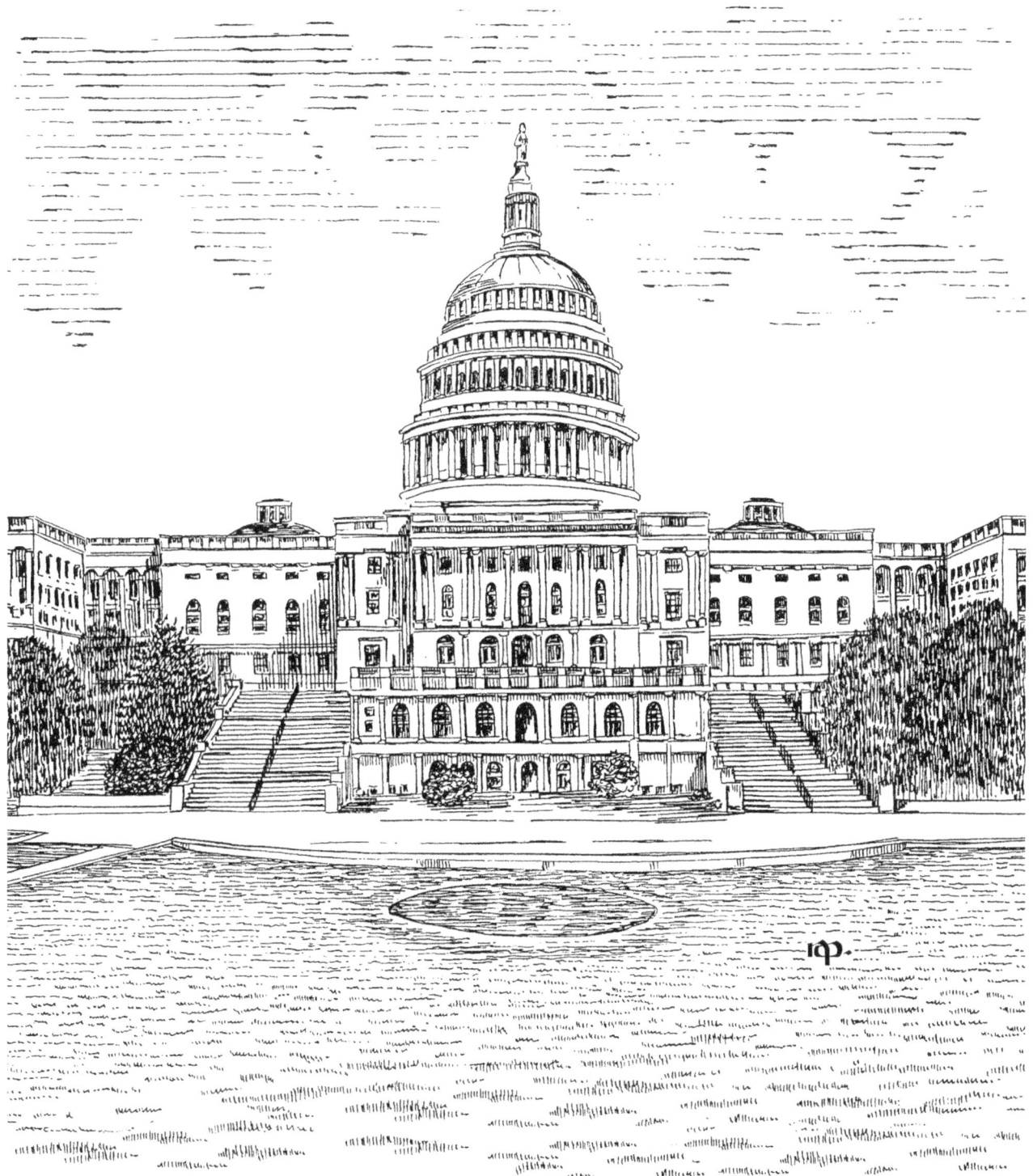

United States Capitol

USS Arizona Memorial

Pearl Harbor, Hawaii

The USS Arizona Memorial, located at Pearl Harbor in Honolulu, Hawaii, marks the resting place of 1,102 of the 1,177 sailors and Marines killed on the USS Arizona during the attack on Pearl Harbor on December 7, 1941 by Japanese imperial forces.

The attack on Pearl Harbor and the island of Oahu was the action that led to the direct involvement of the United States in World War II.

The memorial, built in 1962, is visited by more than one million people annually. Accessible only by boat, it is a 184-foot-long structure which straddles the hull of the battleship sunken in the harbor without actually touching it.

Historical information about the attack, shuttle boats to and from the memorial, and general visitor services are available at the associated USS Arizona Memorial Visitor Center, which opened in 1980 and is operated by the National Park Service.

Remains of the sunken battleship were officially declared as a National Historic Landmark on May 5, 1989.

The Memorial contains a ceremony room, general observation area, and a shrine room, where the names of those killed on the Arizona are engraved on the marble wall.

In 1949, the Territory of Hawaii established the Pacific War Memorial Commission. Pres. Dwight Eisenhower approved the construction of their design in 1958. It was completed in 1961 and dedicated in 1962; it became a national park in 1980. The memorial was designed by Honolulu architect Alfred Preis who had been detained at Sand Island at the start of the war as an enemy of the country because of his Austrian birth.

The United States Navy specified that the memorial be in the form of a bridge floating above the ship, able to accommodate 200 people. It was designed to sag in the center and stand strong at the ends to express initial defeat and ultimate victory.

Every United States Navy, Coast Guard, and Merchant Marine vessel entering Pearl Harbor participates in the tradition of "manning the rails". Personnel serving on these ships stand at attention at the ship's guard rails and salute the USS Arizona Memorial in solemn fashion as their ship slowly glides into port.

The USS Arizona is no longer in commission, but is an active U.S. military cemetery. As a special tribute to the ship and her lost crew, the U.S. flag flies from the flagpole, which is attached to the severed mainmast of the sunken battleship.

USS Arizona Memorial honors all the military personnel killed in the Pearl Harbor attack of 1941.

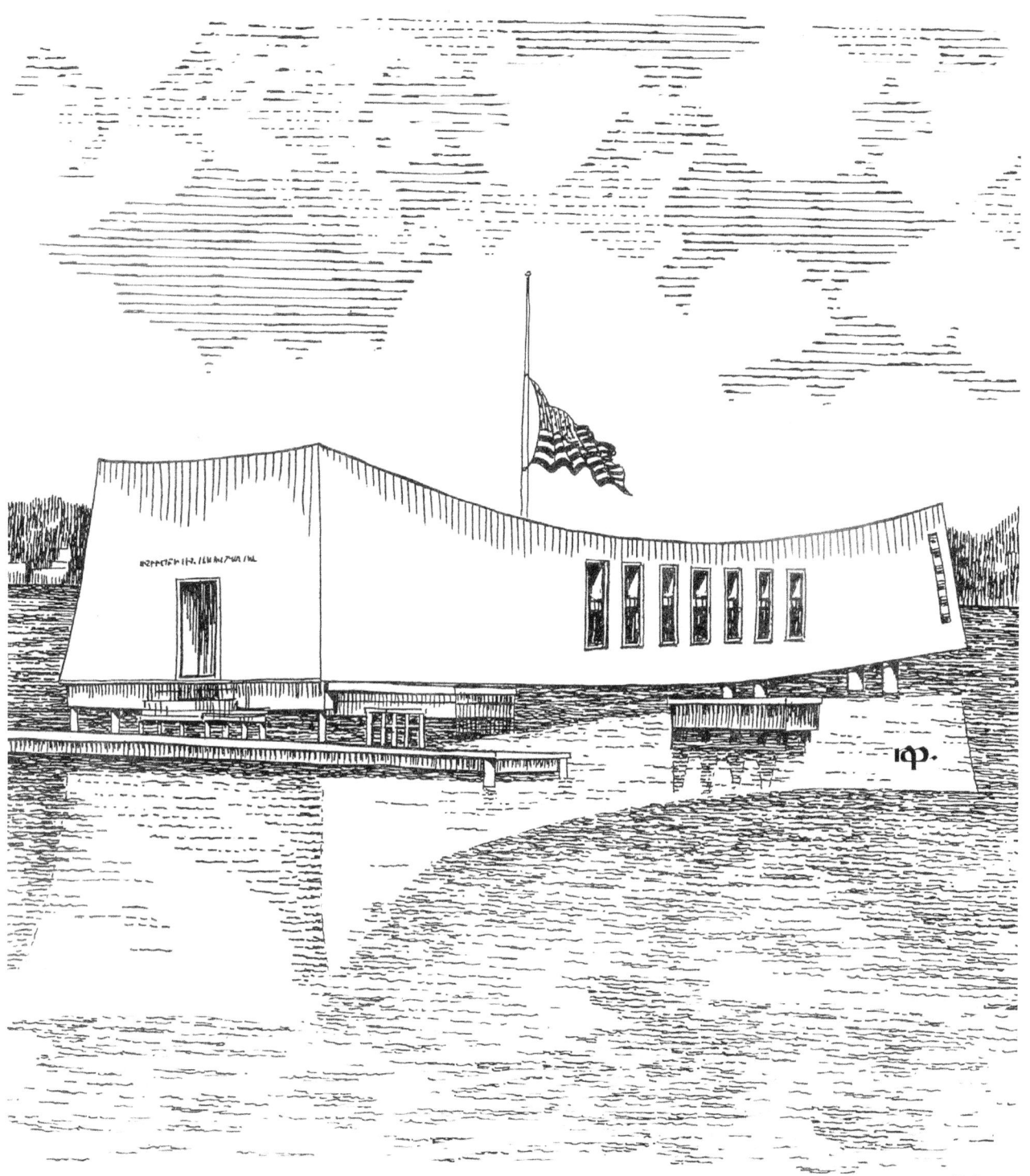

USS Arizona Memorial

USS Constitution

Boston, Massachusetts

The USS Constitution is a wooden-hulled, three-masted heavy frigate of the United States Navy. Named by President George Washington after the Constitution of the United States of America, she is the world's oldest commissioned naval vessel afloat.

Launched in 1797, Constitution was one of six frigates authorized for construction by the Naval Act of 1794; and third to be constructed.

Joshua Humphreys designed the frigates to be the young Navy's capital ships, and so the Constitution and her sisters were larger and more heavily armed and built than standard frigates of the time period.

Built in Boston, Massachusetts, at Edmund Hartt's shipyard, her first duties with the newly formed U.S. Navy were to offer protection for American merchant shipping during the Quasi-War with France and to defeat the Barbary pirates.

Constitution is most famous for her actions during the War of 1812 against Great Britain. She captured several merchant ships and defeated five British warships: HMS Guerriere, Java, Pictou, Cyane and Levant.

The battle with Guerriere earned her the nickname of "Old Ironsides" and public adoration that repeatedly saved her from scrapping.

She continued to serve as flagship in both the Mediterranean and African squadrons, and circled the world in the 1840s. During the American Civil War, she served as a training ship for the U.S. Naval Academy. She carried US artwork and industrial displays to the Paris Exposition of 1878.

Retired from active service in 1881, Constitution served as a receiving ship until designated a museum in 1907.

In 1934 Constitution completed a three-year, 90-port tour of the nation. She sailed under her own power for her 200th birthday in 1997, and again in August 2012, to commemorate the 200th anniversary of her victory over Guerriere in the War of 1812.

Constitution's stated mission today is to promote understanding of the Navy's role in war and peace through educational outreach.

As a fully commissioned US Navy ship, her crew of 60 officers and sailors participate in ceremonies, educational programs, and special events while keeping the ship open to visitors year round and providing free tours.

The officers and crew are all active-duty US Navy personnel and their assignment is considered special duty in the Navy. Command of the vessel is assigned to a US Navy Commander. Constitution is berthed at Pier 1 of the former Charlestown Navy Yard, at one end of Boston's Freedom Trail.

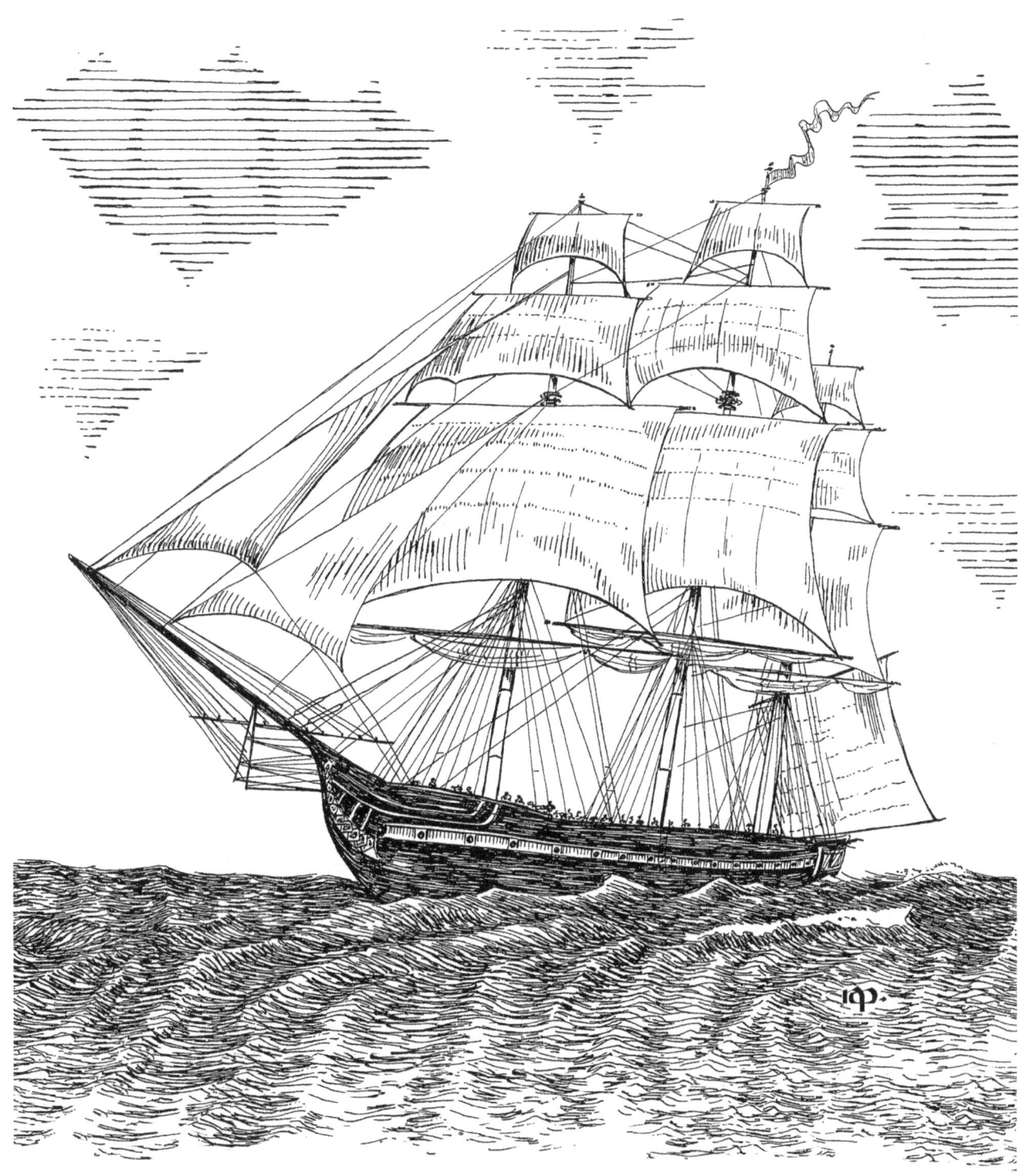

USS Constitution

USS Harlan County

USS Harlan County (LST-1196) was a United States Navy tank landing ship of the Newport-class.

Harlan County (LST-1196) was named after Harlan County, Kentucky as reflected in her unit patch. Her keel was laid on November 7, 1970 at San Diego, California by the National Steel & Shipbuilding Co.

She launched on July 24, 1971, and was commissioned April 8, 1972 with Commander Vernon C. Smith in command.

With a homeport in Little Creek, Virginia, the crew of 32 officers and 591 enlisted men took the ship to virtually every major body of water on this entire planet.

It carried twenty Amphibious Assault Vehicles, which could be off-loaded into another landing craft carrier, pier or beach in a matter of minutes. The ship's flight deck can accommodate most types of US Navy helicopters, which provide protection when delivering AAV's into any hostile areas during a war or skirmish.

She served in the Persian Gulf during Operation Desert Storm/Desert Shield. In 1990 the USS Harlan County helped reestablish the US Navy cooperation with Argentina; she was the first US Navy ship to make an official port visit to Buenos Aires since the Falklands War.

On October 11, 1993, the Harlan County was sent to Port-au-Prince, Haiti to pave the way for an agreed-upon UN intervention.

She was decommissioned in 1995 after a long and very colorful service and transferred to Spain. Her Spanish service ended in 2012 and it was reported that she was sold to Angola as part of a package with the Príncipe de Asturias.

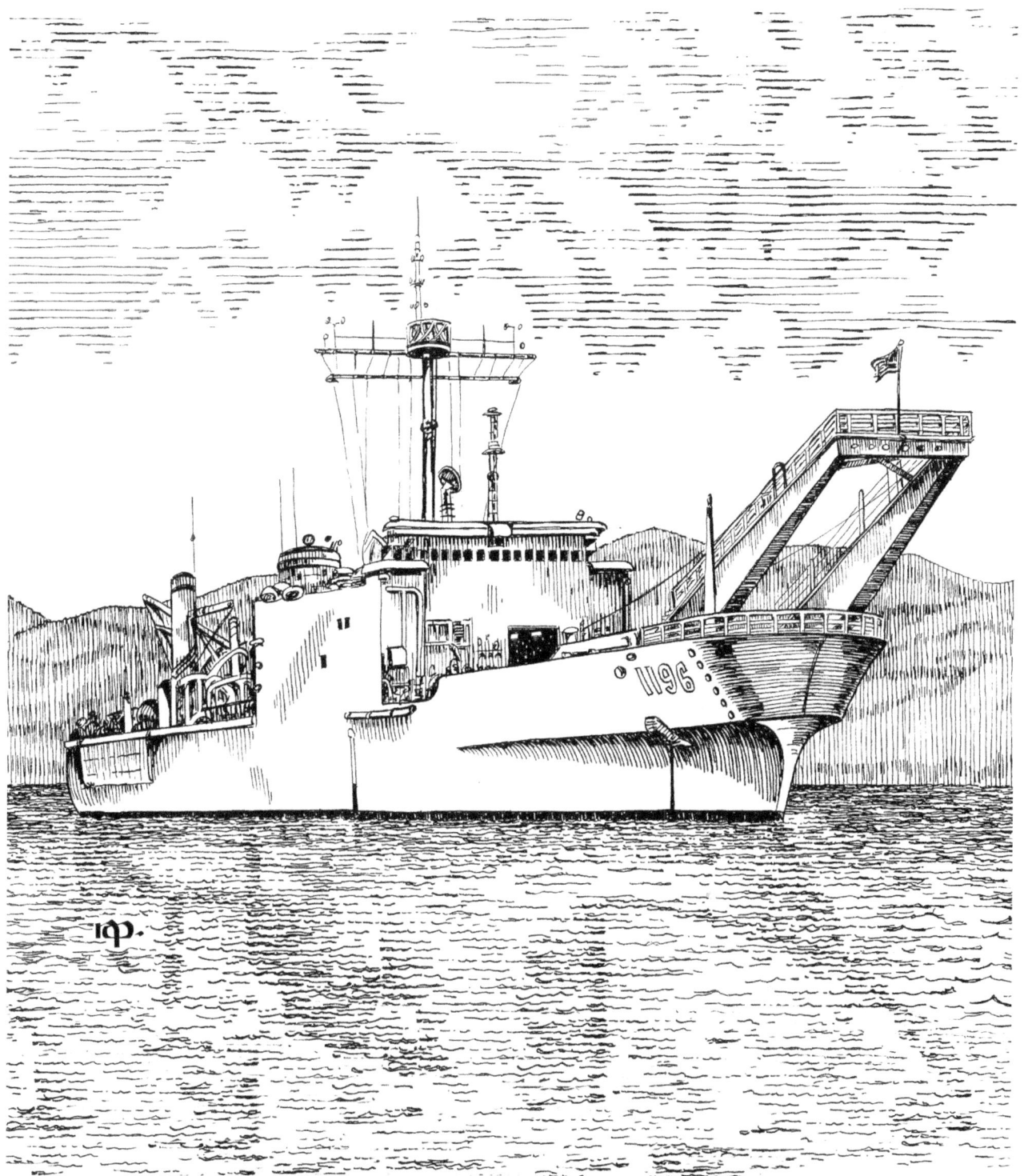

USS Harlan County

Wright Cycle Company
Dayton, Ohio

Dayton Aviation Heritage honors three exceptional men; Wilbur & Orville Wright, and Paul Lawrence Dunbar.

The Wright Cycle Company was home to the Wright brothers' bicycle business from 1895 to 1897. Here the Wright brothers began to manufacture their own brand of bicycles which gave the brothers the mechanical experience and financial resources necessary for their experiments into powered flight.

The Wright Cycle Company was listed as a National Historic Landmark in 1990.

The Wright-Dunbar Interpretive Center is located in the Hoover Block, which was home to Wright & Wright, Job Printers from 1890 to 1895. The Wright brothers began their first business, printing, when Orville was still in high school and they printed small neighborhood newspapers, notecards, bill heads, and circulars.

In their bicycle shop in Dayton, these two men, self-trained in the science and art of aviation, researched and built the world's first power-driven, heavier-than-air machine capable of free, controlled, and sustained flight.

The Wrights also perfected their invention during 1904 and 1905 in their hometown of Dayton. The Wright Cycle company building is one of four structures preserved by the Dayton Aviation Heritage in their National Historical Park complex.

In 1896 the Wright brothers began manufacturing and selling bicycles of their own design, the Van Cleve and St. Claire, named after their ancestors.

They invented the self-oiling hub and the innovation of machining the crank arm and pedal on the left side of the bike with left-hand threads to prevent the pedal from coming unscrewed while cycling.

The brick building at 22 South Williams Street, where the Wrights worked from 1895 to 1897, is the only building on its original foundation and in its original location that housed a Wright bicycle shop.

They built a six-foot wind tunnel on the second floor of their bicycle shop, and conducted pioneering tests in the tunnel of over 200 different shapes of scale-model wings.

In that building they also designed and constructed their gliders and first airplane, the Wright Flyer, which cost under $1,000 to build. They closed their bicycle shop in 1909 and started their aviation company.

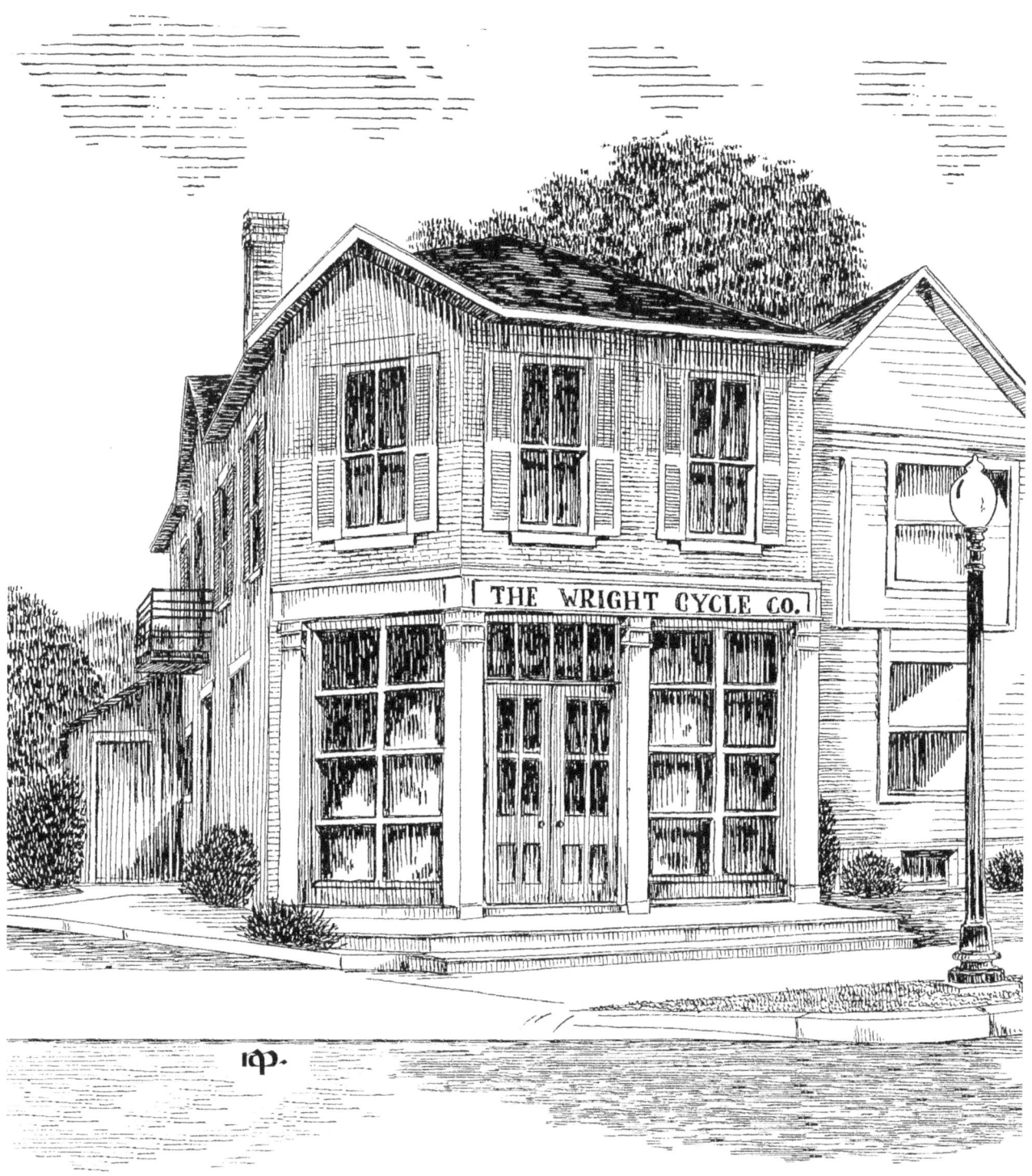

Wright Cycle Company

Zachary Taylor House

Louisville, Kentucky

Located in Louisville, Kentucky, the Zachary Taylor House, also known as Springfield, was the boyhood home of the twelfth President of the United States, Zachary Taylor.

Taylor lived there from 1790 to 1808, held his marriage there in 1810, and returned there periodically the rest of his life. It was also the birthplace for five of his six children, including the son Richard, who was a lieutenant general in the Confederate Army.

Zachary Taylor was born in Orange County, Virginia. He was eight months old when his family moved to a farm on Beargrass Creek just east of the tiny village of Louisville in 1785.

The family began their new life in Kentucky in a small log house, but within five years Richard Taylor built a house at the highest point on his property. He dubbed it "Springfield."

By 1800 Richard Taylor purchased an additional 300 acres, making his property 700 total acres. The property was adjacent to Locust Grove, the farm where George Rogers Clark lived from 1809 until his death in 1818.

Springfield is a 2 1/2-story Georgia Colonial red brick L-shaped house. The western section of the house is the oldest, built around 1790. The eastern section was built between 1810 and 1830. It features a gable roof, a double-parlor, and fireplaces in each room. It was constructed by Richard Taylor and the slaves he owned.

Zachary assisted his father on the farm until 1808, when he received the commission as a second lieutenant in the 7th United States Infantry.

When he married in 1810, Zachary received a gift of 324 acres of land at the mouth of Beargrass Creek, but he still continued to make his residence at Springfield.

When Richard Taylor died in 1829, he specified in his will that Springfield be sold to settle all his debts. Zachary expressed regret that the farm could not have remained in the family.

Upon his death at the White House in 1850, President Taylor's body was brought back to rest in the family burial ground at Springfield. This later served as the nucleus of the Zachary Taylor National Cemetery.

The farm has been subdivided and the house sits on a one-acre lot. It has not undergone any extensive alteration since the time of Zachary Taylor's residence.

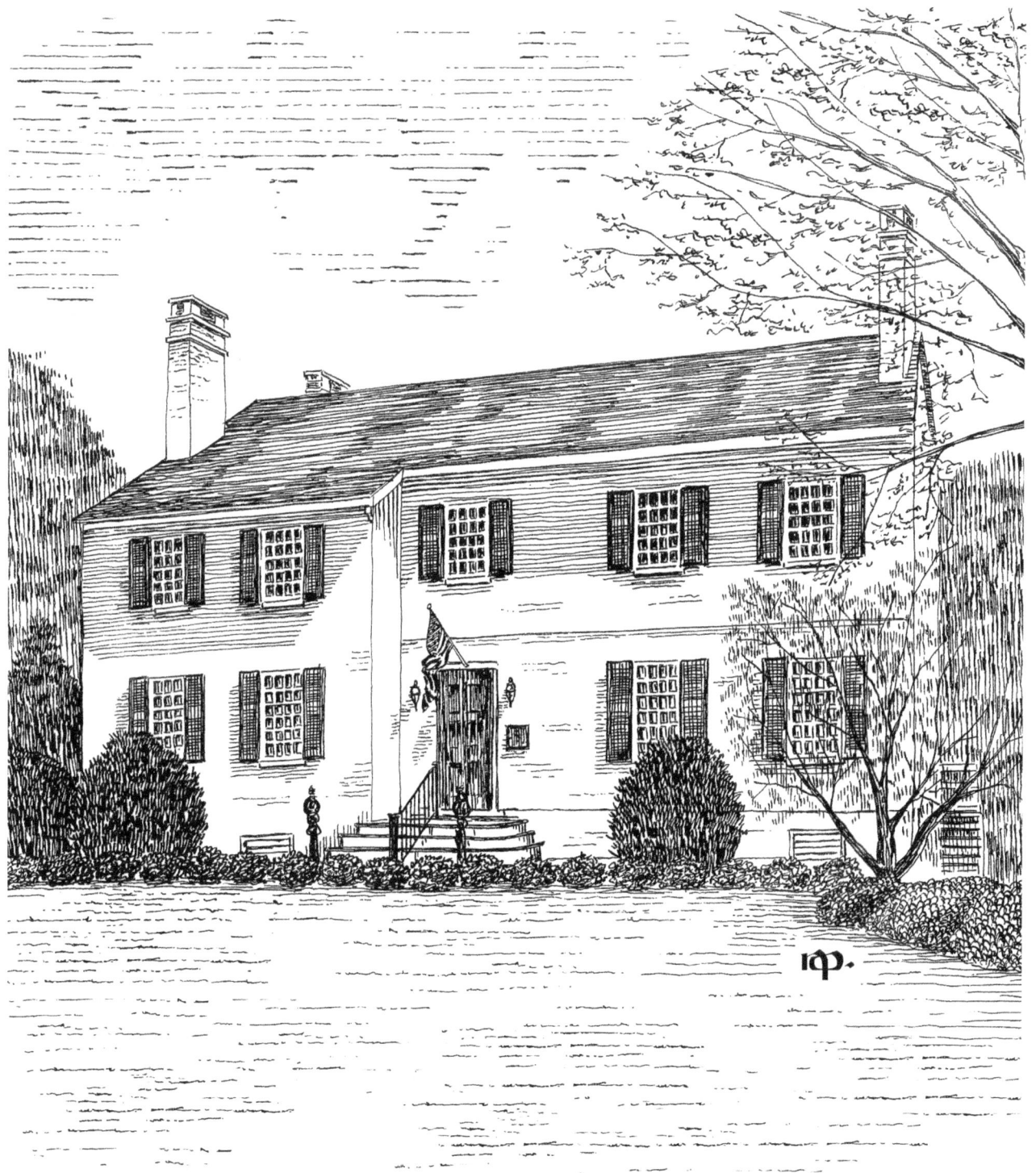

Zachary Taylor House

www.ingramcontent.com/pod-product-compliance
Lightning Source LLC
Chambersburg PA
CBHW080255180526
45167CB00006B/2538